Curiosities

of

British Archaeology

Curiosities

of

British Archaeology

Compiled by
RONALD JESSUP

PHILLIMORE

First published in 1961 by
BUTTERWORTHS
London

Second edition published by
PHILLIMORE & CO. LTD
Shopwyke Hall, Chichester, Sussex
1974

ISBN 0 85033 119 6

Set in Monotype Bembo Type
Printed in Great Britain by
Fletcher & Son Ltd, Norwich

ALBION! o'oer thee profusely Nature showers
Her gifts; with liveliet verdure decks thy soil,
With every mingled charm of hill and dale,
Mountains and mead, hoar cliff, and forest wide;
And thy *Ruins,* where rapt genius broods,
In pensive haunts romantic; rifted *Towers*
That, beetling o'oer the rock, rear the grey crest,
Embattled; and within the secret glade
Conceal'd, the *Abbey's* ivy-mantled pile.

William Sotheby, 1757–83

Archaeology has been and still can be a retreat from harsh reality, but equally it can be and is coming more and more to be an exciting quest to satisfy deep-felt needs of contemporary society . . . Prehistory appeals to individuals not merely as members of societies, but as persons, and it finds complete justification if it enriches the experience of men and helps them to live more abundantly as heirs of all ages and brothers to one another.

Professor Grahame Clark in *Archaeology and Society*, 1960 ed.

FOREWORD

This book of literary curiosities has been compiled from a large collection of pieces, notes, underlinings and extracts which relate in a broad sense to the history and progress of British archaeology. It is, in brief, a prospect of British antiquity. The arrangement is, of course, an arbitrary one, but certain subjects and thoughts seem to gather themselves into obvious categories: the antiquary-archaeologist himself, his tours abroad in the countryside, his digging expeditions, his regard for churches, his discoveries and his attitude to fakes and forgeries, fable and legend, and above all his attention to the grammar of his subject, are the main headings, but it will be seen that some pieces could properly be placed under more than one heading, a few truly perhaps under none.

Again, the selection is a personal one. The range of dates within which authors have been chosen is selective and not representative— no ancient author, for instance, is represented—and no attempt has been made to include a writer merely because he happens to fill a chronological gap. The main link is not chronological sequence but relevance of thought, and sometimes in this grouping one finds unexpected parallels or contrasts. Consider, for short examples, the matter of archaeological illustration as commented upon by Stukeley, James Douglas and the Right Hon. A. J. Beresford Hope, and the wide variety in antiquarian prospect shown by Leland, Camden and Stukeley in their accounts of the city of Exeter. In the items chosen, some telling degree of literary qualification has generally been applied: comments on some feature of the age, some nicety of manner, some strong contrast in a point of view, these too have influenced selection.

Literary curiosities on vellum and parchment, fireside antiquity as it were, would fill a much larger book than this, as would informative and amusing accounts of church crawling and speculative and informed comments on antiquarian myths, fables and legends: a limit had perforce to be set to the present volume.

Readers familiar with the original texts will notice that certain inconsistencies and spelling errors have not been corrected in these extracts.

My grateful thanks are due to my brother Frank W. Jessup, to Brigid Haydon, Professor Stuart Piggott, Dr. Pamela Tudor-Craig and Sir Mortimer Wheeler for helpful suggestions.

RONALD JESSUP

St George's Day, 1961
London, W.1

CONTENTS

ix

ACKNOWLEDGEMENTS

The Author and Publishers wish to express their thanks for permission
to reprint copyright material to the following:

For an extract from *Notes on Archaeological Technique* to the Keeper
of the Ashmolean Museum, Oxford; for an extract from *Field Archae-
ology* to Professor R. J. C. Atkinson and Methuen and Co. Ltd.; for
an extract from *Archaeology and Society* to Professor J. G. D. Clark and
Methuen and Co. Ltd.; to Mr Stanley Wade Baron and Rupert
Hart-Davis Ltd. for an extract from *People and Americans*; to Mr
Bernard Bergonzi for his poem *The British Museum*; to Mr John
Betjeman and John Murray (Publishers) Ltd. for the poem *An
Archaeological Picnic* from Mr Betjeman's *Collected Poems*; for an
extract from *The Elegant Edwardian* to Miss Ursula Bloom and the
Hutchinson Publishing Group; for an extract from *The Ruined Abbeys
of Great Britain* to the representatives of the Author and Gay and
Hancock; for an extract from the late Dr O. G. S. Crawford's *Said and
Done* to George Weidenfeld and Nicolson Ltd.; for an extract from
Florence Desmond, By Herself to Miss Desmond and George G. Harrap
and Co. Ltd.; to Dr J. P. Droop and University Press, Cambridge, for
an extract from *Archaeological Excavation*; for extracts from *Vainglory*
and *Valmouth* to the representatives of the late Ronald Firbank and
Gerald Duckworth and Co. Ltd.; to Mr H. J. Randall and Mr C. M.
Franzero and George Allen and Unwin Ltd. for extracts from *History
in the Open Air* and *Roman Britain* respectively; for an extract from
W. H. Hudson's *Afoot in England* to the Royal Society for the Protec-
tion of Birds and the Society of Authors; for an extract from *Out with
the Cambrians* to the representatives of Evelyn Hughes, and Ernest
Benn Ltd. as successors to Williams and Norgate; to Miss Barbara
Jones and Constable and Co. Ltd. for an extract from *Follies and
Grottoes*, and to Constable and Co. Ltd. for an extract from the
Introduction to *The Goodwin Sands* by G. C. Carter; to Mr Julian
Mitchell for his poem *Excavation*; for extracts from the two works by
William Morris to Longmans, Green and Co. Ltd.; to Mr Alan Ross
for his poem *Clayton Village* and Hamish Hamilton Ltd., publishers of
To Whom It May Concern; to J. M. Dent and Sons Ltd. for extracts
from the Everyman Library edition of *The Letters of Horace Walpole*,
and E. P. Dutton and Co. Inc. for extracts from *Selected Letters of*

Horace Walpole; for an extract from *Aylwin* by Theodore Watts-Dunton to the author's representative and the Hutchinson Publishing Group; for an extract from *Still Digging* to Sir Mortimer Wheeler and Michael Joseph Ltd.; for an extract from *Archaeology from the Earth* to Sir Mortimer Wheeler and The Clarendon Press, Oxford; for an extract from *Digging up the Past* to the representatives of the late Sir Leonard Woolley and Ernest Benn Ltd.

They are also indebted to the Editors of the following periodicals for permission to reprint matter published in their journals: *Antiquity*; *The Connoisseur*; *Daily Sketch*; *Daily Telegraph*; *Evening News*; *Evening Standard*; *Folkestone, Hythe and District Herald*; *Kent Messenger*; *Nottingham Evening Post*; *The Tablet*; *Time and Tide*; and *The Times*.

If any acknowledgements which should have been made here are not specifically made, the Author begs forgiveness for his not intentional discourtesy and, above all else, he remains most dutifully and gratefully indebted to the Society of Antiquaries.

1—THE ANTIQUARY AND ARCHAEOLOGIST

THE ANTIQUARY AND ARCHAEOLOGIST

Aspersion Confuted
Bad Eies
Britain's First Prehistorian?—
—and his Successor
Cure for Antiquaries' Spleen—
—and for Flegme
Delight to be in the Darke
Extasy at Finding It
Footing It
Generous Thought
Habitual Gravity
Infallibility
Jocundissimus
Knowledge of Places, Times and People
Love of the Mouldy
Modest Needs
Nimble Pen
Obstinacy
Prime Duty
Publicity of Wheeler's
Quarrels at Strawberry Hill
Relaxations
Societatis Antiquariorum Londinensis
    The Society of Antiquaries—
        —and an Election Meeting
Talents for Conversation
Tom's Tale: Understanding with Virtue
Women and Antiquity
    Sir John's Wife
    An Obliging Landlady
    Our Fair Countrywomen
    Fine Ladies Soiled
    Propriety
    Out with the Cambrians
    Cure for Marriage
    Apotheosis
Xerophagy Opposed
Your Little Room
Zenith and Ploys

ASPERSION CONFUTED

Travelling long Journeys is costly, at all times troublesome, at some times dangerous: Yet it is both a general and generous Desire of most Men to be acquainted with their native Country.

To satisfy them herein, this Work is set forth ; where thou may'st cross Rivers without Boat or Bridge, climb up Mountains without Pains, and go down without Danger: In a word, thy Eye may safely travel in a few Hours over all England. . . .

Now know this was collected by the Appointment (at the Charge, and for the use) of that worthy Antiquary Sir Henry Spelman . . . who confuted that Aspersion which is generally cast on Antiquaries, that they are either supercilious or superstitious, either proud or popishly affected. . . .

Preface by R.H. to SPELMAN's *Villare Anglicanum*, 1655

BAD EIES

Mr. Edward Bagshawe (who had been second schoole-master of Westminster schoole) haz told me that Mr. Camden had first his place and his lodgings (which is the gate-house by the Queen's Scholars' chamber in Deanes-yard), and was after made the head schoole-master of that schoole, where he writt and taught *Institutio Graecae Grammatices Compendiaria: in usum Regiae Scholae Westmonasteriensis*, which is now the common Greeke grammar of England, but his name is not sett to it. Before, they learned the prolix Greeke Grammar of Cleonard.

'Tis reported, that he had bad eies (I guesse lippitude) which was a great inconvenience to an antiquary. . . .

Mr. Camden much studied the Welsh language, and kept a Welsh servant to improve him in that language, for the better understanding of our antiquities.

Of Mr. Camden: JOHN AUBREY, *Brief Lives*, circa 1680

BRITAIN'S FIRST PREHISTORIAN?—

And here I cannot forget to mention the honest Industry of my old Friend Mr. John Conyers, an Apothecary formerly living in Fleet-street, who made it his chief Business to make curious Observations, and to collect such Antiquities as were daily found in and about London. His character is very well known, and therefore I will not attempt it. Yet this I must note, that he was at great Expence in prosecuting his Discoveries, and that he is remembered with respect by most of our Antiquaries that are now living. 'Tis this very Gentleman that discovered the Body of an Elephant, as he was digging for Gravel in a Field near to the Sign of Sir John Old-Castle in the Fields, not far from Battlebridge, and near to the River of Wells, which tho' now dryed up, was a considerable River in the time of the Romans.

How this Elephant came there? is the Question. I know some will have it to have lain there ever since the Universal Deluge. For my own part, I take it to have been brought over with many others by the Romans in the time of Claudius, and conjecture . . . that it was killed in some Fight by a Britain. For not far from the Place where it was found, a British Weapon made of a Flint Lance like unto the Head of a Spear . . . was also dug up, they having not at that time the use of Iron or Brass, as the Romans had. . . . This conjecture, perhaps, may seem odd to some; but I am satisfied my self, having often viewed this Flint Weapon. . . .

John Bagford's letter relating to the Antiquities of London, in
John Leland's *Collectanea,* 2nd (Hearne's) ed., Vol. 1, 1770

(*This pear-shaped flint hand-axe, found about 1690 and now in the British Museum, was the first stone tool to be recognized as being made by man. It belongs, of course, to the early Stone Age, and the supposed association with the elephants in the invasion forces of the Emperor Claudius is a pleasant eighteenth-century antiquarian fancy.*)

—AND HIS SUCCESSOR

Flint implements discovered at Hoxne, in Suffolk

They are, I think, evidently weapons of war, fabricated and used by a people who had not the use of metals. They lay in great numbers at the depth of about twelve feet, in a stratified soil, which was dug into for the purpose of raising clay for bricks. . . .

The situation in which these weapons were found may tempt us to refer them to a very remote period indeed; even beyond that of the present world; but whatever our conjectures on that hand may be, it will be difficult to account for the stratum in which they lie being covered with another stratum which, on that supposition, may be conjectured to have been once the bottom, or at least the shore, of the sea. The manner in which they lie would lead to the persuasion that it was a place of their manufacture and not of their accidental deposit. . . .

John Frere : Read to the Society of Antiquaries, June, 1797.
Archaeologia, XIII, 1800

(*These 'weapons of war' were flint hand-axes, characteristic tools of the early Stone Age, and John Frere, wise before his time, was one of the first men to challenge the views of creation upheld by the supporters of Archbishop Usher who accepted its happening in 4004 B.C.*)

CURE FOR ANTIQUARIES' SPLEEN—

Some few years back, on the opening of a barrow, I was hurried from my repast, in the company of some friends, by three Irish soldiers, who came running out of breath to me with assurance that they had discovered a perfect skeleton, the enormous size of which they pronouncèd, before I reached the spot, to have been the carcase of a prodigious giant. Eager to transport myself to the spot, I arrived panting for breath, when to my great mortification, and check to a curious avidity, I found the bones not exceeding the ordinary human stature. Vexed from my own disappointment, and the exaggerated account of the Hibernians, I seized a thigh-bone from the grave, and, after having made one fellow stand erect, to measure it by his own, I belaboured the fellows with it for their natural promptness to magnify these casual discoveries into the marvellous. It cured my spleen, and I returned in better humour, though somewhat disappointed, to my friends.

TUMBORACUS [JAMES DOUGLAS], *The Gentleman's Magazine*, July,
1789

—AND FOR FLEGME

He had a kindnesse for me and invited me to his house, and told me a great many fine things, both naturall and antiquarian. . . .

He was much troubled with flegme, and being so one winter at the court at Ludlowe (where he was one of the councesellours), sitting by the fire, spitting and spawling, he tooke a fine tender sprig, and tied a ragge at the ende, and conceited he might putt it downe his throate, and fetch-up the flegme, and he did so. Afterwards he made this instrument of whalebone. I have oftentimes seen him use it. I could never make it goe downe my throat, but for those that can, 'tis a most incomparable engine. If troubled by the wind it cures you *immediately*. It makes you vomit without any paine, and besides, the vomits of apothecaries have *aliquid veneni* in them. . . . It is no paine, when downe your throate; he would touch the bottome of his stomach with it.

Of Walter Rumsey: JOHN AUBREY, *Brief Lives, circa* 1680

DELIGHT TO BE IN THE DARKE

William Harvey, M.D., *natus* at Folkestone in Kent . . . added (or was very bountifull in contributing to) a noble building of Roman architecture (of rustique worke, with Corinthian pillasters) as the Physitians' College, *viz.* a great parlour for the Fellowes to meet in, belowe; and a library, above. All these remembrances and building was destroyed by the generall fire.

He was always very contemplative. . . .

He did delight to be in the darke, and told me he could then best contemplate. He had a house heretofore at Combe, in Surrey, a good aire and prospect, where he had caves made in the earth, in which in summer time he delighted to meditate.

He was wont to say that man was but a great mischievous baboon.

He was far from bigotry.

I remember he kept a pretty young wench to wayte on him, which I guesse he made use of for warmeth-sake as king David did, and tooke care of her in his will, as also of his man-servant.

Of William Harvey: JOHN AUBREY, *Brief Lives, circa* 1680

EXTASY AT FINDING IT

Hugo is a substantial Tradesman, but has a strange Itch for Antiquities. Some Months ago, reading in some old Historian, an Account of a bloody Engagement between one of our Saxon Kings and the Danes and that the Saxon and Danish Princes, whose Bodies were plastred with unslack'd Lime were buried in the Top of a Hill, he attentively remark'd the Places mentioned, purchased proper Materials for his Labour, and in the midst of his busiest Season, out he sets on his Expedition. The Field of Battle was not far from London, and at the nearest Town to it he hired Six Country Fellows to assist him; with them he marches to the Place, and found the Description, exactly answering to what he had read, and immediately order'd them to dig. The Lord of the Manor happening to come by, asked him what he was digging for? Hugo told him; the Gentleman wished him Success, and promis'd to send him a Refreshment; which in two Hours was brought him, with Pen, Ink and Paper, and a Request that he would observe the Nature of the Soil every Foot he dug, assuring him if he discover'd Coals, he would present him with 50 Guineas for his Trouble. Hugo return'd him Thanks, and encouraging his Clowns with a chearing Glass, they set briskly to work. At last they turn'd up some whitish, tough Clay and underneath it lay a Bed of something like Chalk. Hugo immediately cry'd out in an Extasy *I have found it*; and having taken off the outer Crust, there lay, as in a Vault, the Skeleton of a large sized Man at his Length, a Sword of an Unusual Size, on his

6

Right Hand, and at his Feet a Spur. Hugo pack'd up these Royal Fragments in his Sack and carried them Home, and then returning ransack'd the other Mount, and found also the Danish Prince. Possessed of these poor Relicks he is no less proud of the Acquisition, than if he had conquer'd them alive.

The Gentleman's Magazine, February, 1732

FOOTING IT

Edward Norgate . . . was very judicious in Pictures, to which purpose he was imployed into *Italy* to purchase them for the Earl of *Arundel*. Returning by Marseilles he missed the money he expected, and being there unknowing of, and unknown to any, he was observed by a French Gentleman . . . to walk in the Exchange . . . of that City, many Hours every Morning and Evening, with swift feet and sad face, forwards and backwards. To him the civil *Monsieur* addressed himself, desiring to know the cause of his discontent, and if it came within the compass of his power, he promised to help him with his best advise. *Norgate* communicated his condition, to whom the other returned, *Take I pray my Counsel, I have taken notice of your walking more than 20 miles a day, in one furlong upwards and downwards, and what is spent in needless going and returning, if laid out in Progressive Motion, would bring you into your own Country. I will suit you (if so pleased) with a light habit, and furnish you with competent money for a Footman.* Norgate very chearfully consented, and footed it (being accommodated accordingly) through the body of France, (being more then *five hundred English miles*) and so leasurely with ease, safety, and health, returned into *England*. He became the best *Illuminer* or *Limner* of our age. He died at the Heralds Office, *Anno Dom.* 1649.

THOMAS FULLER, *History of the Worthies of England*, 1662

GENEROUS THOUGHT

. . . the Honnour I retain for every gentleman of so usefull a Society! & so learn'd! & my intentions of leaving what I have relating to Antiquities too & this I am verry free to shew under my hand; being sensible in so doing that it is a prudent Act to retain them entire after my decease.

THOMAS BROWNSALL to JOHN ORLEBAR, 4 June, 1743. *Society of Antiquaries Correspondence*, XVIII Century file

HABITUAL GRAVITY

He was a good-looking man of the age of sixty, perhaps older, but his hale complexion and his firm step announced that years had not impaired his strength or health. His countenance was of the true Scottish cast, strongly marked, and rather harsh in features, with a shrewd and penetrating eye, and a countenance in which habitual gravity was enlivened by a cast of ironic humour. His dress was uniform, and of a colour becoming his age and gravity; a wig, well dressed and powdered, surmounted by a slouched hat, had something of a professional air. He might be a clergyman, yet his appearance was more that of a man of the world than usually belongs to the Kirk of Scotland, and his first ejaculation put the matter beyond question. . . . Amid this medley, it was no easy matter to find one's way to a chair, without stumbling over a prostrate folio, or the still more awkward mischance of overturning some piece of Roman or ancient British pottery.

SIR WALTER SCOTT, *The Antiquary*, 1816

INFALLIBILITY

It is rather strange that the labours of Dr Borlase, in investigating and describing Cornish antiquities, did not incite a similar desire in other Cornishmen . . . so implicit was the faith in him that it was considered he had described everything in the county worthy of notice. A practical illustration of this sentiment occurred not long ago. In a western parish of Cornwall, some labourers were employed in enclosing waste land, when they came across a stone circle, and suspecting it to be akin to others popularly held in veneration, they hesitated to destroy it, and appealed for advice to a mine captain, who decided that if noticed in Borlase it should be preserved, if not, it should be demolished. The doctor's 'Antiquities' being referred to, and no mention of the circle found, it was at once cleared away.

J. T. BLIGHT, *The Gentleman's Magazine*, July, 1865

JOCUNDISSIMUS

Some years ago the Noviomagian Society visited Cobham Hall, and I went there to meet them. When I arrived they were departing to dine at Gravesend. . . . I at once got into one of the carriages . . . and resigned myself to whitebait, champagne and old friends. . . .

June 30, 1849. The Anniversary of the Noviomagian Club of which I have now been some years a member. . . . We breakfasted with T. Crofton Croker at his house, 3 Gloster Road, Old Brompton. This Society has now been founded twenty-one years, and originated in a meeting of antiquaries at Keston Heath, in Kent, at which the late A. J. Kempe presided on the opening of some ruins and tumuli, an account of which is published in the *Archaeologia*. The bringing together of a few friends of congenial tastes was found to be so very pleasant, that it was determined to meet in London in winter. The Club (named after the Roman Station, Noviomagus, at Keston) was founded at Wood's Hotel, Portugal Street, Lincoln's Inn Fields, Croker President. Today we visited Hampton Court . . . and afterwards dined at the Star and Garter, Richmond Hill.

CHARLES ROACH SMITH, *Retrospections Social and Archaeological*, i, 1883, quoting the *Journey Book of F. W. Fairholt*

(*The Noviomagian Club, or the Noviomagian State as it liked to call itself, was governed by a President, a Vice-President, Secretary and Treasurer, and each ordinary member was given a title which in some way reflected his interests or profession. In 1844, for instance, the Club included a Father Confessor, Lord Chancellor, Chinese Professor, Lord Seneschal, Comptroller General, Phoenician Professor, Architect, Extraordinary Physician, Draftsman-in-Ordinary, and Lord High Admiral. The High President's chair, an interesting piece of Elizabethan furniture, stands on the stairs of the Society of Antiquaries' apartments in Burlington House. The Club was dissolved in 1908. An extract from its Minutes in 1844 appears on pages 27 and 98.*)

KNOWLEDGE OF PLACES, TIMES AND PEOPLE

William Somner . . . was born on the 30. day of *March* 1606 within the Parish of *St Margaret's* in the City of *Canterbury*. A fit birth-place for an Antiquary: *this being one of the most ancient Cities in England*. And like a true Patriot, he prov'd his natural affection, and repaid his nativity by giving it a new birth. He restor'd the perisht ruines, and brought back all its pristine glories. *For his thoughts and affections having ever much inclin'd him to the search and study of Antiquities, he did more particularly, as bound in duty and thankfulness, apply himself to the Antiquities of Canterbury.*

He was so well pleas'd with his lot of breathing first in this fair ground, that neither mind nor body could be mov'd to any distance from it. . . .

Fashions he despised abroad, and learning he would have at home. So that here in studious content, he took up his cradle, his mansion, and his grave.

He lov'd much, and much frequented the *Cathedral* services; where after his devotions were paid, he had a new zeal for the honour of the *House*, walking often in the *Nave*, and in the more recluse parts, not in that idle and inadvertent posture, nor with that common and trivial discourse, with which those *open Temples* are vulgarly prophan'd: but with a curious and observant eye, to distinguish the age of the buildings, to sift the ashes of the dead; and, in a word, to eternise the memory of things and Men. His visits within the City were to find out the Ancestors, rather than the present inhabitants; and to know the genealogy of houses, and walls, and dust. When he had leisure to refresh himself in the Suburbs and the fields, it was not mearly for digestion, and for air; but to survey the *British bricks*, the *Roman ways*, the *Danish hills* and *works*, the *Saxon Monasteries* and the *Norman Churches*. At the digging up foundations, and other descents into the bowels of the earth, he came often to survey the Workmen; and to purchase from them the treasure of Coins, Medals, and other buried Reliques. . . . Whenever he relaxt his mind to any other recreation, it was to that of shooting with the long bow.

This was his diversion: but his more constant delight was in *classic Historians*, in old *Manuscripts, Leiger-books, Rolls* and *Records*. . . . And truly I know no one part of humane learning, than can render any Man a more agreeable Companion, and a more beneficial friend, than this knowledge of places, times, and people.

WHITE KENNETT, 1693, in a Preface to WILLIAM SOMNER'S *Gavelkind*, 1726

LOVE OF THE MOULDY

He is a man strangely thrifty of time past, and an enemy indeed to his maw, whence he fetches out many things when they are now all rotten and stinking. He is one that hath that unnatural disease to be enamoured of old age and wrinkles, and loves all things (as Dutchmen do cheese), the better for being mouldy and worm-eaten. He is of our religion, because we say it is most ancient; and yet a broken statue would almost make him an idolater. A great admirer he is of the rust of old monuments, and reads only those characters, where time hath eaten out the letters. He will go you forty miles to see a saint's well or a ruined abbey; and there be but a cross or a stone foot-stool in the way, he'll be considering it so long, till he forget his journey. His estate consists much in shekels, and Roman coins; and he hath more pictures of Caesar than James or Elizabeth. Beggars cozen him with musty things which they have raked from dunghills, and he preserves their rags for precious relics. He loves no library, but where there are more spiders' volumes than authors', and looks with great admiration on the antique work of cob-webs. Printed books he contemns, as a novelty of this latter age, but a manuscript he pores on everlastingly, especially if the cover be all moth-eaten, and the dust make a parenthesis between every syllable. He would give all the books in his study (which are rarities all) for one of the old Roman binding, or six lines of Tully in his own hand. His chamber is hung commonly with strange beasts' skins, and is a kind of charnel-house of bones extraordinary; and his discourse upon them, if you will hear him, shall last longer. His very attire is that which is the eldest out of fashion, and his hat is as antient as the tower of Babel. He never looks upon himself till he is grey-haired, and then he is pleased with his own antiquity. His grave does not fright him, for he has been used to sepulchres, and he likes death the better, because it gathers him to his fathers.

JOHN EARLE, *Microcosmographie or A Piece of the World Discovered in Essays and Characters*, ed. ED. BLOUNT, 1628

MODEST NEEDS

Romano British 2nd century face mask incinerary urn. Perfect condition. Exchange gold Omega Seamaster.

The Times, November 19, 1958

Sedan chair required to enable two old people to visit each other, Wiltshire; museum pieces and fancy prices not entertained.

The Times, March 14, 1949

Wanted for decorative purposes, five human skulls. Also massive ornate inexpensive Victorian cast-iron garden furniture in Gothic and Rustic designs.

The Tablet, June 5, 1949

. . . his last request was to be buried at Mucking, Essex, where the rubbish his firm collected was disposed of on the marshes.

Evening News, February 17, 1952

NIMBLE PEN

A most remarkable [parish] clerk lived at Grafton Underwood in the eighteenth century, one Thomas Carley, who was born in that village, in 1755, having no hands and one deformed leg. Notwithstanding that nature seemed to have deprived him of all means of manual labour, he rose to the position of parish schoolmaster and parish clerk. He contrived a pair of leather rings, into which he thrust the stumps of his arms, which ended at the elbow, and with the aid of these he held a pen, ruler, knife and fork, etc. The register books of the parish show admirable specimens of his wonderful writing. . . . He died in 1823.

P. H. DITCHFIELD, The Parish Clerk, 1907

OBSTINACY

The late Mr Gostling, of Canterbury, was a worthy man, and well respected for his good-nature and pleasantry; but, at the same time, he was very sanguine, and not a little opinionated, insomuch that, when he had taken a thing into his head, it was not an easy matter to drive it out. He was a great collector of antiquities; and, in a long life, had amassed a considerable number of curious antique articles. Amongst other matters, he had gotten a piece of household furniture, of copper, which he was pleased to call a *curfew*; and his friends, on account of his years and good-humour, did not care to contradict him. . . .

T. ROW, The Gentleman's Magazine, August, 1779

PRIME DUTY

The prime duty of the field archaeologist is to collect and set in order material with not all of which he can deal at first hand. In no case will the last word be with him; and just because that is so his publication of the material must be minutely detailed, so that from it others may draw not only corroboration of his views but fresh conclusions and more light. . . . It is true that he may not possess any literary gifts, and that, therefore, the formal presentation of results to the public may be better made by others; but it is the field archaeologist who, directly or indirectly, has opened up for the general reader new chapters in the history of civilised man; and by recovering from the earth such documented relics of the past as strike the imagination through the eye, he makes real and modern what otherwise might seem a far-off tale.

SIR LEONARD WOOLLEY, Digging Up the Past, 1930, Ernest Benn Ltd.

PUBLICITY OF WHEELER'S

Our more conventional archaeological friends sometimes raised their eyebrows and sniffed a little plaintively at 'all this publicity of Wheeler's'! But we were not deterred, and we were right; right not merely because this same public was incidentally contributing in gifts no small part of our considerable funds, but because I was, and am, convinced of the moral and academic necessity of sharing scientific work to the fullest possible extent with the man in the street and in the field. Today, in 1954, he is in fact our employer. Today, ninety per cent of the money spent on field-archaeology in Great Britain comes from our rates and taxes. That was not so in 1934; it might easily not be so now had we, and others like us, not deliberately built up a popular mood to which such expenditure was no longer wholly alien. It was not the least of the results of Maiden Castle that this mood of sympathy and half-understanding was by 1937 in the ascendant. Earlier phases had been manifest at Caerleon and elsewhere, when competitive journalism had whipped up public interest as a rather exotic stunt. Now the public was beginning to come to us of its own volition, the mountain was coming to Mahomet. But it did not come through the unprovoked force of gravity!

SIR MORTIMER WHEELER, *Still Digging—Interleaves from an Antiquary's Notebook*, 1955, Michael Joseph Ltd.

QUARRELS AT STRAWBERRY HILL

Strawberry Hill, July 28, 1772.

I am anew obliged to you, as I am perpetually, for the notice you give me of another intended publication against me in the *Archaeologia*, or *Old Woman's Logic*. By your account, the author will add much credit to their Society! For my part, I shall take no notice of any of his *handycrafts*. However, as there seems to be a willingness to carp at me, and as gnats may on a sudden provoke one to give a slap, I choose to be at liberty to say what I think of the learned Society; and therefore I have taken leave of them, having so good an occasion presented as their council on Whittington and his Cat, and the ridicule that Foote has thrown on them. They are welcome to say anything on my writings, but that they are the works of a fellow of so foolish a Society.

H. W. *The Letters of Horace Walpole*, LXXXIX, The Antiquarian Society, to The REVD WILLIAM COLE. Everyman ed., 1948 printing, 132, J. M. Dent and Sons Ltd.

13

RELAXATIONS

I rather think the *Aqua Fortis* which I use copiously in my copper plates has at times injured my health—and by way of relaxation from the dry study of antiquity I have published two small works of 3 vols. each. It has been a kind of *novel mania* in which I have been engaged—but thank God I hope I am now effectually cleared of the delirium—at least I promise you that I am now a convalescent. One of the works is called *Fashionable Infidelity* and the other the *Maid of Kent*. In this latter I have made a Sir Simon Hales the Hero. A very accidental thing—I assure you—I had no kind of personal [torn] whatever to the Kentish family of that name [torn] had printed the first volume before I had [torn] that such a family did recently exist in the county. I trust it will not be taken as [illegible] but if it should be, I dare say the similarity of character will not fit. These books I have published with a good intent of introducing a better kind of a thing for the amusement of families than the stupid trash which circulating libraries teem with. But whether I have been successful I must leave to veteran critics, or rather the *blue stocking club* to decide.

JAMES DOUGLAS to H. G. FAUSSETT, 5 May, 1790. Society of
Antiquaries *Manuscript* 723

SOCIETATIS ANTIQUARIORUM LONDINENSIS
The Society of Antiquaries—

The antiquarian society is conducted on a very extensive plan, and it is now become one of our most fashionable rendesvous's—Instead of old square toes you now behold smooth faces, and dainty thin shoes with ponderous buckles on them. Our precedent is My Lord Leicester.

I wish, my Dear Sir, you would take a trip to town and enquire how these things are—I do not know any one who I should be so heartily glad to see.

JAMES DOUGLAS to H. G. FAUSSETT, 4 February, 1785. Society of
Antiquaries *Manuscript* 723

—and an Election Meeting

We have had much serious business debated at our Society on this last Council election, etc. I was honoured with a *Scrutatorship* and kept seven hours without my dinner casting up votes till my eyes struck fire and the colic seized my bowels for the want of food. This aerial repast you may say is bad for an hungry antiquary—but what of that, my zeal, my zeal! and oh my patience under such affliction of long and fustian speeches amply rewarded my labours—we sat down at ½ past eight I should say 9 to a good dinner and plenty of wine carousing till ½ past one at the Devil Tavern—and as a certain wit replied on that occasion, that the Society *was broke up and gone to the devil.*

JAMES DOUGLAS to H. G. FAUSSETT, 25 April, 1785. Society of Antiquaries *Manuscript* 723

(*The Bicentenary of the Society's Royal Charter was celebrated in 1957.*)

TALENTS FOR CONVERSATION

In London several regular and known meetings are held of literary characters, who converse upon philosophical subjects, new discoveries, etc. One of the chief of them takes place between the hours of seven and nine every Thursday evening, during the meeting of the Royal and Antiquarian Societies, in an outer room of the apartments in Somerset-House, appropriated for their reception, and it is exceedingly interesting to every intelligent stranger, who feels any degree of scientific and literary curiosity. About seven those gentlemen drop in who mean to assist at the meeting of the Society of Antiquaries. The members of the Royal Society enter at eight, when the conversations, turning chiefly on philosophical subjects, are renewed and prolonged till nine. A stranger may be introduced to these conversations by any member of either of the two societies. He will not elsewhere obtain so advantageous an idea of the union of politeness, scientific intelligence, and talents for conversation, in the English character.

N. PHILLIPS, *Mirror of London*, 1804

TOM'S TALE: UNDERSTANDING WITH VIRTUE

Some antiquarians grave and loyal,
Incorporate by charter royal,
Last winter, on a Thursday night, were
Met in full senate at the Mitre.
The president, like Mr. Mayor,
Majestic took the elbow chair;
And gravely sat in due decorum,
With a fine gilded mace before him.
Upon the table were display'd
A British knife without a blade,

15

A comb of Anglo-Saxon real,
A patent with King Alfred's seal
Two rusted mutilated prongs,
Suppos'd to be St. Dunstan's tongs,
With which he, as the story goes,
Once took the devil by the nose.

Awhile they talk'd of ancient modes,
Of manuscripts, and Gothic codes,
Of Roman altars, camps and urns,
Of Caledonian shields and churns;
Whether the Druid slipt or broke
The misletoe upon the oak?
If Hector's spear was made of ash?
Or Agammemnon wore a sash?
If Cleopatra dress'd in blue,
And wore her tresses in a queue?

At length a dean who understood
All that had pass'd before the flood,
And could in half a minute shew ye
A pedigree as high as Noah
Got up, and with a solemn air,
First humbly bowing to the chair,
'If aught,' says he, 'deserves a name
Immortal as the roll of fame,
This venerable group of sages
Shall flourish in the latest ages,
And wear an amaranthine crown
When kings and empires are unknown.
Perhaps e'en I whose humbler knowledge
Ranks me the lowest of your college,
May catch from your meridian day
At least a transitory ray:
For I, like you, through ev'ry clime,
Have trac'd the step of hoary Time,
And gather'd up his sacred spoils
With more than half a cent'ry's toils.
Whatever virtue, dead, or name,
Antiquity has left to fame,
In ev'ry age, and ev'ry zone,
In copper, marble, wood, or stone,
In vases, flow'r-pots, lamps, and sconces,

16

Intaglios, cameos, gems, and bronzes,
These eyes have read through many a crust
Of lacker, varnish, grease, and dust;
And now, as glory fondly draws
My soul to win your just applause,
I here exhibit to your view
A medal fairly worth Peru,
Found, as tradition says, at Rome,
Near the Quirinal Catacomb.'

He said, and from a purse of satin,
Wrapp'd in a leaf of monkish latin,
And taught by many a clasp to join,
Drew out a dirty copper coin.
Still as pale midnight when she throws
On heaven and earth a deep repose,
Lost in a trance too big to speak,
The Synod ey'd the fine antique;
Examin'd ev'ry point and part,
With all the critic skill of art;
Rung it alternate on the ground,
In hopes to know it by the sound;
Apply'd the tongue's acuter sense
To taste its genuine excellence,
And with an animated gust
Lick'd up the consecrated rust:
Nor yet content with what the eye
By its own sun-beams could descry,
To ev'ry corner of the brass
They clapp'd a miscroscopic glass;
And view'd in raptures o'er and o'er
The ruins of the learned ore.

Pythagoras, the learned sage,
As you may read in Pliny's page,
With much of thought, and pains, and care,
Found the proportions of a square,
Which threw him in such frantic fits
As almost robb'd him of his wits,
And made him, awful as his name was,
Run naked through the streets of Samos.
With the same spirits Doctor Romans,
A keen civilian of the Commons,

Fond as Pythagoras to claim
The wreath of literary fame,
Sprung in a phrensy from his place
Across the table and the mace,
And swore by Varo's shade that he
Conceiv'd the medal to a T.
'It rings,' says he, 'so pure, and chaste,
And has so classical a taste,
That we may fix its native home
Securely in imperial Rome,
That rascal, Time, whose hand purloins
From science half her kings and coins,
Has eat, you see, one half the tale,
And hid the other in a veil:
But if, through cankers, rust, and fetters,
Mishapen forms, and broken letters,
The critic's eye may dare to trace
An evanescent name, and face,
This injur'd medal will appear,
As mid-day sunshine, bright and clear.
The female figure on a throne
Of rustic work in Tiber'stone,
Without a sandal, zone, or boddice,
Is Liberty's immortal goddess;
Whose sacred fingers seem to hold
A taper wand, perhaps of gold;
Which has, if I mistake not, on it
The Pileus, or Roman bonnet:
By this the medallist would mean
To paint that fine domestic scene,
When the first Brutus nobly gave
His freedom to the worthy slave.'

   When a spectator's got the jaundice,
Each object, or by sea, or land, is
Discolour'd by a yellow hue,
Though naturally red, or blue:
This was the case with 'squire Thynne,
A barrister of Lincoln's Inn,
Who never lov'd to think or speak
Of any thing but ancient Greek:
In all disputes his sacred guide was
The very venerable Suidas;

And though he never deign'd to look
In Salkeld, Littleton, or Coke,
And liv'd a stranger to the fees
And practice of the Common-Pleas:
He studied with such warmth, and awe,
The volumes of Athenian law,
That Solon's self no better knew
The legislative plan he drew;
Nor could Demosthenes withstand
The rhet'ric of his wig, and band;
When, full of zeal, and Aristotle,
And fluster'd by a second bottle,
He taught the orator to speak
His periods in correcter Greek.

 'Methinks,' quoth he, 'this little piece
Is certainly a child of Greece:
Th' AErugo has a tinge of blue
Exactly of the Attic hue:
And, if the taste's acuter feel
May judge of medals as of veal,
I'll take my oath the mould and rust
Are made of Attic dew and dust.
Critics may talk, and rave, and foam,
Of Brutus, and imperial Rome,
But Rome, in all her pomp and bliss,
Ne'er struck so fine a coin as this.
Besides, though Time, as is his way,
Has eat the inscription quite away,
My eye can trace, divinely true,
In this dark curve a little Mu:
And here, you see, there seems to lie
The ruins of a Doric Xi.
Perhaps, as Athens thought, and writ
With all the pow'rs of style, and wit,
The nymph upon a couch of mallows
Was meant to represent a Pallas;
And the baton upon the ore
Is but the olive-branch she bore.'

 He said—but Swinton, full of fire
Asserted that it came from Tyre:

A most divine antique he thought it,
And with an empire would have bought it,
He swore the head in full profile was
Undoubtedly the head of Belus;
And the reverse, though hid in shade,
Appear'd a young Sidonian maid,
Whose tresses, buskins, shape, and mien,
Mark'd her for Dido at sixteen;
Perhaps the very year when she was
First married to the rich Sichaeus.
The rod, as he could make it clear,
Was nothing but a hunting spear,
Which all the Tyrian ladies bore,
To guard them when they chac'd the boar.
A learned friend, he could confide on,
Who liv'd full thirty years at Sidon,
Once shew'd him, 'midst the seals and rings
Of more than thirty Syrian kings,
A copper piece, in shape and size,
Exactly that before their eyes,
On which in high relief was seen
The image of a Tyrian queen;
Which made him think this other dame
A true Phoenician, and the same.

The next a critic, grave and big,
Hid in a most enormous wig,
Who in his manners, mien, and shape was
A genuine son of Esculapius,
Wonder'd that men of such discerning
In all th'abstruser parts of learning,
Could err, through want of wit or grace,
So strangely in so plain a case.

'It came,' says he, 'or I will be whipt,
From Memphis in the Lower Egypt;
Soon as the Nile's prolific flood
Has fill'd the plains with slime and mud,
All Egypt in a moment swarms
With myriads of abortive worms,
Whose appetites would soon devour
Each cabbage, artichoke, and flow'r.
Did not some birds, with active zeal,

Eat up whole millions at a meal,
And check the pest, while yet the year
Is ripening into stalk and ear.
This blessing, visibly divine,
Is finely pourtray'd on the coin;
For here this line, so faint and weak,
Is certainly a bill or beak;
Which bill or beak, upon my word,
In hieroglyphics means a bird,
The very bird whose num'rous tribe is
Distinguish'd by the name of Ibis.
Besides the figure with the wand,
Mark'd by a sistrum in her hand,
Appears, the moment she is seen,
An Isis, Egypt's boasted queen.
Sir, I'm as sure as if my eye
Had seen the artist cut the die,
That these two curves which wave and float thus,
Are but the tendrils of the Lotus,
Which, as Herodotus has said,
Th' Egyptians always eat for bread.'

He spoke, and heard, without a pause,
The rising murmur of applause;
The voice of admiration rung
On ev'ry ear from ev'ry tongue:
Astonish'd at the lucky hit,
They star'd, they deify'd his wit.

But ah! what arts by fate are tried
To vex, and humble human pride?
To pull down poets from Parnassus,
And turn grave doctors into asses!
For whilst the band their voices raise
To celebrate the sage's praise,
And echo through the house convey's
Their paeans loud to man and maid;
Tom, a pert waiter, smart, and clever,
Adroit pretence who wanted never,
Curious to see what caus'd this rout,
And what the doctors were about,
Slyly stepp'd in to snuff the candles,
And ask whate'er they pleas'd to want else.

Soon as the Synod he came near,
Loud dissonance assail'd his ear;
Strange mingled sounds, in pompous style,
Of Isis, Ibis, Lotus, Nile:
And soon in Romans' hand he spies
The coin, the cause of all their noise,
Quick to his side he flies amain,
And peeps, and snuffs, and peeps again;
And though antiques he had no skill in,
He knew a sixpence from a shilling;
And, spite of rust, or rub, could trace
On humble brass Britannia's face,
Soon her fair image he discries,
And, big with laughter, and surprise,
He burst—'And is this group of learning
So short of sense, and plain discerning,
That a mere halfpenny can be
To them a curiosity?
If this is your best proof of science,
With wisdom Tom claims no alliance;
Content with nature's artless knowledge;
He scorns alike both school and college.'

More had he said—but, lo! around
A storm in ev'ry face he found:
On Romans' brow black thunders hung,
And whirlwinds rush'd from Swinton's tongue;
Thynne lightning flash'd from ev'ry pore,
And reason's voice was heard no more,

The tempest ey'd, Tom speeds his flight,
And, sneering, bids 'em all good night;
Convinc'd that pedantry's allies
May be too learned to be wise.

JAMES CAWTHORN, 1721–61

(*The Society of Antiquaries met at the Mitre Tavern, Fleet Street, from 1718 to 1726, then, as now, on a Thursday. The 'fine gilded mace' must have been that sixteenth century military mace which by 1819 had become too shabby for official use and therefore discarded.*)

22

WOMEN AND ANTIQUITY
Sir John's Wife

When his daughter-in-lawe returned home from visiting her neighbours, he would alwaies aske her what of antiquity she had heard or observed, and if she brought home no such account, he would chide her (jestingly).

Of Sir Henry Spelman: John Aubrey's *Brief Lives*, *circa* 1680

An Obliging Landlady

At All-Saints, or Lower Glisset, there was a small ale-house, and the only one hereabouts (The Rose): my old landlady after some discourse preparatory, informed me that at Boroston, a mile lower upon the river, had been an old city; and that strangers had come out of their way on purpose to see it; that ruins and foundations were there; that it had seven parish-churches, which were beaten down in the war time; that many old coins had been ploughed up when she was a girl, which the children commonly played withall; but the case at present was plainly the same with that of old Troy, described in the ballad upon her wall, where she showed me these passionate verses,

> *Waste lie those walls that were so good,*
> *And corn now grows where Troy towers stood.*

This account, so natural, satisfied me that *Vindogladia* must here be fixed, and Wimbornminster robbed of that honour, where the tide of antiquarians have hitherto carried it, for no other reason but name sake; the distances and road being repugnant. I suppose the name signifies the white river, or vale; *vint*, white; *gladh*, a river; whence our glade, or valley where a river runs. This place being not capable of affording me a proper mansion, I left the more particularly scrutiny of it for another opportunity.

William Stukeley, *Itinerarium Curiosum*, 1776 ed., Iter VII

Our Fair Countrywomen

Although the morning of Tuesday was lowering and extremely unpropitious for opening the Saxon barrows, agreeably to the arrangements of the General Committee as stated in the Programme—nevertheless, nearly two hundred ladies and gentlemen assembled about eight miles from Canterbury, at Breach Down, where there is a range of tumuli, eight of which were to be opened and minutely examined.

23

. . . The situation of these tumuli is one of eminent beauty: commanding a vale, of which the boundaries are charmingly varied by graceful woods and undulating hills; while a gentle *Bourne* meandering through pastures and gardens—amongst which occasionally peeps a cottage or a steeple—gives light and life to a landscape, possessing in rare perfection, all those rural and quiet graces so characteristic of English scenery.

The down was barren—where lay the tumuli—the lone half-obliterated memorials of the existence of a race who once with bounding pulses were the dwellers on the heights and in the glens of this vicinity. The viewless wind, as it swept in fitful gusts over the burial-place of the slumberers beneath, seemed to whisper of the deeds which 'they in mortal coil had done' and an impending storm also might be imagined to be a token of disapprobation from

'The guardian phantom of the spirits of the grave'

at the proceedings of the disentombers. The spell of fancy once in action, associations connected with that spot of ground invariably crowded upon the mind—and pictured scenes of grief and agony—the ebbing of the full tide of earthly emotions—the extinguishment of the fire of ardent passion—the severance of ties of parental affection and the devotedness of friendship—as the chill silence of the obstructive tomb inclosed the remains of some much-loved dear ones. . . .

Hardly were the examinations commenced, when a thick mist spread over the valley below—which shortly after was succeeded by a general drenching rain. In despite of this untoward occurrence, the unsheltered archaeologists, through whom

'the storm riddled right merrilie'

unflinchingly pursued those investigations after

'Remnants of things which have passed away'

which many of them had travelled hundreds of miles to witness. Nor was the gentler sex deterred by the *contretemps* from anxiously hovering at the brink of the graves, lest they should miss any discovery of articles

'fashioned by long-forgotten hands'.

Vainly did the noble president entreat the ladies to seek the only shelter the bleak downs afforded—that of a windmill—he was met with the observation 'that the loss of a dress which could easily be replaced was of trifling consideration compared with the equally interesting and instructive researches in which they were engaged'. . . .

It was indeed delightful to notice the feeling with which our fair

24

countrywomen, made for once participators in an intellectual pursuit with their husbands, fathers, brothers and friends, examined every ancient memorial disenterred from the universal Mother, Earth. When the sky cleared up . . . those few ladies who had embraced the miller's offer, crowded round the tumuli and almost passionately expressed their gratification, as beads, and the wire on which they were strung, or amulet, or ring, or armlet was handed to them for inspection. Report of the Proceedings of the British Archaeological Association at the First General Meeting, Canterbury, 1844. Edited by ALFRED JOHN DUNKIN, 1845

(For further remarks on this archaeological beanfeast, see pages 25-27, 143 and 202.)

Fine Ladies Soiled

The First Archaeological Congress
The Meeting of the British Archaeological Association at Canterbury
September, 1844

My dear brother Bob,
  This is the scud, that took place in the mud,
    While we sat and looked on from the carriage;
  Such a dash was not seen, such a splash has not been,
    My dear Bob, since the day of my marriage.

  Fine ladies so soiled, as onward they toiled,
    While Professors so grave grubbed away;
  Would have made you declare, had you only been there,
    It was ten times as good as a play.

  There were clergy in cloaks, cutting all kinds of jokes,
    (For many were far from their homes;)
  There were 'cutters' and 'pasters' and some sketch-book wasters,
    All intending to make weighty tomes.

  My Lady Montresor, was pleased beyond measure,
    And the President-esses no less;
  Such fun was ne'er seen, on Breach Down or Green,
    Since the rollicking days of Queen Bess.

  Such draggling of skirts! such giggling of flirts,
    As you see in a storm in Hyde Park;
  With no end of umbrellas, to shelter the Fellows,
    Who seemed bent upon digging till dark.

25

The 'Buckland' Professor, a very great messer,
　　In clay, and in rubble, and chalk;
Jumped into a grave, some relick to save,
　　And there held a pretty long talk.

Sir William Beetham, of course too was with'em,
　　It's nothing without 'Ulster King';
How he handled the thigh-bones, and other queer dry bones,
　　Sometimes shouting out—'No such thing!'

There were Nancy and Sally (not she of 'our alley'),
　　But the fat, fair, and frisky, Miss Tibbs;
A rale antiquary, (so said Irish Aunt Mary),
　　Since the moment she left off her bibs.

Then the chuckles o'er buckles, as down on their knuckles,
　　They picked up little odd bits of brass;
The clowns standing round, asking what they had found,
　　If coins? and they thought they would pass.

Of the two Secretaries, we heard nothing but 'Where is—'
　　Their names being lost in the bustle;
I rather suppose they were absent, because,
　　They liked not with Boreas to tussle.

While sly Pettigrew (for he very well knew
　　It would rain) kept his mummy away,
Having promised on Friday, that should it prove wet or dry day,
　　Mummy HAR should then moisten his clay.

So there we sat still, half a mile from the mill,
　　And a 'right merrie' trio we were;
And when to the Bourne, all horses they turn,
　　Why we were the first to be there.

Shall I tell you for why? we saw by the sky
　　There would be no change in the weather;
So instead of staying last, we chose to ride fast,
　　And not all come to luncheon together.

The best of good feeding, with true courtly breeding,
　　Was prepared for us all at Bourne Park;
Had the party been weeded, to say truth it needed,
　　We could gladly have staid there 'till dark.

But all things must end, and so, my dear friend,
  Did this very enjoyable day;
Should kind fate, my dear brother, grant me such another,
  May you not be miles far away.

Minutes of the Noviomagian Club, December 18, 1844
(For the Noviomagian Club, see page 9.) *(Mr Pettigrew added to the company's delight by obligingly unwrapping a mummy after dinner.)*

Propriety

By way of epilogue I may perhaps venture a short word on the question much discussed in certain quarters, whether in the work of excavation it is a good thing to have cooperation between men and women. I have no intention of discussing whether or no woman possesses the qualities best suited for such work: opinions, I believe, vary on the point, but I have never seen a trained lady excavator at work, so that my view if expressed would be valueless. Of a mixed dig, however, I have seen something, and it is an experiment that I would be reluctant to try again. I would grant if need be that women are admirably fitted for the work, yet I would uphold that they should undertake it by themselves.

My reasons are twofold. . . . In the first place there are the proprieties . . . not only of those that rule in England or America, but those of the lands where it is proposed to dig . . . the work of an excavator on the dig and off it lays on those who share in it a bond of closer daily intercourse than is conceivable . . . between men and women, except in chance cases, I do not believe that such close and unavoidable companionship can ever be other than a source of irritation; at any rate I believe that however it may affect women, the ordinary male at least cannot stand it . . . mixed digging I think means loss of easiness in the atmosphere and consequent loss of efficiency. A minor . . . objection lies in one particular form of constraint . . . moments will occur on the best regulated dig when you want to say just what you think without translation, which before the ladies, whatever their feelings about it, cannot be done.

J. P. Droop, *Archaeological Excavation*, 1915, Cambridge University Press

Out with the Cambrians

Long ago when I first made my appearance among those learned people who journey so slowly in wagonettes I remember that an experienced friend urged me 'to keep with the Cambrians', by which she meant to keep well to the front when lecturers were speaking, or enthusiasts were taking rubbings of inscriptions or examining effigies, and recognised authorities on early camps were exhibiting plans; and never to lag behind with jolly camp followers who regarded archaeological excursions in the light of a picnic. But to 'keep with Cambrians' and be a Cambrian requires strength in addition to enthusiasm, for a true Cambrian never finds it wearisome to descend from a motorcoach only five minutes after taking a seat which promises to be comfortable; nor should such a one find it exhausting to climb under the midday sun to the highest point of a hill-fort like Caer Twr, which crowns a rocky height above the Irish Sea; and should be cheerfully ready to scale any number of stone walls in order to reach the remains of early British dwellings. Moreover, a Cambrian should never grow weary of looking at celts, cinerary urns or beakers, and certainly should never wander off to search for a gipsy's grave when there is a chance of entering a chambered tomb. And naturally such an enthusiast never misses a single excursion or evening lecture, and should be amongst the first away from the breakfast-table in order to secure a front seat on a leading motor-coach.

EVELYN HUGHES, *Out with the Cambrians*, 1934, Williams and Norgate Ltd.

Cure for Marriage

June 19th 1908. At Billesley on the site thought to be that of the old church, was found a stone coffin, with two skulls, and one a woman. The first skull, a man's, supposed to be from the Crusades, and some five or six other coffins were found. She remembered the skeleton with the gold armlet, but that was elsewhere. . . . The tumulus was made by her mother, Miss Fortescue, afterwards Mrs Jackson, between 1828–30. Their father objected to the girls marrying, and let them interest themselves in research, hoping to keep them from becoming loved by some man. . . .

Extract from *Harvey Bloom's Diary* in URSULA BLOOM, *The Elegant Edwardian*, 1957, Hutchinson

Apotheosis

For the rest, something like a hundred assistants and students were associated with the excavation during each of the four seasons. . . . Among these grateful mention must be made of Mrs Aylwin Cotton and Miss K. M. Richardson, who acted as seconds-in-command during the last two seasons . . . of Miss Leslie Scott (Mrs Peter Murray-Threipland), Miss Joan du Plat Taylor, Miss Margaret Whitley, Miss Veronica Seton-Williams, Miss Nancy Champion de Crespigny (Mrs H. Movius), Miss M. Collingridge, Miss Delia Parker, Miss Ione Gedye, Miss Margaret Clay (Mrs J. Lister), Miss Rachel Clay (Mrs A. R. Maxwell-Hyslop). . . .

Extract from a Research Report of the Society of Antiquaries,
1943

XEROPHAGY OPPOSED

A Dinner of the Kent Archaeological Society

Saumons à la Mayonnaise

Salades de Homard à la Rachael

Galantines de Volaille

Anguilles en Aspic

Salad de Saumon à la Tartar

Galantine de Veau

Cotes de Boeuf roti

Quartiers d'Agneau

Pressed Beef

Galantine de Dindon

Pigeon Pies

Veal and Ham Pies

Tongues

Hams

Roast Fowls

Braised Fowls à la Creme

. . . . .

Wine Jelly
Cremes Françaises

. . . . .

Champagne (Roederer)	10s. od.
Moselle	8s. od.
Still Hock	7s. od.
Bucellas	6s. od.
Claret	6s. od.
Sherry	6s. od.
Port	7s. od.

The Bull Hotel, Dartford, Kent. 25th July, 1867

YOUR LITTLE ROOM

Heppington, March 25, 1763

Good Sir,

In return for the favours and civilities I received at Bethnal Green, I have taken the liberty to beg your acceptance of a fibula vestiaria, and some beads, all dug up by myself, about a year ago, at Ash, in this county. If you think they deserve a place in your very valuable and curious collection of antiquities, I shall think myself happy; as, indeed, I shall ever do, if, in consequence of my future searches, I shall be enabled to contribute anything else worthy of your notice.

The only merit these remains pretend to, is their being undoubtedly Roman, and truly genuine; which circumstance, however, makes me prefer them to everything else in my otherwise trifling collection; and, indeed, these I can hardly look upon with pleasure, since I saw your inestimable museum.

I have also presumed to throw my mite into your Dactylotheca. It is a ring, with a small head of the old Pretender; it is reckoned to be very like, and well done; it has been many years in my family. A little picture of Charles II, which, I suppose, was also formerly set in a ring, bears it company; as also a coin, which I look upon to be very curious, and fell into my hands but yesterday. It is an half-penny of the old gentleman above-mentioned, struck in the year 1719, a year before the death of James II. It was found in the pocket of one of the rebels who fell at the battle of Culloden.

If, when you come to put your little room on the top of the stairs to right, you meet with anything which you may think unworthy of a place amongst the great many curiosities it contains, I shall think myself greatly obliged to you for it; as I shall also for any duplicates or refuse coins which may chance to come to your hands; and I shall be glad to purchase from you any such as are more valuable, of which you may happen to have duplicates.

I am sincerely glad to find, by Mr Gretton, that you are so much better; and hope that the course of physic which you are now in, and the return of warm weather, will perfectly restore your health. I shall think it long till I have the pleasure of seeing you in Kent, and hope you will give me as much of your company at Heppington as you can spare.

The four uppermost beads in the box are of amber, and on that account are the more rare. I think it proper to mention to you that they are very brittle, that you may handle them accordingly.

Mrs Faussett joins me in compliments, best wishes, etc.,

I am, Sir,

your obliged humble servant,

Bryan Faussett.

The REVD BRYAN FAUSSETT to EBENEZER MUSSELL: letter in JOHN NICHOLS, *Illustrations of the Literary History of the Eighteenth Century*, v, 1828

(*Mr Ebenezer Mussell who lived near Aldgate and also had a house on Bethnal Green was known to his contemporaries as 'a skilful collector of books and other curiosities'. He re-erected part of the old Aldgate from the City of London close to his house at Bethnal Green, the courtyard of which was paved with bricks from the Roman fort at Richborough.*)

ZENITH AND PLOYS

As archaeologists, then, we are at the same time collectors and interpreters. The obvious next question is, What do we collect and seek to interpret? The question lands us at the outset in a minor quandary from which escape is urgent. Throughout these chapters the term archaeology has been used in the widest possible sense, including equally the study of eolithic choppers and of Victorian gas-lamps. Others are, I am afraid, sometimes less catholic in their usage. The French appear to have evolved a hierarchical distinction between *l'archéologie* and *la préhistoire* that is subtle enough to escape the average foreigner, but we have our British counterpart. From time to time one hears the term 'archaeologist' and 'antiquary', or even that hideous and unnecessary pseudo-noun 'antiquarian', used with a sense of divergence significantly akin to that of 'sheep and goats', or 'chalk and cheese'. The antiquary, it seems, is the more genteel of the two; he sits in a chair and uses a quizzing-glass, or in moments of supreme afflatus crashes upon his knees and rubs a brass. The archaeologist, on the other hand, wears corduroy shorts, strides about on draughty landscapes with a shovel and an odorous pipe, and is liable to be an undergraduate. To

31

these divergent types, might be added a third, the anthropologist, vaguely interested in flagrantly un-British 'natives'. Of course all this dichotomy or trichotomy is nonsense; but there does lurk behind it a nucleus of actuality of a not wholly desirable kind. The common tendency to discriminate archaeologists as prehistorians and antiquaries as medievalists does good to nobody. If anything, it attempts on the one hand to rob prehistory of a little of the humanity that comes more easily to the Middle Ages; and on the other hand to deprive medieval studies excessively of the cold and calculating objectivity that is attributed to the prehistorian. Recently, after training the young members of the staff of one of our Historical Monuments Commissions on a typical prehistoric site, I was glad to see them proceed with the excavation of a medieval site by the identical technique, with fruitful results ranging in period from the eleventh to the seventeenth centuries. And yet how rarely has that simple and obvious procedure been attempted! Let it be agreed that the two words 'archaeologist' and 'antiquary' shall in future be exactly synonymous, rooted in a common discipline and striving by the same or closely similar methods to the same end.

. . . the archaeologist is digging up, not *things*, but *people*.

In a simple direct sense, archaeology is a science that must be lived, must be 'seasoned with humanity'. Dead archaeology is the driest dust that blows.

Sir Mortimer Wheeler, Archaeology from the Earth, 1954,
The Clarendon Press

ANCIENT JAWBONE

An American woman tourist has bought an ancient jawbone found on the site of a Roman township at Northfleet, to take home as a gift for her dentist.

Evening Standard, September 25, 1968

2—ARCHAEOLOGY IN THE OPEN AIR OR, ANTIQUARY ON TOUR

ARCHAEOLOGY IN THE OPEN AIR
OR, ANTIQUARY ON TOUR

All among the Barrows
The face of the country
Hints to the Travelling Antiquary
Too much Travel?
Sunset any Hour
The Wonders of Wilt-shire: Stone-henge
Stonehenge: a catastrophe
  The Kentish View of it
  The Remedy for It
A Roman road at Woodyates
An Honest Topographer
Preservation of Antiquities—
  —a Saxon cross
  —at Newcastle-upon-Tyne
  —and from bombed London
A potte of brasse
Saint in a Barrow
Evil Doers in a Barrow
A Choice Morsel of Antiquity
Mr Wordsworth's *Sonnet*
Stukeley in the field
To dine and lie at a Roman town
Leland's Exeter
Camden's Exeter
Stukeley on Exeter
Walpole on Tour
A Corner of Wales
  (1) Cairarvonshire and Merionithshire
  (2) Pwlh heli
  (3) Ladies from Portland, Oregon
  (4) Ogs and his Shorts
A British Earthwork
A Dorset Trackway
The Romans in London (1)
The Romans in London (2)
The Romans in Leicester
That Marvellous Palimpsest

ALL AMONG THE BARROWS

The third Summer Meeting was held on Thursday, August 20th. The party numbered about 70. . . .

All among the Barrows. Who would not be there! Nevertheless, at this time of the year the path often lies through nettles and thistles. . . . The route is now along the summit of the ridge, towards Blackdown, and for more than half the distance runs on the short grass of the chalk, between barrows on either hand, twenty in number, with near views of multitudes more, including two rows of seven and four, respectively, at right angles to the ridge.

Proceedings Dorset Natural History and Antiquarian Field Club,
vol. XXIX, 1908

THE FACE OF THE COUNTRY

No true history can be written without documents; they are the life-blood of the study. As Lord Acton explained so clearly, history became scientific as it passed from the age of the chronicles to the age of the documents. But there is one document that no historian can neglect except at grave peril, and that is the face of the country. It is not easy to read; to many it conveys neither message nor meaning. The man who would read it must own the tools of the trade. He must have assimilated the main facts of stratigraphical geology and be able to apply them. He must know the principles of transport by water and by land, and what forms of movement are natural and easy, and what are distasteful and difficult. He must know the principles of strategy and tactics, and the conditions that govern the movements of bodies of men. He must have an eye for a military position, and an eye for a commercial position. He must know where and how men lived at different levels of civilization, the conditions that attracted them and the reasons therefor. Above all he must be able to read a map, to appreciate what is significant in geographical control, to have an eye for country and a feeling for landscape. He must love the high places of the earth and have felt 'the tangle of the isles'. And he must remember that this knowledge can be gained in one way and one way only—by tramping the country on his own feet.

But the matter is a still deeper significance. The English people are a people of the open air. From the time of their first landing they avoided towns and sought open villages. The real English stock has never taken kindly to towns, even when circumstances have forced urban life upon it. The Mediterranean type of town has never become acclimatized here. Even now the ideal of English town-planning is the garden-city—

a town that is made to look as little like a town and as much like a bit of the country as it possibly can. So the conclusion is plain. The true life of England is a life of the great spaces and the open air, and the historian who would portray that life rightly must be a man of the open air.

H. J. RANDALL, *History in the Open Air,*
Allen and Unwin Ltd., 1934

HINTS TO THE TRAVELLING ANTIQUARY

If our reader proposes to travel by the first class, and to see the scenery and antiquities, we recommend him to take his seat with his back to the engine, on the far side of the carriage near the window. If it be summer time he may feel no inconvenience from sitting with his face towards the locomotive, especially if he select a carriage as near to the engine as possible; but in dry, hot weather, the hind part of the train is in a cloud of fine penetrating dust, which is irritating to the nose and the lungs. In winter time, when the weather is severe and the landscape shrouded in mist, the centre seat, with the back to the engine, is the most comfortable. If part of a journey is to be performed during darkness, we strongly advise the purchase of a railway lamp. The most perfect one in existence is sold by TUCKER AND SON, OF THE STRAND; it completely answers the intended purpose, and by an ingenious contrivance, the cover of the lamp is a powerful reflector to throw light on the book, and a shade to protect the eyes of the old gentleman in the opposite corner, who, but for this contrivance, would be blinking like an owl in the sunshine; the three hooks securely hold on to the back or door of the carriage, and a screw fastens it, when so required, to the arm of the seat. The portability is extraordinary. . . .

The secret of reading in railway carriages—and the writer has studied several thousand pages while whirled along the iron way—is to prevent the communication of the vibrations of the carriages to the arms and book. The elbows should not, therefore, be rested on the solid parts of the carriage, but the book should be held in both hands, and supported by muscular power; the full elasticity of the arms from the shoulders downwards, acting like carriage springs to the volume; while the head, being balanced on the neck, or at least not pressed or rested against the solid sides of the compartment, is equally free from communicated vibration. When the traveller desires to see much of the country through which the line passes, he cannot do better than select for his conveyance a third-class or parliamentary train, to which first and second class carriages are always attached.

One of the most agreeable means of whiling the tedium of railway travelling is to meet with a sociable fellow-passenger, from whom much information may be derived. . . . Ample topics of conversation will be found in the subject of railways themselves, which at almost every mile present some interesting feature either in the construction of the line itself, or in natural scenery, with its ever-varying character.

GEORGE MEASOM, *The Official Guide to the South-Eastern Railway*,
1858

TOO MUCH TRAVEL?

The art of book-making is rising to the rank of a great social evil. It is one of the worst features of the literary condition of the present age, that such an art should flourish as it appears to do, judging by the specimens which are each week laid upon our table. Whether the evil arises from deficient taste on the part of readers whose appetite is rather vigorous than judicious, and who care not much of what nature be the intellectual food they swallow, so they enjoy an unstinted quantity; or whether it be that the mass of such trash offered to the publishers is so great as to defy all precautions against its admission, and compel them, in spite of all their vigilance, to allow a portion of what is thrust on their attention to be flung upon a literary market by no means understocked . . . we will not attempt to determine. Certain it is, that this book-manufacture is a nuisance which ought not to be inflicted on the public, and an injustice towards authors of a higher and more conscientious class. . . . Travellers enjoy especial facilities for this kind of manufacture. They are always provided with the skeleton into which they may weave the more or less flimsy fabric of their work. They have gone over a certain amount of ground, travelled in vehicles more or less uncomfortable, and seen many places more or less insignificant, about each of which it is possible to say a good deal. Then they have probably visited several inns, and enjoyed a few minutes converse, agreeable or angry, with the landlord of one or more. . . . Then they are tolerably sure of readers, however few.

The Economist, November 20, 1858

SUNSET ANY HOUR

SCENERY, however extensive, viewed through the IMITATION SUNSET GLASSES, appears as if glowing in a beautiful Sunset. Invaluable little boons for viewing scenery.

37

It is better to use two glasses—one to each eye. Post-free by return: the pair, 36 stamps; in best black or white ivory, 60 stamps. Single Glass, 18 and 30 stamps.

G. F. MORTON, ISLINGTON GREEN, LONDON, N.

These glasses have a most beautiful effect at the Crystal Palace, inside and outside the Palace

Advertisement in MURRAY's *Hand-Book to Kent & Sussex*, 1858

THE WONDERS OF WILT-SHIRE: STONE-HENGE

After so many wild and wide conjectures of the Cause, Time, and Authors hereof, why, when and by whom this monument was erected, a *Posthume-book* comes lagging at last, called *Stone-henge restored* [by Inigo Jones, 1655] and yet goeth before all the rest. It is questionable, whether it more modestly propoundeth, or more substantially proveth this to be a *Roman* work, or *Temple* dedicated to *Coelus* or *Coelum*, (son to *Aether* and *Dies*) who was *senior* to all the *Gods* of the *Heathen*.

That it is a *Roman* design he proveth by the *Order*, as also by the *Scheame* thereof, consisting of *four* equilateral Triangles, inscribed within the Circumference of a Circle, an *Architectonicall Scheam* used by the *Romans*; Besides the *Portico* or entrance thereof, is made double, as in the *Roman* ancient Structures of great Magnificence. Not to say that the *Architraves* therein are all set without Morter, according to the *Roman Architecture*, wherein it was ordinary to have *Saxa nullo sulta glutino*.

No less perswasive are his Arguments to prove a *Temple* dedicated to *Coelum*; First, from the *Scituation* thereof, standing in a *plain*, in a free and open Ayre, remote from any village, without woods about it. Secondly, from it's *Aspect*, being *sub dio*, and built without a *roof*; Thirdly, from the *Circular Form* thereof, being the proper Figure of the Temple of *Coelus*; Not to mention his other arguments, in which the Reader may better satisfy himself from the Originall Author, then my second-hand relation thereof.

THOMAS FULLER, *History of the Worthies of England*, 1662

STONEHENGE: A CATASTROPHE

A considerable change has taken place in the position of the stones which form an extraordinary relick of the ancient superstitions of our countrymen. This is attributed to the rapid thaw which succeeded a very hard frost. Some people employed at the plough, near Stonehenge, January 3, remarked that three of the large stones had fallen, and were apprised of the time of their fall by a very sensible concussion, or jarring of the ground. These stones prove to be the western of those pairs, with their imposts, which had the appelation of *Trilithon*; and had long deviated from its true perpendicular. There were, originally, five of these trilithons, two of which are even now still remaining in their ancient state. It is remarkable, that no account has ever been recorded of the falling of the others, and, perhaps, no alteration has been made in the appearance of Stonehenge for three centuries prior to the present tremendous downfall. . . . The destruction of any part of this grand oval we must particularly lament, as it was composed of the most stupendous materials of the whole structure.

The Gentleman's Magazine, January, 1797

The Kentish View of it

Alas, Stonehenge, where were the Genii of the Druidical Temple, while a few rabbets were undermining the stones that had continued upright for no one can tell how many centuries? For, to this cause, and not to a rapid thaw after a high frost, is this catastrophe attributed in a Kentish Gazette.

The Gentleman's Magazine, February, 1797

The Remedy for It

But not all of the fallen stones are in this sense sacrosanct. Within the two outer stone circles, respectively of large local sarsens and small 'bluestones' brought from Wales, are two elements of horseshoe plan, the outer again of sarsen and the inner of bluestone. The sarsen horseshoe consisted of five pairs of huge upright stones, each pair united at the top by a carefully fitted lintel. Of the resultant 'trilithons,' as the eighteenth-century antiquary William Stukeley called them, two are complete, two are incomplete, and the remaining one in its entirety lies prostrate. These great trilithons dominated the whole monument as do their survivors even now; but how much has been lost is demonstrated in an admirable engraving by D. Loggan of about 1675–1700 in the Blackmore Museum at Salisbury.

The engraving shows the now prostrate trilithon still standing as it was built, and shows too how greatly it added to the dignity and intelligibility of the whole scheme. In fact, the trilithon continued to stand until January 3, 1797, when it fell with 'a very sensible concussion, or jarring of the ground,' after a period of gradual subsidence. It is this relatively recent accident that is now to be set right, with all the combined skill of the architects and archaeologists best qualified to undertake such work. The task should be completed by the end of June, and it may be revealed confidentially that the technical operation-order ends with the laconic sentence 'Leave the site perfect'.

SIR MORTIMER WHEELER, Work in Progress at Stonehenge,
The Times, February 26, 1958

A ROMAN ROAD AT WOODYATES

I continued the Roman road for two or three mile, where it is rarely visited: it is very beautiful, smooth on both sides, broad at the top, the holes remaining whence it was taken, with a ditch on each hand: it is made of gravel, flint, or such stuff as happened in the way, most convenient and lasting. There are vast numbers of barrows upon these downs, just of such manner and shapes as those of Salisbury Plain: at the first and most considerable group I came to, there was a most convincing evidence of the Roman road being made since the barrows. . . . Now so it fell out, that the line of direction of the Roman road necessarily carried it over part of one of these *tumuli*, and some of the materials of the road are dug out of it: this has two little tumps in the centre.

WILLIAM STUKELEY, Itinerarium Curiosum, 1776 ed., Iter VII

AN HONEST TOPOGRAPHER

Reader, I am sorry that having not hitherto seen the Cathedral of *Hereford*, I must be silent about the building in this County.

Reader, I must confess myself sorry and ashamed, that I cannot do more right to the Natives of this County [Westmorland] so far distanced North, that I never had yet the opportunity to behold it . . . *Time*, *Tide* and a *Printers-Press*, are *three unmannerly things*, that will *stay for no man*, and therefore I request, that my *defective indeavours* may be well accepted.

I am sorry I have never seen the Cathedrall of *Worcester*, so that I cannot *knowingly* give it a due commendation, and more sorry to hear that our late Civil Wars, have made so sad an Impression thereon.

THOMAS FULLER, History of the Worthies of England, 1662

PRESERVATION OF ANTIQUITIES—
—a Saxon cross

In Willughby town is a handsome cross of one stone, five yards long: in the time of the reforming rebellion the soldiers had tied ropes about it to pull it down; but the vicar persuaded them to commute for some strong beer, having made an harangue to show the innocence thereof.

WILLIAM STUKELEY, *Itinerarium Curiosum*, 1776 ed., Iter V

—at Newcastle-upon-Tyne

Archaeology has now become so favourite a study, and so many young energetic societies have recently engaged in its pursuit, that there is a danger of the older institutions being left behind, if their members do not use their best exertions to keep pace with the rapid advance of this interesting study.

The exertions of the Society have likewise been directed to the preservation of the monuments of antiquity in the neighbourhood. The opening out of the roadway from the High Level Bridge to St. Nicholas' Square has exposed fully to view the well known 'Black Gate', one of the main entrances to the Castle of this town. It was at one time much to be feared that this fine structure would fall a sacrifice to modern convenience, and would be swept away with the surrounding buildings. Against the proposed destruction of this venerable edifice, the Society most energetically appealed to the Corporation, and your Council is happy to report, with signal success. Not only did the Corporation determine to retain the Black Gate entire, but they offered a reward of £50 for the best design for the approach in question, with a clause specially insisting on the preservation of the Black Gate.

Archaeologia Aeliana, new series vol. I, 1857

—and from bombed London

The raids on London continued with the same fierce intensity. Every street was piled high with debris, and this gave Charles an idea. As fast as London was knocked down he bought up loads of brick and stone rubble and had it taken out to the farm, to fill up pot-holes and a pond, to level the farmyard. It made a substantial foundation over which cement and straw could be laid. There were also broken-down walls which had to be repaired, and the services of Mr Hardy were enlisted, who, besides being a first-class builder and handyman, was

41

quite artistic. He could not bear to see the gargoyles and other decorative stone carvings from some of the fine old buildings in London being laid down with the rest of the rubble for the cattle to walk on. Instead he picked out the choicer specimens and mounted them in the cement facings of the walls he was repairing. It looked slightly incongruous to see gargoyles and pious saints' heads of stone, which for centuries had decorated and dignified historic buildings, now cemented into farmyard walls, and looking for all the world as if their bodies had been walled up, leaving only their heads as evidence.

FLORENCE DESMOND, *Florence Desmond, by Herself,* 1953, George G. Harrap and Co. Ltd.

A POTTE OF BRASSE

An old man of Ancaster told me that by Ureby, or Roseby, [Rauceby] a plough man tooke up a stone, and found another stone under it, wherein was a square hole having Romaine quoin in it. He told me also that a plough man toke up in the feldes of Harleston a 2. miles from Granteham a stone, under the wich was a potte of brasse, and an helmet of gold, sette with stones in it, the wich was presentid to Catarine Princes Dowager. There were bedes of silver in the potte: and writings corruptid.

JOHN LELAND, *Itinerary* in 1535–43, Hearne's 2nd ed., 1744–5

SAINT IN A BARROW

Erat itaque in predicta insula tumulus agrestibus glebis coacervatus quem olim avari solitudinis frequentatores lucri gratia illic acquirendi scindebant defodientes, in cuius latere velut cisterna inesse videbatur, in quo vir beate memorie Guthlac desuper imposito tugurio habitare coepit.

FELIX, *Vita S. Guthlaci* in W. DE GRAY BIRCH, *Memorials of S. Guthlac,* 1881

EVIL DOERS IN A BARROW

On the roll of the justices in eyre who sat at Oxford in the year 1261 (Public Record Office, Assize Roll 701, m. 22) is an entry of some archaeological interest:

Duo homines extranei inventi fuerunt occiso sub hoga de Cudes-
lowe. . . . Et testatum est per xii quod malefactores latitant in concavitate
illius hoge, et ibi plures roberie et homicidia fuerunt. Ideo preceptum
est vicecomiti quod prosterni faciat hogam illam.

Two strangers were found killed under the 'how' of Cutteslowe.
The hundred jury testify that evil doers are wont to lurk in the
hollow of the 'how', and that many robberies and homicides have
been committed there. Therefore the sheriff was commanded to
level the 'how'.]

Cutteslowe, today a part of Wolvercote, but formerly a parish of
itself, in Wotton Hundred, lies immediately to the north of Oxford,
between the Cherwell and the main road running from Oxford to
Banbury. . . .

HELEN M. CAM, Antiquity, March 1935

A CHOICE MORSEL OF ANTIQUITY

Travelling lately through Hertfordshire, I was shown a drawing . . .
of the British *torques*; . . .

This choice morsel of antiquity was found in May, 1787, by one
Izaac Bennett, a labourer, upon a farm near Mardox, about 2½ miles
from Ware, in 'hollow ditching,' a piece of land called the Brick-
ground. He discovered it about 2 feet below the surface, lying in a bed
of strong clay, and, through haste in taking it up, broke it.

In a few days after the discovery of this ornament, the labourer
brought it to a watch-maker in Ware; who, desirous of knowing the
fineness of the gold before purchasing it, sent a specimen to London
for the purpose of having it assayed. In the interim, perhaps from a fear
of having it claimed by the lord of the manor, the poor fellow sold his
prize to a Jew for £20 (scarce half its value in metal); and being instantly
consigned to the crucible, every trace of this great curiosity had been
lost; but, fortunately, the watch-maker made a correct drawing of it
while in his possession, preserving also the memoranda from which the
present account is principally composed.

The Gentleman's Magazine, September 1800

MR WORDSWORTH'S SONNET

How profitless the relics that we cull,
Troubling the last holds of ambitious Rome,

Unless they chasten fancies that presume
Too high, or idle agitations lull!
Of the World's flatteries if the brain be full,
To have no seat for thought were better doom,
Like this old helmet, or the eyeless skull
Of him who gloried in its nodding plume,
Heaven out of view, our wishes, what are they?
Our fond regrets, insatiate in their grasp?
The Sages theory? the Poet's lay?
Mere fibulae without a robe to clasp;
Obsolete lamps, whose light no time recalls;
Urns without ashes, tearless lachrymals.
MR WORDSWORTH, in the Album of LORD ALBERT CONYNGHAM.

The Athenaeum, September 21, 1844

STUKELEY IN THE FIELD

Aukborough I visited, because I suspected it the *Aquis* of the Romans,
in *Ravennas*, and I was not deceived; for I presently descried the Roman
castrum. There are two little *tumuli* upon the end of the road entering
the Roman town. The Roman castle is square, three hundred foot
each side, the entrance north: the west side is objected to the steep cliff
overhanging the Trent, which here falls into the Humber; for this
castle is very conveniently placed in the north-west angle of Lincolnshire, as a watch-tower over all Nottinghamshire and Yorkshire, which
it surveys. Here you see the Ouse coming from York, and downward
the Humber mouth, and all over the isle of Axholme. Much salt-marsh
is gained from all these rivers, though now and then they reclaim or
alter their course. Then they discover the subterraneous trees lodged
here at the Deluge in great abundance, along the banks of all the three
rivers: the wood is hard and black and sinks like a stone. Here are likewise other plentiful reliques of the Deluge in the stones, viz. seashells
of all sorts, where a *virtuoso* might furnish his cabinet: sometimes a
stone is full of one sort of shell, sometimes of another; sometimes of
little globules like the spawn of fishes: I viewed them with great
pleasure. I am told the camp is now called Countess Close, and they
say a countess of Warwick lived there; perhaps owned the estate;
but there are no marks of building, nor I believe ever were. The *vallum*
and ditch are very perfect: before the north entrance is a square plot
called the Green, where I suppose the Roman soldiers lay *pro castris*:
in it is a round work, formed into a labyrinth, which they call Julian's
Bower. The church is of good stone, has a square tower, but the choir

ruinous, excluded by a wooden partition: between it and the marshes, a good spring rising out of the cliff. I dare say no antiquary ever visited this place since the Romans left it: for the people were perfectly ignorant of any matters we could enquire about; and as to finding coins, &c. they would make us no other answer than laughing at us, but I heard since, from other good hands, that they have been found here in great numbers.

WILLIAM STUKELEY, *Itinerarium Curiosum*, 1776 ed.

TO DINE AND LIE AT A ROMAN TOWN

From hence I determined to proceed to London all the way on the Roman road, which perhaps has not been so scrupulously travelled upon for this thousand years: the intent, which I executed, was to perform the whole sixth journey in Antoninus his Itinerary; of which I shall give as complete an account as can be expected, considering how totally most of the stations here are erased, and that I was resolved so far to imitate an ancient traveller, as to dine and lie at a Roman town all the way if possible, and sometimes in danger of faring as meanly as a Roman soldier: I doubt not but the reader's candour will overlook the errors or imperfections of this simple narration, of what I could observe myself, and fish out from the uncouth relations of the country people, who, for one half of the way, had never heard of enquiries of this sort since memory, and were too apt to be morose upon that occasion, thinking I had some design upon their farms in my inquisitiveness.

WILLIAM STUKELEY, *Itinerarium Curiosum*, 1776 ed., Iter V

LELAND'S EXETER

The town of Excester is a good mile and more in cumpace, and is right strongly waullid and mainteinid.

Ther be diverse fair towers in the toun waul bytwixt the south and the west gate.

As the waulles have be newly made, so have the old towers decayed.

The castelle of Excester standith stately on a high ground bytwixt the est gate and the north.

Ther be 4. gates in the toune by names of est, west, north and south.

The est and the west gates be now the fairest and of one fascion of building; the south gate hath beene the strongest.

45

There be diverse fair streates in Excester, but the high streate, that goith from the west to the est gate, is the fairest.

In this streate be *castella, aquaeductus, et domus civica.*

There be xv. paroche chirchis in the towne.

The cathedrale chirch of S. Peter and Paule: the cimiterie wherof having 4. gates is environid with many fair housis.

The college house, wher the cantuarie prestes lyith, made of late tyme by John Rese Deane of St. [Bu]rianes.

The Vicares College.

The Carnarie chapelle in [the cemi]tery, made by one John Tr[esurer of] the cathedrale chirch of Ex[cester].

A chapelle/paroch chirch/in the cimiterie.

There was a priorie of S. Nicolas, a celle to Bataille-Abbay, in the north side of the toune.

Joannes de Grandisono Bisshop of Excester made an hospitale of S. John, and endowid it with landes. This hospitale is hard by the est gate.

There is an other poore hospitale in the toun wherin yet sik men be kepte.

There was an house of Gray Freres betwixt the north and west gate neere the towne waulle, now a plain vacant ground caullid Frerenhay.

Bytten Bisshop of Excester remevid thens the Gray Freres, and buildid them an house a litle without the south gate.

There was an house of Blake Freres in the north side of the cemiterie of the cathedrale chirch, but without the close.

The Lorde Russelle hath made hym a fair place of this house.

There appere 2. fragmentes of inscriptions of the Romaines sette by chaunce of later tymes in the towne waulle renewid on the bak side of [this] house sumtyme longging to the Blak Freres. One of the[m stan] dith in a tower of the waul, the other is in [the waull hard by the tower].

The suburbe that lyith without the est gate of Excester is the biggest of al the suburbes of the towne, and berith the name of S. Sithewelle, where she was buried, and a chirch dedicate ther to her name.

The suburbe without the north gate is caullid S. David downe, *alias* . . .

The suburbe without the west gate is caullid S. Thomas suburbe.

In this suburbe is a greate stone bridge of 14. arches over Ex river.

The suburb without the south gate is caullid by the name of S. Magdalene.

Bridges on Ex.

Excester Bridg of xiiii archis

Cowley a mile and more upward, having xii archis undre the Gut and Causey.

Thorberton about a 4. miles upper.

Tuverton Bridge a v. miles upper.

Tuverton Town is on the est ripe of Exe ryver.

JOHN LELAND, *The Itinerary* in 1535–1543, Lucy Toulmin Smith's
ed., 1907

*(Leland also noticed the Cathedral Charter, the books in its Library, its tombs, and
compiled a list of bishops of Exeter.)*

CAMDEN'S EXETER

And now the *Isc* is grown bigger; but dividing into many streams
very convenient for mills, it flows to the City *Isca*, to which it leaves it's
name. Hence Alexander Necham;

> *Exoniae fama celeberrimus Iscia nomen*
> *Praebuit.*

To Exeter the famous *Ex* gives name.

This city is call'd *Isca* by Ptolemy, by Antoninus *Isca Dunmoniorum*
for *Danmoniorum*, by others falsly *Augusta*, as if the second Legion
Augusta had quarter'd there: whereas that was garrison'd in the *Isca
Silurum*, as shall be said hereafter. It was nam'd by the Saxons Exan-
ceaster and *Monketon* from the monks; now at this day it is called
Excester, by the Latins *Exonia*, by the Welsh *Caer-isk, Caer-uth* and
Pen-caer, that is, a chief city. For *Caer* (that I may once for all note it)
signifies a City, in British; hence they call Jerusalem, *Caer Salem*:
Paris, *Caer Paris*; Rome, *Caer Ruffayne*. So Carthage in the Punick
tongue, as Solinus testifies, was call'd *Cartheia*, that is to say, a *new City*.
Among the Syrians likewise I have heard that *Caer* signify'd a city; and
seeing it is took for granted, that the whole world has been peopl'd by
them, it may seem very probable, that they also left their tongue to
posterity, as the mother of future languages. *This city* (as Malmesbury
says) *tho' the ground about it be wet and filthy, and will scarce bear a crop
of bad oats, and often yielding empty ears without grain in them; yet by reason
of it's stateliness, the richness of the citizens, and resort of Strangers, all kind
of merchandise is so plentiful in it, that one need lack nothing there that is
necessary.* It stands on the east side of the *Isc*, upon a hill of easie and
gentle rise to the eastward, and falling again to the west; encompass'd
with a ditch and very strong walls, having many towers between them.
The town is a mile and half in circuit, with suburbs shooting out here
and there for a long way: It contains 15 Parish-Churches, and in the
highest part near the East-gate, has a castle call'd *Rugemount*, formerly

the seat of the West-Saxon Kings, afterward of the Earls of Cornwall; which now has nothing to recommend it, but its antiquity and situation. For it commands the city underneath it, and the country on all sides; and has a very pleasant prospect to the sea. In the east part of the city stands the Cathedral, in the midst of fine houses quite round, built by King Athelstan (as the private history of this place witnesses) in honour to S. Peter, and fill'd with Monks: at last the Monks being remov'd to Westminster, Edward 3 grac'd it with the dignity of being an Episcopal See, having transferr'd the Bishopricks of *Cornwall* and *Kirton* hither; and made *Leofric* the Britain first Bishop of it; whose successors have improv'd the Church both by buildings and revenues. And *William Bruier*, the ninth Bishop after him, in lieu of the displac'd Monks, brought in a Dean and twenty four Prebendaries. In that age, flourish'd *Josephus Iscanus*, who owes his birth and name to this place: a Poet of very lively wit, whose pieces were so highly approv'd of, that they met with as much applause even as the ancients. For his poem of the *Trojan war* has been twice publish'd in Germany under the title of *Cornelius Nepos*.

When *Isca* first fell under the Roman Jurisdiction, does not plainly appear; I am so far from thinking it conquer'd by *Vespasian*, as Geoffery of Monmouth asserts, when under *Claudius* the Emperour, Suetonius tells us he was first shown to the world; that I should think it was hardly then built. Yet in the time of the *Antonines* it was probably very famous; for Antoninus continues his *Itinerary* in these parts to this City and no farther. It fell not absolutely under the dominion of the Saxons before the year after their coming into Britain 465. For then, Athelstan forc'd the Britains, who before that liv'd in the city in equal power with the Saxons, out of it, drove them beyond Tamar, and encompass'd the city with a ditch, a wall of square stone, and bulwarks: since that time, our Kings have granted it many privileges, and among the rest (as we read it in the Book of William the Conqueror) *This city did not geld but when London, York, and Winchester did; that was half a mark of silver for a Knight's fee. And in case of an expedition by land or sea, it serv'd after the rate of five hides.* It hath also from time to time undergone much misery; once spoil'd by an out-rage of the Danes in the year of our redemption 875, but most dismally by *Sueno* the Dane, in the year 1003, being betray'd by one *Hugh* a Norman the governour of the city: when it was laid level from the east to the west-gate: and had scarce begun to recruit, till William the Conqueror laid close siege to it; at which time the Citizens not only shut up their gates against him, but gall'd him with many bitter reflections; however, a part of their wall happening to fall down, (which the Historians of that age attribute to the hands of Providence) a surrender soon follow'd; at this time (as

48

it is in the said Survey-book) *the King had in this city 300 houses: it paid 15 pounds a year. Eight and forty houses were destroy'd after the King came into England.* After this it was press'd by three sieges, yet easily escap'd them all. First by *Hugh Courtney* Earl of Devonshire in the civil war between the houses of York and Lancaster: again, by *Perkin Warbeck* a sham and counterfeit prince, who being a young man, and of mean descent, by pretending to be *Richard* Duke of York, the second son of K. Edward 4, rais'd a very dangerous war: thirdly, by the seditious Cornish, in the year 1549, when the citizens, tho' under a most sad want of all sorts of provisions, continu'd loyal, till John Baron *Russel* rais'd the siege.

But *Exeter* has not suffer'd so much by these enemies, as by certain heaps (*Wears* as they call them) which *Edward Courtney* Earl of Devonshire, in an out-fall with the citizens, threw into the chanel of the river *Isc*; which hinders ships from coming to the town, so that all merchandize is brought thither by land from *Topesham,* a little village three miles from the city. Nor are these heaps remov'd, tho' it is commanded by Act of Parliament. From these, a small village hard by is call'd *Weare,* but formerly *Heneaton,* which belong'd heretofore to Austin de *Baa,* from whom by right of inheritance it came to *John Holand,* who in a seal that I have seen, bore a *lion rampant gardant among flower de luces.* The government of this City is administer'd by 24 of whom one yearly is chosen Mayor, who with four Bayliffs manages all publick affairs. As for the position, the old Oxford-Tables have defin'd its longitude to be 19 degrees, 11 minutes. It's latitude 50 degrees, 40 minutes.

WILLIAM CAMDEN, Britannia, 1586, ed. Gibson, 1695

STUKELEY ON EXETER

Exeter is the famous *Isca Dumnoniorum* of the Romans, the last station this way in Antoninus his Itinerary; *pen cair* of the Britons, the capital: it is a large and populous city, built upon a pleasant eminence on the eastern bank of the river *Ex* or *Iscu* when latinised. I suppose the original word signifies no more than waters, like the French *eaux,* a collection of them, or several rivers, or branches of rivers, running parallel; and that whether it be wrote *Ax, Ex, Ix, Ox* or *Ux*; of which many instances all over England. This river is navigable up to the city, but the tide comes not quite so high. The walls take in a very great compass, being a parallelogram of 3000 Roman feet long, 200 broad; having a gate on every side: it lies oblique to the cardinal points of the compass, and objects its main declivity to the south-west. What adds to its wholsomeness and cleanliness, is that the ground is higher in a ridge along the middle of its length, declining on both sides: further, on the south-west and north-west sides it is precipitous: so that, with the river, the walls, the declivity of ground and ditch without side, it was a place of very great strength, and well chose for a frontier against the ancient *Corinavii*: it was built with a good omen, and has been ever in a flourishing condition. The walls are in pretty good repair, having many lunettes and towers, and make a walk round the city, with the advantage and pleasure of seeing the fine country on the opposite hills, full of wood, rich ground, orchards, villages and gentlemen's houses. The beauty of the place consists mainly of one long street, running the length of the parallelogram, called High-street, broad and straight: the houses are of a very old but good model, spacious, commodious, and not inelegant: this street is full of shops well furnished, and all sorts of trades look brisk. The people are industrious and courteous; the fair sex are truly so, as well as numerous; their complexions, and generally their hair likewise, fair: they are genteel, disengaged, of easy carriage and good mien. At Mr Cole's the goldsmith I saw an old ground-plot of this city in queen Elizabeth's time; there has since been a vast increase of buildings within and without the city: the situation renders it of necessity clean, dry and airy. The soil hither from Honiton was sandy rather than stony, whence it must needs be very healthful; and it is of a convenient distance from the sea. They drive a great trade here for woollen manufacture in cloths, serges, stuffs, &c. all along the water-side innumerable tenters or racks for stretching them. Here is a good face of learning too; many booksellers' shops: I saw a printed catalogue of an auction of books to be sold there. I saw the coloss head of the empress Julia Domna dug up near Bath, in Dr. Musgrave's garden, which his father calls *Andromache*: the head-dress is like that of her times, and her bust at Wilton; nor is the manner and carving despis-able: the graver has not done it justice. It is the noblest relique of British antiquity of this sort that we know: it is twenty-one inches from the top of the attire to the chin, and belonged to a statue of twelve foot proportion, set upon some temple or palace originally. In the same place is the inscription of Camillus published by him: I saw his library, a very good collection of books, coins, and other antiquarian *supellex*; likewise a treatise, ready for publication, of the original gout, which he wrote thirty years ago, before his other two. The doctor had made this particular distemper his particular view through his long practice; and this country remarkably abounds with patients of that sort, which he attributes in a great measure to the custom of marling the lands with lime, and the great use of poor, sweet cyder, especially among the meaner people.

In the northern angle of the city, and highest ground, is Rugemont castle, once the royal residence of West-Saxon kings, then of the earls of Cornwall: it is of a squarish figure, not very large, environed with a high wall and deep ditch: there is a rampire of earth within, equal in height to the top of the wall at present, and makes a terrace-walk overlooking the city and country. In the morning, the air being perfectly serene, and the sun shining, I observed from this place all the country southward, between the sea and Exeter, covered with a very thick fog; the west side of the city and the country beyond it very clear. In this place is the assize-house and a chapel. In the wall of this castle is a narrow cavity quite round, perhaps for conveyance of a sound from turret to turret. Dr. Holland supposes this to have been a Roman work originally; and it is not unlikely that it was their *praetorium* or garrison. Beyond the ditch is a pleasant walk of trees, and a little intrenched hill, called Danes castle.

The cathedral is a good pile of building: two old towers stand on the north and south transept of the most ancient part: the organ is remarkably large; the diapason pipes fifteen inches in diameter, and set against the pillars of the church: the west front of the church is full of old statues. Many religious foundations in the city are converted into streets and houses, full of numerous families and thriving inhabitants, instead of lazy monks and nuns. King Edward I in Saxon times founded the monastery of Exeter, anno 868: Athelstan enlarged it for the Benedictines in 932: Edward Confessor translated those monks to Westminster, and made this an episcopal see, not Edward III as Mr. Camden says. Leofricus a Briton was the first bishop and founder of the cathedral: he was chaplain to Edward the Confessor, anno 1046: he gave his lands at Bampton in Oxfordshire to this church: he has a monument in the southern transept. Warewast, the third bishop, began to build the choir, 13 Henry I. Bishop Brewer created the dean and the prebends in the time of Henry III. Bishop Quivel built the body of the church to the west end, 13 Edward I he instituted the sub-dean and singing men. Bishop Grandison lengthened the cathedral by two arches, and is buried in a little chapel in the west end: bishop Lacy began the chapterhouse; bishop Nevil finished it: bishop Courtney built the north tower, or rather repaired it, and gave that large bell called *Peter*: the dean and chapter built the cloysters. St. Mary's chapel, at the end of the choir, is now turned into a library: this, I suppose, is what bishop Leofric built. The bishop's throne in the choir is a lofty Gothic work. Here are many monuments of bishops in the cathedral.

The present deanery, they say, was a nunnery. The monastery of St. Andrew at Cowic was founded by Thomas Courtney earl of Devon; a cell to Bec abbey in Normandy: it was dissolved in the time of Edward III. Roger Holland, I suppose duke of Exeter, lived in it in the time of Edward VI. St Nicholas' priory was a cell to Battle abbey: St John's was of Augustine friers: Polesloe, a mile off, dedicated to St Catherine, a nunnery of the Benedictine order: Marsh was a cell to Plympton: Cleve was a monastery of Black canons; St. Jame's priory of Cluniac monks: Grey friers, without South-gate, were Franciscans; Gold-hays, without West-gate Black friers: the Bear inn was the abbot of Tavistock's house; the Black-lion too was a religious house; Lathbier another, near the new river below Radford mount. Thus had these holy locusts well nigh devoured the land.

In Corry-lane, over against St. Paul's church, is a little old house called King Athelstan's, said to have been his palace, built of large square stones, and circular arches over the doors: it seems originally indeed to have been a Roman building, though other later works have been added to the doors and windows: over the door in the street is a very small niche crouded into the wall, as if it had been converted into a religious house: in the yard, a winding stone stair-case is added. One arch of South-gate seems to be Roman. No doubt the walls of the city are upon Roman foundations for the most part, and great numbers of antiquities have been found here. In digging behind the guild-hall in Pancras-lane, they found a great Roman pavement of little white square stones eight foot deep. A pot of Roman coins of two pecks was dug up, two years ago, near St. Martin's church: I saw some of them in Dr. Musgrave's possession, of Gordian, Balbinus, Philippus, Julia Maesa, Geta, Gallienus, and the like. Mr. Loudham, surgeon in this city, has many of them among his curious collection of antiquities, manuscripts, &c. Mr. Reynolds the schoolmaster is a great collector and preserver of such learned remains. St. Mary Arches church, and St. Stephen's Bow, by their names seem to have been built out of Roman temples.

The bridge over the *Isca* is of great length, and has houses on both sides and both ends; a considerable void space in the middle: there is a church upon it with a tower-steeple. In the Guild-hall are the pictures of a General Monk, and the princess Henrietta Maria, born at Bedford-house, a palace in this city, during the civil wars. The composition of the stone of this country is intirely made of little black pebbles, incrusted in a sandy matter of a red colour, and mouldering nature.

WILLIAM STUKELEY, *Itinerarium Curiosum*, 1776 ed., Iter VI

WALPOLE ON TOUR

Wentworth Castle, August, 1756

I always dedicate my travels to you. My present expedition has been very amusing, sights are thick sown in the counties of York and Nottingham; the former is more historic, and the great lords live at a prouder distance: in Nottinghamshire there is a very Heptarchy of little kingdoms elbowing one another, and the barons of them want nothing but small armies to make inroads into one another's parks, murder deer, and massacre park-keepers. But to come to particulars: the Great Road as far as Stamford is superb; in any other country it would furnish medals, and immortalise any drowsy monarch in whose reign it was executed. It is continued much farther, but is more rumbling. I did not stop at Hatfield and Burleigh to see the palaces of my great-uncle-ministers, having seen them before. Bugden palace surprises one prettily in a little village; and the remains of Newark castle, seated pleasantly, began to open a vein of historic memory. I had only transient and distant views of Lord Tyrconnel's at Belton (in Lincolnshire) and of Belvoir. The borders of Huntingdonshire have churches instead of milestones, but the richness and extent of Yorkshire quite charmed me. Oh! what quarries for working in Gothic!

This place is one of the very few that I really like; the situation, woods, views, and the improvements, are perfect in their kinds; nobody has a truer taste than Lord Strafford. The house is a pompous front screening an old house; it was built by the last lord on a design of the Prussian architect Bott, who is mentioned in the King's Memoires de Brandenburg, and is not ugly: the one pair of stairs is entirely engrossed by a gallery of 180 feet, on the plan of that in the Colonna palace at Rome: it has nothing but four modern statues and some bad portraits, but, on my proposal, is going to have books at each end. The hall is pretty, but low; the drawing-room handsome; there wants a good eating-room and staircase: but I have formed a design for both and I believe they will be executed—that my plans should be obeyed when yours are not! I shall bring you a ground-plot for a Gothic building, which I have proposed that you should draw for a little wood, but in the manner of an ancient market-cross. Without doors all is pleasing: there is a beautiful (artificial) river, with a fine semicircular wood overlooking it, and the temple of Tivoli placed happily on a rising towards the end. There are obelisks, columns, and other buildings, and, above all, a handsome castle in the true style, on a rude mountain, with a court and towers: in the castle-yard, a statue of the late lord who built it. Without the park is a lake on each side, buried in noble woods. Now contrast all this, and you may have some idea of Lord Rockingham's. Imagine a most extensive and most beautiful modern front erected before the great Lord Strafford's old house, and this front almost blocked up with hills, and everything unfinished round it, nay within it. The great apartment, which is magnificent, is untouched: the chimney-pieces lie in boxes unopened. The park is traversed by a common road between two high hedges—not from necessity. Oh! no; this lord loves nothing but horses, and the enclosures for them take place of everything. The bowling-green behind the house contains no less than four obelisks, and looks like a Brobdignag nine-pin-alley: on a hill near, you would think you saw the York-buildings water-works invited into the country. There are temples in corn-fields; and in the little wood, a window-frame mounted on a bunch of laurel, and intended for an hermitage. In the inhabited part of the house, the chimney-pieces are like tombs: and on that in the library is the figure of this lord's grandfather, in a night-gown of plaster and gold. Amidst all this litter and bad taste, I adored the fine Vandyck of Lord Strafford and his secretary, and could not help reverencing his bed-chamber. With all his faults and arbitrary behaviour, one must worship his spirit and eloquence: where one esteems but a single royalist, one need not fear being too partial. When I visited his tomb in the church (which is remarkably neat and pretty, and enriched with monuments) I was provoked to find a little mural cabinet, with his figure three feet high kneeling. Instead of a stern bust (and his head would furnish a nobler than Bernini's Brutus) one is peevish to see a plaything that might have been bought at Chenevix's. There is a tender inscription to the second Lord Strafford's wife, written by himself; but his genius was fitter to coo over his wife's memory than to sacrifice to his father's. . . .

During my residence here I have made two little excursions, and I assure you it requires resolution; the roads are insufferable; they mend them—I should call it spoil them—with large pieces of stone. At Pomfret I saw the remains of that memorable castle 'where Rivers, Vaughan, and Grey lay shorter by the head;' and on which Gray says—

> *'And thou, proud boy, from Pomfret's walls shalt send*
> *A groan, and envy oft thy happy grandsire's end!'*

The ruins are vanishing, but well situated; there is a large demolished church, and a pretty market-house. We crossed a Gothic bridge of eight arches at Ferrybridge, where there is a pretty view and went to a large old house of Lord Huntingdon's at Ledstone, which has nothing remarkable but a lofty terrace, a whole-length portrait of his grandfather in tapestry, and the having belonged to the great Lord Strafford. We saw [Kippax Park] that monument of part of poor Sir John Bland's extravagance, his house and garden, which he left orders to make without once looking at either plan. The house is a bastard Gothic, but of not near the extent I had heard. We lay at Leeds, a dingy large town; and through very bad black roads (for the whole country is a colliery, or a quarry), we went to Kirkstall abbey, where are vast Saxon ruins, in a most picturesque situation, on the banks of a river that falls in a cascade among rich meadows, hills, and woods: it belongs to Lord Cardigan: his father pulled down a large house here, lest it should interfere with the family seat, Deane. We returned through Wakefield, where is a pretty Gothic chapel on a bridge, erected by Edward IV in memory of his father, who lived at Sandal castle just by, and perished in the battle here. There is scarce anything of the castle extant, but it commanded a rich prospect.

Letters of HORACE WALPOLE, LXXXII, To RICHARD BENTLEY, Everyman edition, 1948, J. M. Dent and Sons Ltd.

A CORNER OF WALES

(1) *Cairarvonshire and Merionithshire*

Gaflogeon hundrede goith from the ende of Uwch Mennith in commot mayne towarde Traithmaur as far as Abreerche. In this commot is Pulthely . . . Pollele Bay a poore market, now a late *statio opt. carinis.* The prince had a place there, as yet apperith.

Harlauche Castel and market toune yn this hundrede. . . . Towarde the se side and low partes is summe good corne. Meate good plenty of wood in this commot.

JOHN LELAND, *Itinerary,* Hearne's 2nd ed., 1744

(2) *Pwlh heli*

(Lhyn) affords but two small towns worth our notice: the innermost at the bay of *Pwlh heli,* which name signifies the *Salt Pool*; and the other by the Irish Sea . . . call'd *Nevin.* . . . If any more towns flourish'd here, they were then destroy'd when *Hugh* Earl of Chester, *Robert* of Rutland, and *Guarin* of Salop (the first Normans that advanced thus far) so wasted this promontory, that for seven years it lay desolate.

WILLIAM CAMDEN, *Britannia,* 1586, Gibson's ed., 1695

(3) *Ladies from Portland, Oregon*

Is that how you pronounce it? Well what do you know? Isn't that cunning, Mary Jane? Pi-Thel-li. I just love these names.

And then we can go on to Portmadoc, which is quite a sweet little town as I remember.

That's a good enough idea. And what about this down here, isn't that Harlech? Goodness we musn't miss Harlech! Well now look here we'll head for Harlech and then you'll be figuring out where we go from there. I think this will be a lovely day's driving.

STANLEY WADE BARON, *People and Americans*, 1953,
Rupert Hart-Davis Ltd.

(4) *Ogs and his Shorts*

The members of the Cambrian Association in those days were a motley crew of amateurs who had inflated ideas of their own importance, a survival of Victorian times. They paid a formal visit *en masse* to the excavations during their summer meeting [1919]. The site was rather inaccessible, being in an open moorland. I was living on the spot in a tent and my usual dress was shorts and a sweater, and it never occurred to me that any more formal attire would be thought necessary to receive them in. They duly arrived and were conducted round the sites; in one place it was necessary to climb over a wall, but it was surmounted without accident by the members of the party, which included Professor Boyd Dawkins, then doyen of British archaeology, Canon Fisher, the editor of *Arch. Camb.*, and a local M.P. whose name I forget. Long afterwards I heard that there had been disapproving comments on my informal dress; that a man of thirty-two should wear shorts on so solemn an occasion seemed rather shocking. But good old Boyd Dawkins defended me stoutly—I had 'had a hard time as a prisoner of war and perhaps had not yet completely recovered my balance'.

O. G. S. CRAWFORD, *Said and Done*, 1955, George Weidenfeld
and Nicolson Ltd.

A BRITISH EARTHWORK

(*An Archaeologist speaks*)

The grassy downs of Dorset,
Rising o'er our homes of peace,
E'er teem with life and riches
In the sheep and precious fleece:
And charm the thoughtful roamer
When, like us, he climbs to scan
Their high-cast mounds of war—the works
Of Britain's early man,
Whose speech, although here lingers yet
His mighty works of hand,

Has ceased a thousand years to sound
  In air of this green land,
And startled may it be to hear
  The words of British kin—
      An gwaliow war an meneth
      An caer war an bryn.

Their breastworks now are fallen,
  And their banks are sunken low;
The gateway yawns ungated,
  And unsought by friend or foe.
No war-horn calls for warriors,
  And no clear-eyed watchmen spy
For tokens of the foe, around
  The quarters of the sky.
No band, with shout and singing,
  Sally forth with spear and sword,
Staying foes at wood or hill,
  Or at the waded river ford;
Or else to take the hill, and fight
  To win, or die within
      An gwaliow, etc.

There were lowings of the cattle
  By the rattling spears and swords;
There were wails of weeping women
  And grim warriors' angry words—
'Be every Briton fearless, or
  For ever live in fear;
And bring his ready weapons out—
  His bow, and sword, and spear!
For what have we to fight the foe?
  Our children and our wives!
For whom have we to fight? For those
  Far dearer than our lives!
And we, to shield them all, will die,
  Or else the battle win,
      Yn an gwaliow war an meneth
      Yn an caer war an bryn!'

But now, in sweet, unbroken peace
  May Dorset land-folks sleep;
In peace may speed the gliding plough,
  In peace may graze the sheep;

57

In peace may smoke our village tuns;
   And all our children play;
And may we never need high banks
   To keep the foe at bay!
And blest be lord or farmer
   Of the land, who wins our thanks
By sparing from the spade and sull
   These olden British banks,
And nor destroying, for a crown,
   Or pound that he might win,
      An gwaliow, etc.

(*An gwaliow war an meneth*—the ramparts on the mountain; *An caer war an bryn*—the stronghold on the hill.)

THE REVD WILLIAM BARNES, 1877

A DORSET TRACKWAY

Well, people say this hollow track
   Was never made for wheels and springs;
   But worn by packhorses in strings,
With wares, on ev'ry horse a pack.

Before, by yonder plain and ridge,
   The road was stean'd two-waggons wide,
   Where wheels now spin and horsemen ride,
On high-cast bank and high-bowed bridge.

The road clim'd up, onwinding deep
   Beside the ashes on the height,
   Where elderflow'rs are hanging white
O'er yonder crowds of cluster'd sheep.

And up at Holway men would shout
   'Hold hard,' or else would blow a horn
   On their side of the way, to warn
Oncomers back, till they were out.

And then it struck along the glades
   Above the brook, to Rockley spring,
   And meads, where now you hear the ring
Of mowers' briskly-whetted blades.

And then it sunk, the slope to dive
    Through Pebbleford, where uncle took
    His way across the flooded brook,
But never reach'd his home alive.

And then it touch'd the ridgy ground
    With marks of walls, where Deanton stood;
    Though now the houses, stone and wood,
Are gone, with all their tongues and sound.

Our elders there, as we are told,
    Had once their homes, and doors to close
    Between warm hearths and winter snows;
And there play'd young, and there grew old.

THE REVD WILLIAM BARNES

THE ROMANS IN LONDON (1)

In 1852 an excavation made for a cellar on the east side of Trinity Place on Tower Hill disclosed the solid foundation of one of the bastions of the eastern section of the Roman town wall. Among the broken stones were sculptured architectural mouldings from a building or monument of some magnitude. There was in particular a block of stone which contained most of the three top lines of a finely-cut sepulchral inscription which was thought to be in memory of one Fabius Alpinus Classicianus.

By a chance discovery some eighty-three years later, the fascinating story of Classicianus could be completed. Part of the Roman wall and bastion was exposed in the same place by engineers of the London Passenger Transport Board who were preparing foundations for a new sub-station. The site was investigated by the Society of Antiquaries, and in the foundation course of the bastion, where it had been re-used as building stone, was found a large block of Cotswold oolite on which were three lines of a sepulchral inscription. There were many ways in which this stone corresponded with the inscribed panel previously found at the same place, and it was indisputably part of the same monument. The new discovery was presented to the British Museum by the London Passenger Transport Board, and a facsimile of the whole inscription and explanatory plaques were placed in the wall of the sub-station.

A new restoration of the monument in the British Museum has recently been completed. The inscription may be translated:—

59

'To the gods of the underworld [and in memory] of Caius Julius Alpinus Classicianus, of the Fabian tribe, son of Caius . . . Procurator of the Province of Britain, [his] wife, Julia Pacata Indiana, daughter of Indus, made [this monument.]

A fortunate historical reference enables this Julius Classicianus to be identified with some certainty. In the Annals of Tacitus, (XIV, 38) there is mention of the appointment of a new Procurator of Britain, Julius Classicianus, after the rebellion of Boudicca, an event which took place in A.D. 61. His wife Julia was probably the daughter of the Julius Indus who in A.D. 21 stemmed a revolt among the people of his own Gaulish tribe, the Treveri, and the British Museum authorities have reconstructed the London tomb on the basis of monuments of the same kind found in that part of Gaul.

R. F. JESSUP, *Notes on Roman London, Daily Mail* Publications, 1958

THE ROMANS IN LONDON (2)

Here's proof that the people of Norfolk never forget a benefactor.

To-morrow they will lay wreaths at the feet of a man who saved their orphans and widows from death in the year A.D. 61. Their saviour was a Roman procurator, Caius Alpinus Classicianus.

Classicianus's noble deed came to light when a statue erected to him in A.D. 65 was found among the remains of the Roman Wall near Tower Hill during excavations for the London Underground system. The original statue is now in the British Museum.

Boy Scouts and Girl Guides from Norfolk will lay wreaths at the replica of the statue which has been erected in Trinity-place, Tower Hill.

Mr and Mrs Frederick Cawsey, members of the church parochial council, will be dressed as the Roman Procurator and his wife to greet the Scouts.

The vicar . . . will supervise the day's celebrations. . . .

Evening News, October 31, 1958

THE ROMANS IN LEICESTER

Two hours later I made a halt in Leicester, whose name was Ratae Coritanorum, or more simply Ratae, and was what we call to-day a prosperous provincial city.

Before the church of St Nicholas, exactly at No. 50 of St Nicholas Street, is a shop which sells corsets and brassieres. When you have made sure that nobody is watching you going in (in the provinces, alas, people are such gossips!) you cross the threshold of the shop, and when you have explained to a proprietoress of Amazonian stature, who bears most effective testimony to the efficiency of her corsets, what you want, she will emit a yodelling call. From the back parlour comes out the Herculanean consort of the prepossessing 'corsetière'; and, having exacted the fee of threepence, he will guide you through the parlour and kitchen and courtyard, down several steps, until you land in a large and spotless subterranean chamber, the walls of which are lined with shining white tiles, like a public convenience. But down on the floor your eyes open wide at two stupendous mosaics designed in brilliant colours, and you think of the cheerfulness of that rich flooring in the comfortable living-room of a prosperous merchant of Ratae. The white tiles and the electric light—so explains the custodian—have been added by the Town Council, which authorises him to pocket the threepence as a token for the thoroughness with which the good fellow polishes the Roman floor.

In the Leicester Museum I had been tempted to linger before a fragment of terracotta upon which an amorous bard had engraved: 'Verecunda, actress—Lucius, gladiator': no doubt the forgotten leading lady was the image of her own name.

C. M. FRANZERO, *Roman Britain*, 1935, Allen and Unwin Ltd.

THAT MARVELLOUS PALIMPSEST

The face of the country is the most important historical document that we possess. Upon the map of England—'that marvellous palimpsest' is written much of English history; written in letters of earth and stone, of bank and ditch, of foliage and crop. As is the case with every map, the writing is not such as he that runs may read. It needs patience to discover, knowledge to decipher, insight, sometimes amounting to genius, to interpret. But the writing is there, all else awaits the competence of the reader.

The idea has grown slowly, and historians have assimilated it more slowly still. To many it is entirely repugnant; to others it is completely alien. There are historians whom it would be inequitable to disparage and dangerous to neglect, to whom documents are documents and men are just men, affected neither by ancestry nor environment. To these the face of the country is meaningless, and the influence of physical conditions a fond thing vainly imagined. Some go so far as to recognize that the men of the forest are somehow different from the men of the desert, but beyond distinctions of this kind their insight does not penetrate.

H. J. RANDALL, *History in the Open Air*, 1934, Allen and Unwin Ltd.

1500-YEAR-OLD NEWS FLASH

On Deepfield Way (Coulsdon, Surrey), excavating foundations, we've found what appears to be an early Saxon burial ground. It may be earlier.

Various items have come to light, and we're holding up building while the local archaeological society conducts a dig.

A viewing platform will be erected so that visitors will have a fair view. Come and see to-day; and let's hope the weather holds fine.

A lot of interesting things happen when Wates build; but we haven't had this before.

An advertisement by Wates the Builders,
June 15, 1969

3—TREASURE FOR PLEASURE
OR, ANTIQUARY WITH A SPADE

TREASURE FOR PLEASURE
OR, ANTIQUARY WITH A SPADE

Persuasion and a little brandy
The way to open a Barrow
The impertinence of passengers
Much time and pains
The carriage full of gold
Summer day
November night
Snow and candle light
A bit of barrow-digging
A Roman barrow?
Fate of a Roman pavement—
　—and of another
Alienation of a Roman pavement
The Ravaged Villa
The spirit of the times
Saxon Obsequies
Research in the Cheviots
Bones and the Archaeologist (1)
Bones and the Archaeologist (2)
Salt on a corpse
A nice Relish of Antiquities
A jurisprudential enquiry
Treasure-Trove
Horace Walpole's mahogany model
Canons of Excavation
Long-barrow funerals
Selective or total?
They see when hypnotised
Using the Virgula Divina
The Magic Box
Excavation

PERSUASION AND A LITTLE BRANDY

At a place commonly called GILTON TOWN, in the parish of Ash, next Sandwich, in the county of Kent, on the right hand side of the high road leading from Canterbury to Sandwich, and about a quarter of a mile short of Ash-Street, is a large and deep sand-pit, in which from time to time for a great many years past, whenever sand has been dug within three or four feet of the surface, or whenever the surface has rushed down after frost or rain, as it usually does, many antiquities of different sorts have been discovered and picked up, either by the servants of the farmer who used the land, who have often been employed in carrying out the sand to manure the farm, or by the inhabitants of the village of Ash, or, perhaps, more particularly, by the servants of a miller, who has two large windmills on the west side of and close to this sand-pit.

Happening to be at Ash in the end of the year 1759, for the purpose of copying the monumental inscriptions in that church among others, and inquiring, as I always do on such occasions, whether there were any antiquities or other remarkables in the neighbourhood, I was informed of this famous sand-pit, and of the particulars above mentioned.

I immediately visited the place, and after having looked about it and examined it for some little time, one of the miller's servants came into the pit to me and shewed me something sticking out, about three or four inches out of the sand, about three feet from the surface of the eastern and deepest part of the pit. It appeared to me to be nothing more than some piece of stick or some root; but he assured me it was the head of a spear; and said he was certain there was a grave there from the colour of the sand, which, in a small line of about eighteen inches in length, and parallel to the surface, and about two inches in thickness, appeared in that place of a much darker tinge than the rest of the sand. He told me also, that, if I were pleased he would get a ladder and a spade and see what was in it.

It was now pretty late in the day, which made me object to his proposal, imagining that he would not have time to go through with his work. However, on his assuring me that he had been used to the work, and that by the help of another miller, his fellow-servant, he should soon rifle it (for that was his expression), my curiosity prompted me, though at a considerable distance from home, to set them about the business and to wait the event.

The miller and his companion immediately produced two ladders and as many spades; and with these began to delve in a very rough manner into the sand rock in an horizontal manner, as if they had designed to have made an oven. The head of the spear (for such indeed it proved) they, at the first or second stroke of their spades, contrived to break all to pieces. Indeed it was very brittle. At the next stroke or two, part of a skull and a few vertebrae of the neck (all much decayed) were indescriminately with the soil cast down into the pit, without the least care or search after anything. That concern, they said, they left to me and my servant at the bottom, who were nearly blinded with the sand falling on us, and in no small danger of being knocked on the head, if not absolutely buried, by the too zealous impetuosity of my honest labourers.

I found, in short, that this method of proceeding would not do; but that if the grave did chance to contain anything curious, it must, most likely, be lost and overlooked. I therefore desired them to desist, and advised them rather to open the ground above, till they should get down to the skeleton, and then carefully to examine the bottom of the grave. This advice, having been used to proceed oven-fashion, if I may so call it, they did not at first at all relish; but after a little persuasion and a little brandy (without which nothing, in cases such as the present, can be done effectually), they very cheerfully approved and very contentedly followed, so that in a very short time they got to the skeleton, I mean to what remained of it. And though I then went into the grave myself, and very carefully examined every handful of the above mentioned discoloured sand (namely, where the body had lain and rotted), I found nothing but some soft spongy remains of decayed bones. It was now too near night to think of doing anything more at that time, and too late in the season, to attempt anything further that year. But I promised myself the pleasure of returning to the work, and making a further and more diligent search, as early as the weather and length of days of the ensuing spring would give me leave.

THE REVD BRYAN FAUSSETT, *Inventorium Sepulchrale*, 1757–73,
ed. by CHARLES ROACH SMITH, 1856

THE WAY TO OPEN A BARROW

The way to open a barrow, is either to remove the mound of earth entirely, or to make a section through it at least six or eight feet wide from north to south, or from east to west, or to sink a shaft down the centre from top to bottom. Sir R. C. Hoare, invariably adhered to the latter mode with a desire not to injure the external form. The greatest caution should be used in removing the earth, especially when charcoal and fragments of pottery appear intermingled with it; for it not unfrequently happens that relics or interments are found near the surface, or round the outsides of a Barrow. With respect to the Deposits, Mr Cunnington, first discovered and established contrary to the theory of Dr Stukely, that the primary interment is always on the floor of a

Barrow or in a cist dug in the chalk beneath it. In one instance Sir R. C. Hoare, after immense labour found a simple interment of burnt bones at the depth of fifteen feet. The interments are generally found about two, three, four, five, or six feet below the surface of the natural soil. When a wall or heap of flints closely arranged together present themselves, they should be removed with the hand, because a pick-axe, crow-bar, or spade at such a crisis has often destroyed an Urn, by making an irruption into the cist. On arriving at the cist, the operations should be conducted slowly around its edge either with a trowel or a knife. Want of success at first should never terminate in abandoning a Barrow until it has been thoroughly examined.

THE REVD CHARLES WOOLS, notes to *The Barrow Diggers*, 1839

THE IMPERTINENCE OF PASSENGERS

I had often cast a wishful look at them [nine small burial mounds at Bishopsbourne, near Canterbury], and from time to time had promised myself the future pleasure of examining their contents. But, on account of the smallness of their size and number, and their proximity to so public a road (by means of which last circumstance I knew myself liable to be pestered with a numerous set of troublesome spectators), I did not set about opening them until the 16th of July, 1771; on the morning of which day, arriving at this spot in my way to Kingston Down rather earlier than usual, and being provided with plenty of labourers for that day's intended work, I thought that a good opportunity of putting my intentions with regard to these so publicly situated tumuli into execution. So setting ourselves immediately to the business, we finished our work in little more than two hours; during which time, it being so early in the day, we had very little or no interruption, either from the curiosity or impertinence of passengers, or other idle spectators, the teazingness and plague of whose ill-timed attendance in business of this sort, is not to be conceived but by those who, like myself, have had the disagreeable experience of it.

THE REVD BRYAN FAUSSETT, *Inventorium Sepulchrale*, 1757–73, ed. by CHARLES ROACH SMITH, 1856

(*The excavation record of this parson-antiquary was thirty-one barrows in one day on 29th July, 1771.*)

MUCH TIME AND PAINS

We this day spent much time and pains (no less than five men for eight hours having been employed upon it), in endeavouring to overturn a very large mound, or tumulus, at the east corner of this burial ground, next Barham Down, and close to the road leading from Kingston to Ileden, on the left hand. It was about eighteen paces diameter, and about six feet in perpendicular height above the surface of the natural soil. When we had got about half way through it, we found (as indeed I before suspected from some sinkings on its top) that it had been opened before. For we met with nearly a whole tobacco-pipe, of that sort which were used when first tobacco was used in England, viz., with a large and short strig, and a very small and narrow bowl. This lay nearly at the bottom of the highest part of the tumulus. We may, therefore, from this circumstance conclude that this mound was opened not long after the reign of king James the First, or perhaps in it.

THE REVD BRYAN FAUSSETT, *Inventorium Sepulchrale*, 1757–73, ed. by CHARLES ROACH SMITH, 1856

THE CARRIAGE FULL OF GOLD

His son, Henry Godfrey Faussett, was born at the vicarage of Abberbury in 1749, a short time only before the return of his family into Kent. Companion in his childhood in all his father's archaeological rambles and researches, he may be said to have been born and bred an antiquary; and it was his boast through life that he had himself discovered, as he superintended the opening of one of his father's barrows on Kingston Down, that famous fibula, which was the gem of his collection, and it still is, I believe, of all Anglo-Saxon tumular antiquities. The story of its discovery, by the way, will give some idea of the astonishment and prejudice which antiquaries of the day had to encounter. On finding it, he carried it with great glee to his father, who was in his carriage hard by, suffering under an attack of his old enemy [gout]: his father drove off with it; and next day a report was spread that the carriage had been so full of gold that the wheels would scarcely turn; and the lord of the manor prohibited all further excavation on these downs.

Letter: THOMAS GODFREY FAUSSETT of Heppington, to JOSEPH MAYER, August 5, 1854

SUMMER DAY

Outside the embankments are vast tracts of 'saltings' which have been, since the Roman occupation of Britain, separated from the mainland by the gradual encroachment of the waters upon this portion of the county. The saltings are intersected by countless creeks, dykes, and rills, but at high tide are entirely submerged. Now it has been clearly proved by the researches of Mr Roach Smith, who has written exhaustively on the subject, that during Roman times, the saltings, and a vast tract of marshland, was the site of, perhaps, the most extensive potteries that have hitherto been discovered in this country. This can, at the present day, be demonstrated to those who are in earnest, and enthusiastic enough to wade knee-deep along the mud flats at low water. [The Librarian of the University of Cambridge] when first introduced by the writer to the Upchurch potteries (Easter Monday, 1879) grappled with the difficulties of the situation by converting his trousers into knickerbockers, and plunging through the ooze all day with bare feet. I myself have a vivid recollection of stepping into an anchor hole, nearly leaving my waterman's boots behind, or rather *below* me, in my endeavours to extricate my legs. All these petty annoyances, however, were compensated for by the information gained of the past history of this outlying district.

. . . our party on this enjoyable day (21st July, 1882) included Mrs. Payne, Miss Claypole, and Mr Roach Smith. Luncheon was served at the mouth of Otterham Creek, upon the greensward, as the tide was rising, and afterwards our distinguished friend entertained the ladies with anecdotes of past experiences, and sang to them from one of Planché's extravaganzas, while Mr. Dowker and the writer prosecuted further research. . . . Our day ended with a refreshing tea at the Crown Inn, Upchurch, and a pleasant drive to Sittingbourne.

GEORGE PAYNE, *Collectanea Cantiana*, 1893

NOVEMBER NIGHT

Men were employed in dragging furze from an adjoining spot and it was a fine subject for the talent of an artist to have described the Urn smoking at the flame, while a red and flickering gleam played upon the countenances of the labourers, who speaking in low and subdued tones, and having their eyes fixed upon the flames and dead Men's bones were afraid to look into the surrounding darkness. The swell of the passing breeze as it fanned the fire raised them from their reverie, or roused their attention from some direful story of goblin damned, which was gravely related and as faithfully believed. The effect produced by the narrative of the village thatcher added most strongly to the horror of their situation as he gravely declared that his father and elder brother had been most cruelly dragged about and beaten by some invisible hand on the very Down on which we stood.

There was no danger of a Deserter from my party, as fear kept them together, and our group was augmented by the curiosity of the passing peasants, who deviating from their homeward course wondered why a fire blazed upon the unfrequented Down, a spot on which it is more than probable no fire had ever gleamed since the last Deposit was pompously and religiously placed in the Barrow just explored, save at the May-eve rites. But now how changed the scene. The Urn when it was last seen by man, so hallowed, so venerated, the form, the features of the chief whose ashes it contained, fresh to the minds and perhaps dear to the memories of those who assisted at the sepulchral ceremonies, now after the lapse of many hundred years, calmy reeked before a burning faggot to the rude gaze of an astonished peasant.

W. A. MILES in THE REVD CHARLES WOOLS,
notes to *The Barrow Diggers*, 1839

SNOW AND CANDLE LIGHT

. . . on Tuesday I opened a barrow near Chollerton. Found two (?burnt) bodies, one in an urn, sadly broken & decayed, with a central cist, in which were the very trifling remains of (?an unburnt) body. Nothing had been buried with any of these bodies. The snow was 6 inch. deep on the Ground, & a high wind, so you may imagine that the work was done under difficulties. The cist was examined by candle-light, & the scene was a very picturesque one, the workmen standing round in the partial light, some fine old bushes waving above us, & myself on my knees, with a candle held in front of me, discussing the mouldering remains. . . .

CANON WILLIAM GREENWELL to ALBERT WAY, December 6, 1847.
Society of Antiquaries Correspondence, 1844–8

A BIT OF BARROW-DIGGING

Danby Parsonage, Grosmont, York.
. . . a bit of barrow-digging I undertook at Lord Falkland's request as far back as last May. My barrow is of much interest. I think Greenwell will be likely to endorse the view I am disposed to take. The investigation is not complete yet: but I have, as I think, ascertained this much:—There is a grave, and I am 18 inches down into it: but the grave is an insertion in an older and much smaller barrow, the contents of which were a burial after cremation, bits of the urn being met with in the filling in of the grave, and the disturbed calcined bones being found at a higher level and in diverse places. Over the interment in this

inserted grave a large accumulation of fresh matter was added, leading to the extension of the barrow to more than twice, perhaps three times, its original area and general dimensions. This is, in few words, the only theory that accounts for the ascertained facts. The digging of the grave most certainly was not done from the summit of the howe as it now is. There had been certainly no disturbance of the upper two feet and three quarters, or three feet, of the soil above the grave, and proportionately over the surface of the mound generally. I go tomorrow, all well, to complete the examination. Would you like an account for your Society?

J. C. ATKINSON to ST. JOHN HOPE, September 30, 1889. *Society of Antiquaries Correspondence*

A ROMAN BARROW?

The following Accident has given occasion for variety of Opinions here & sh'ld be glad to have that of the Learn'd with you.

A Person lately going into a gravel pit a short mile S.E. of this Citty in search for Fossils, observed a great variety of fragments of Urns scattered about the bottom of the pit, he brought some of them to Me, and I went along with him to view the place, & observed as follows.

The pit is in the centre of a high piece of ground, not so high but more extended than the Tumuli in general are, yet resembling one, when you are in the pit you see about two feet of earth, before you come att the stratum of Gravell, & along one side of the pit, betwixt the Earth's Gravel, runs a layer of very black Earth three or four inches in breadth, intermixed with pieces of burnt wood, this is separated from the stratum of Gravell, by a layer or kind of pavement of Oyster Shells, which have a very regular appearance. In the middle of the pit stands a hillock of the same height with the sides of the Pitt which was left by the Workmen, in this burnt Earth & Oyster Shells appear the same as in the sides of the Pitt, many fragments of Urns lay scattered about, & amongst the rest several of the fine red ones resembling Coral.

I went several times with a hand Trowel, & dug into the burnt Earth, & found many bottoms of the Coraline Urns with names stamped upon the middle, as OFRONI, CAIUS etc. There was only one whole Urn found, of the coarse grey sort full of Earth & Pebbles; many fragments of large Vessels were dug out. I have the neck of one which hath held several Gallons, these were generally of a white coarse Clay, there were several pieces of Craters or Pateras of the fine red, with figures in relief or vine Branches, Ivy, Lions, Tigers, & upon one are two Satyrs & Fawns, one playing upon a double Flute, there is onely the back of the other ? dancing? both in an antic posture.

Amongst the burnt Earth there was a surpriseing quantity of Teeth, which I take to be Horses, many Horns of young Bulls, & Bones of Birds, particularly that of a Cock's Leg with the Spur on.

We were equally surprised with the quantity of large Iron Nails, one near two feet in length haveing a round head in proportion. There were also Iron Instruments of different kinds, one resembling the Sacrificing Knife, & a large flatt Copper Needle.

As lease could not be obtained to open further the side of the Pitt, We were much confined in our researches. I am sorry the ground is not the propperty of One whose Curiosity wod urge Him to open the Sides a few feet each way, as no Doubt some further discoveries might be made.

WILLIAM WHITE, Surgeon, of York, to B. BARTLETT, June 29, 1770.
Society of Antiquaries Correspondence, XVIII century file, 3

FATE OF A ROMAN PAVEMENT—

Through the Park [Woodstock] we crossed again the Akeman-street, which runs all along with a perfect ridge made of stone, dug every where near the surface: it bears between north-east and east: it is a foot-path still through the Park with a stile, and a road beyond it which passes to Stunsfield, where are marks of an intrenched work, once a Roman station: and in the place they found (the 25th Jan. 1712) a most curious tesselated pavement, for bulk and beauty the most considerable one we know of: it was a parallelogram of thirty-five foot long and twenty foot wide, a noble room, and no doubt designed for feasting and jollity: in one of the circular works was Bacchus represented in stones properly coloured, with a tiger, a *thyrsus* in his hand enwrapped in vine leaves. This admirable curiosity deserved a better owner; for the landlord and tenant quarreling about sharing the profits of showing it, the latter maliciously tore it in pieces. When the earth was first laid open on its discovery, they found it covered a foot thick with burnt wheat, barley and pease: so that we may guess upon some enemy's approach it was covered with those matters to prevent its being injured, or was turned into a barn and burnt.

WILLIAM STUKELEY, *Itinerarium Curiosum*, 1776 ed., Iter II

—AND OF ANOTHER

October 14. One Mr Daniel Reeves of West Dean [Wilts] attended with the entire centre of the pavement lately found there, about 4 feet square superficies.

Society of Antiquaries *Minutes*, 1741–2

ALIENATION OF A ROMAN PAVEMENT

The Honorary Secretary read communications he had received from antiquaries with regard to the report that the Rev. S. E. V. Filleul, rector of All Saints, proposed to present a Roman pavement found in All Saints' glebe to the inhabitants of Dorchester, Boston, Mass., U.S.A.

The Rev. W. Miles Barnes said he supposed that the pavement, if not sent to America, would be destroyed. The nature of the cement seemed to have gone, and the tesserae were so loose that one could take them up by the handful. Laying these pavements was a costly work, and he did not think that the Museum had funds enough to lay the pavement if offered to them. Therefore it seemed that sending the pavement across the Atlantic really saved it from oblivion.

Proceedings Dorset Natural History and Antiquarian Field Club,
vol. XXIV, 1903

THE RAVAGED VILLA

In shards the sylvan vases lie,
    Their links of dance undone,
And brambles wither by thy brim,
    Choked fountain of the sun!
The spider in the laurel spins,
    The weed exiles the flower:
And, flung to kiln, Apollo's bust
    Makes lime for Mammon's tower

HERMAN MELVILLE, 1819–1891

THE SPIRIT OF THE TIMES

It was in the latter part of the August of 1844 that I accompanied Lord Albert Conyngham (now Lord Londesborough) on a visit to the Friars at Aylesford, for the purpose of opening a large Roman

73

barrow or sepulchral mound in the adjoining parish of Snodland. On the northern boundary of this parish the ground rises into a bold knoll, the summit of which bears the appearance of having been cut into an encampment. Just beneath the brow of the hill, looking towards the south, is the barrow which is the object of our visit. In the fields on the slope of the hill, descending from it, we picked up bits of Roman tile and pottery, which showed that the spot had been formerly occupied by that people; and at the foot of the hill is a small hamlet, which, with the hill, is named Hoborough, or Holborough. In ancient documents the word is written Holanbeorge, Holanberghe, &c. which would seem to mean the hollow borough, or the borough with a hollow or cave. The word which has usually been corrupted into borough, or bury, was generally applied by our Saxon forefathers to a fortified station, though in some cases it is merely another form of the word barrow, applied to a sepulchral mound. Here, however, it has probably its more usual meaning, which would confirm our suspicion that the top of the knoll owes its fortified appearance to the hands of man. The barrow, which was a large one and very near the top of the hill, commands a magnificent view over the vale of Maidstone, which spreads itself in a rich panorama around.

Our party at the 'digging' consisted of our kind and hospitable host and hostess, Mr. and Mrs. Charles Whatman of the Friars, Lord Albert Conyngham, the Rev. Lambert B. Larking of Ryarsh, the Rev. Mr. Phelps of Snodland, and two or three other ladies and gentlemen from the neighbourhood. As the barrow was of large dimensions, we had engaged some twelve or fourteen labourers, and, having determined to cut a trench of about six feet wide through the centre of the barrow from east to west, we commenced both ends of the trench at the same time, and divided the men between the two excavations. A rough sketch which I took on the spot, when the excavation was tolerably advanced on the east side, will give the reader some idea of the method on which we went to work. It was the labour of four long days to cut entirely through the barrow; but we who were not absolutely diggers contrived to pass our time to the full satisfaction of all the party. We had hired one of the boats which are used in this part of the country for carrying the amateur toxophilites along the Medway to their archery meetings; and each morning, after an early breakfast, we were rowed several miles down the river, which is here picturesque and singularly tortuous, to the place of landing. A plentiful supply of provisions had been procured for pic-nicing on the hill, and we remained by the barrow all day, watching and directing the operations. Unfortunately, it was one of those large barrows which do not repay the labour of cutting through them; and, although the final result was interesting in itself, we all felt somewhat of disappointment as our men laboured hour after hour, and no sepulchral chamber presented itself, and not even a burial-urn could be found to reward our patience. Two or three small fragments of broken pottery were all the articles which occurred in the body of the mound, until we came to the floor on which it had been raised. We contrived to pass our time, at intervals between digging and pic-nicing, in games of various descriptions—not exactly such as those which the builders of the mound celebrated when they laid the deceased on his funeral pile—and in other amusements. The season was fortunately exquisitely fine, and it was only once or twice that we were visited with a heavy shower from the south-west, when the only shelter near was afforded by the hole we had ourselves dug on the western side of the mound, in which we managed so to interlace parasols and umbrellas—much as the Roman soldiers are said to have joined together their shields when advancing to the attack of a fortress—as to form a tolerably impenetrable roof over our heads. The neighbourhood was not very populous, and during the first three days our visitors were few—some children from the village below, a gypsy woman or two, with dark eyes, who carried off a few halfpence, and perhaps a chance passer-by. But, although we found little, report had magnified our findings in no ordinary degree, and we afterwards learnt that it had gone over the country around that we had dug up a great treasure of gold. It was not, therefore, surprising if, on the last day of our excavation, we saw from our elevated position men on horse and men on foot making their way towards us from all points of the compass, and we were told that after our departure the top of the hill was crowded with visitors. We had uncovered the floor on which the mound was raised through the whole extent of the trench, and our observations held out no promise of any further discoveries if we cut into the mound in other directions. We had therefore determined to proceed no further, when an unexpected accident put a stop to our labours. The mound was twenty feet high, made of fine mould, and the workmen had imprudently cut the walls of the trench perpendicular; the consequence of which was that in the afternoon of the fourth day the upper part on one side fell in, and one of the labourers escaped narrowly with his life.

The trench we had cut through the barrow was in different parts from five to seven feet wide, and, from the discoveries made in the excavation, it appeared that the barrow had been raised over the ashes of a funeral pile. A horizontal platform had first been cut in the chalk of the hill, and on this a very smooth artificial floor of fine earth, about four inches deep had been made, on which the pile had been raised, and which we found covered with a thin coating of wood-ashes. The surface of ashes was not less than twenty feet in diameter. The barrow was twenty feet high from this floor of ashes. From the nature of the ground it was difficult to fix the exact limits of its circumference; a rough measurement before the barrow was opened gave a circumference of somewhat more than two hundred feet, and a subsequent measurement through the trench gave a diameter of ninety-three feet; but this perhaps included a part of the raised ground which did not strictly belong to the mound itself. In the floor of ashes were found scattered a considerable number of very long nails (which had probably been used to fasten together the framework on which the body was placed for cremation), with a few pieces of broken pottery which had evidently experienced the action of fire. A part of a Roman fibula was also found. Our impression was that this mound had been the monument of some person of rank, whose body, like that of the Emperor Severus, was burnt on the funeral pile, and his ashes carried home perhaps to Italy. The barrow was raised on the site of the pile, as a sort of cenotaph to his memory.

THOMAS WRIGHT, *Wanderings of an Antiquary*, 1854

SAXON OBSEQUIES

The Hon. R. C. Neville has for some weeks employed a number of labourers in excavating a locality near Great Wilbraham, in Cambridgeshire, long since known as the site of a Saxon Burial Ground. Various interesting remains have been from time to time discovered there, but it appears that they have hitherto rather served to gratify the avidity of collectors than promote the ends of antiquarian research, which is Mr Neville's aim in making a systematic investigation, and taking advantage of the opportunities it affords of getting at facts. As the mounds which at one time covered the graves have been long since levelled, trenches have been cut, in order to ascertain the position of the tumuli. We are informed that the skulls of the skeletons which are found in most of the graves are of two very decided characters, and of very distinct periods; that the older graves contain but few and rude beads and that the skulls in these are of remarkable flatness, the orbits of the eyes being almost at the top of the head, which is long and most deficient in size; that, in the other class of graves which furnish beads, swords, knives, spear-heads, and fibulae in profusion, the skulls are high and well developed in front. This is the popular ethnological view of the result of the discoveries. But we do not see why the absence of frontal space in the skulls decides them to be anterior in date to the others; and we shall look for that rigid attention to authenticated facts which is necessary before theories can be maintained, and which we make no doubt Mr Neville has adopted the proper means to secure. Upwards of a hundred urns of dark-coloured unbaked earth are said to have been exhumed. In some graves have been found thin bronze dishes and a wooden bucket or pail, hooped and ornamented with bronze, with a handle still attached. This is a rather important discovery, which does not square with the opinions of those who saw in a very similar object, found some time since at Wilbraham, a Saxon crown or diadem. In several graves umboes of shields were found; within one of these the handle yet remained, grasped by the finger-bones of a human hand. The skeletons of a man and horse occupied one grave, with a sword placed between them. In another, as many as four fibulae were found, together with sixty-four beads of various materials. One of the swords discovered is said to be of a very superior description; the blade as usual of iron, but the handle ornamented with bronze.

The Gentleman's Magazine, November, 1851

RESEARCH IN THE CHEVIOTS

Consecutive explorations of an unusual character have been made during the summers of the last and present years in the Cheviot district. On these lofty hills, which are sealed for so many months of the year with snow, a veritable tract of ancient Britain has been laid bare: a walled town, several fortlets, scattered hut-circles and tumuli have been disencumbered of the earth that has been accumulating over them for nearly two thousand years; and many interesting facts have been thus disclosed respecting the Celtic tribes whom Caesar found in possession of the land. It would appear that the Cheviot hills were well populated in those remote times. Huge circles of masonry overgrown with herbage are seen on most of them, sometimes on the slopes, sometimes on the summits, and within many of these there are smaller circles of turf-covered stones marking sites of huts. In all these ramparts and dwellings, blocks of the porphyry of the district have been used as the sole building material.

On the southern slope of a hill, locally distinguished as Greenlaw, great masses of ruin promised a rich reward to the spade of the excavator. Here three walled enclosures, connected with one another by a roadway, have been brought to light. Within these enclosures traces of as many as seventy stone huts can be counted. Most of the entrances into these face the east, and the floors of those that have been dug into are found to have been rudely flagged with flat stones. The largest of the enclosures has been strengthened with two ramparts; against the inner of these walls is a hut which has a flue—the earliest evidence of the use of chimneys we possess. In several of the huts charred wood was found in the floors, as well as broken pottery; in one a glass bead, in another a stone seat, in others a fragment of a glass armlet, part of the horn of the red deer, and three bottom stones of hand-mills. The Celtic remains on Broughlow, Chesters, and Ingram Hill have also been examined. The most recent diggings have been made on Yeavering Bell, of which we have already printed a detailed account.

The Gentleman's Magazine, December, 1862

BONES AND THE ARCHAEOLOGIST (1)

The real Antiquary will always respect the Skeletons, Ashes, and Bones of the dead, which he may discover in his subterranean excavations. With hallowed feelings sanctified by the knowledge that the dry bones shall live, he will do unto them as he would wish should be done unto his own remains when he has passed away and has been forgotten; for in opening Barrows it is not the Antiquary's object to violate the receptacles of the Dead, but from the relics which may be found in them, to trace the manners and the customs of the Early Britons, as the spade is almost their only historian. When the Antiquary meets with Skeletons near the surface of the earth he will bury them deeper than they were before they were denuded. When he opens a cist he will not disturb its contents unnecessarily. The Ashes and Bones of the Dead he will collect together with reverential awe, and he will never fail to restore those circling mounds of earth over them, which pointed out to him as they will point out to future Antiquaries, if not destroyed, the Tumuli of the Ancient Britons.

Finis Coronat Opus

THE REVD CHARLES WOOLS, notes to The Barrow Diggers, 1839

BONES AND THE ARCHAEOLOGIST (2)

The remains of the skeletons, and especially the skulls, of the early races of men inhabiting the British Islands, have become objects of interest to those who have made them their particular study. It unfortunately, however, happens that persons engaged in opening barrows, and making excavations for antiquities, even those well instructed in other respects, generally fail in procuring skulls in such a state as to be of any use for purposes of science. . . . It must be recollected that it is the whole of the bones of the head and face, including lower jaw and teeth, which the anatomist requires for his researches, not a few fragments, or the mere brain-case: at the same time, where the bones are fractured or disjointed, if every fragment, or nearly every fragment, be recovered, he will be able to rejoin them, and re-construct the cranium.

Whether it be barrow, cairn, or cemetery of any kind that is undergoing examination, as soon as a proximity to the skeleton is ascertained, and it is always advisable to proceed from the feet towards the head, the pickaxe and shovel should be laid aside; the stones and soil must be carefully removed with a garden trowel, the digger employed by entomologists, and the hand, so as to expose the head perfectly.

No attempt should even now be made to lift up the skull, until the earth has been cautiously removed all round it, so as to make it entirely free; it may then be gently raised up, and placed upon a sheet of soft paper, the superfluous soil picked out, the bones wrapped up immediately, and the package tied with string.

Where the skull has been fractured by the pressure of the earth, and the bones of the face crushed and displaced (for it is these which yield first, yet in most cases they are merely dislocated, not destroyed), every fragment, however small, and every tooth, should be diligently gathered up, and the whole wrapped in a sheet of paper, as before.

> '*All, all, have felt Time's mighty wand,*
>   *And, brought again to light,*
> *Defaced, despoil'd, can scarce withstand*
>   *The touch, however slight*'

It is best to inscribe immediately on these packets the name of the barrow, and a number, to distinguish each skull disinterred, which may at first be done with a pencil. As soon as possible afterwards this should be written in ink, and the same number marked with the pen upon the skull, or on two or three of the fragments where it is broken.

In all cases the position in which the skeleton lies should be accurately observed and noted down, whether extended on the back or side, or flexed, that is, with the knees drawn up, and the direction of the compass in which the head is laid. The relics accompanying the body, whether urns, implements, weapons, lamps, coins, etc., should always be carefully preserved, as they frequently indicate the people and the period to which the interment has belonged.

The safest mode of transmitting ancient skulls is to pack gently and neatly any number of the parcels, made in the manner above directed, in a box with a little hay. The elasticity of this substance is a perfect protection to the fragile bones during carriage.

J. BARNARD DAVIS, Hints for the Collecting and Preserving the Bones of Ancient Skulls, *Gentleman's Magazine*, October, 1853

SALT ON A CORPSE

It is apprehended that what your correspondent . . . describes as found in St Mary's churchyard at Leicester, and imagines a plate once charged with salt, and laid on a corpse was a *patten* intombed in the coffin of some priest or incumbent of that church.

The custom of putting a plate of salt on the belly of a deceased corpse, is desired to be accounted for. Is it to prevent any discharge from the navel after death? or, is it still retained?

I will venture to inform your correspondent after I have bid him recollect that the place of the interment was in church, that it was a custom in Leicester and its shire, yet continued, to place a dish or plate of salt on a corpse, to prevent its swelling and purging, as the term is. To account for the partial corrosion of the pewter, that it prevailed chiefly on the margin of the plate, and so slightly in its calix, we may suppose it was protected by its saline contents from the action of the morbid matter; for the effluvia of salt may pervade or overflow its container or charger, as readily as magnetic virtue; and the lips of the plate possessing little or no preventive salt, the sanies was at liberty, *there*, to effect the greater impression.

The Gentleman's Magazine, August, 1785

A NICE RELISH OF ANTIQUITIES

The Report of this Discovery [of Roman graves at Crundale in Kent] brought the Right Honourable Colonel Heneage Finch (now Earl of Winchelsea) whose inquisitive Genius inclines him to a curious Search after Antiquities, and of which he hath a nice Relish, and is an excellent Judge, to come and examine this Place more narrowly; which was done the same year; and in digging we found two Bodies of Persons full grown and another of a Child, lying side by side without any Urns with them.

JOHN HARRIS, *The History of Kent*, 1719

A JURISPRUDENTIAL ENQUIRY?

In a [Saxon] barrow, opened in Bourne Park, were some bones found, belonging to a male, who was in the prime of his life when he died. These bones lay within but a few inches of the surface, and Dr Pettigrew, who had long experience as a teacher of anatomy, would unhesitatingly assert that the body belonged to recent times, and had not lain underground half a century. In travelling that morning to

Breach Downs, he had noticed the sign of a house (Black Robin's Corner) which was a memorial of the spot where a notorious robber and murderer had committed his unholy and atrocious deeds. Though he was unwilling to say that the man whose skeleton they had discovered had been murdered, still he asserted that there was every probability of his not having received a legitimate burial. He was a man in the prime of life, between thirty and forty years of age—had been buried within fifty years, and the fact afforded curious matter for an enquiry in a jurisprudential point of view.

Report of an Evening Lecture by Dr. W. J. PETTIGREW to the British Archaeological Association at Canterbury, 1844

TREASURE-TROVE

There is also amongst other things a grave attempt against the king and his dignity and his crown . . . for instance the fraudulent hiding of treasure-trove, as if a person should be accused that he had found treasure, for instance, gold or silver or any other kind of metal, in whatever place . . . presumptions may be of this kind, as if he has exhibited more wealth than usual in his dress or in other ornaments, in his food or in his drink, and such like . . . and it does not matter in what place this kind of treasure has been found according to modern times, although in ancient times it was otherwise observed.

But treasure is an ancient deposit of money or some other metal, respecting which memory exists not, so that it has no owner, and so of natural right, it becomes the property of him who has found it, so that it shall not belong to another. Otherwise if anyone shall have hidden any thing under the ground for the sake of gain, or of fear, or of custody, it shall not be treasure of which a theft is made. Treasure is believed to be a gift of fortune, and no one ought to seek for treasure by the labour of serfs, nor to dig up the ground for treasure, but if he was engaged at work upon one thing, and fortune gave him another. Since therefore treasure is in nobody's goods, and of ancient time it was by natural right the property of the finder, it is now by the law of nations the property of the lord the king himself.

HENRY DE BRACTON, De Legibus et Consuetudinibus Angliae, circa 1256, Second Treatise of the Third Book, iii

HORACE WALPOLE'S MAHOGANY MODEL

At Gen. Conway's, Park-place, a new structure is reared: a Druid Temple, sent piece-meal from the States of Jersey, where it was lately

81

found by the Governor, Gen. Conway, as new ground was raising for their defence. The magnitude of the stones is such, that the mechanick wonders. Those who look to objects higher than are obtainable by the mechanical powers, will not here look in vain.

The druidical temple from Jersey is the same of which Gen. Conway and Mr Molesworth communicated an account to the Society of Antiquaries, published in their *Archaeologia* VIII, 383, 386. Two models were also made in mahogany, one of which, if I mistake not, is in the possession of Mr H. Walpole.

The Gentleman's Magazine, December, 1788

CANONS OF EXCAVATION

The examination of ancient sites can no longer be regarded, as was unhappily the case in former days, as a mere search for antiquities. The thing found is of value, whether to history, art, or science, but the circumstances of its finding are of even more evidential worth. The ideal excavation is one in which all the evidence is recognized and recorded, a task which demands no ordinary degree of knowledge and experience. It follows that such work should not be lightly undertaken, for with the best of intentions it is easy to do more harm than good. The choice of a site should not be at haphazard, but made with a particular problem in view. No work should be begun without the supervision of an archaeologist competent by reason of his experience and general knowledge to direct every detail. Provision must be made for complete and accurate record by measurements, drawings, and photographs of all evidence disclosed. Supervision must be continuous, and a necessary condition of all such work is that its results should be published as promptly and completely as possible. Where an excavation extends over a series of years, annual reports of the progress made should be issued, leaving the final conclusions to appear at the close of operations.

Archaeological excavation is only possible at a very considerable expense of time and money. The excavator who obtains his results with the least expenditure of either is to be commended, but only on the understanding that the results are really obtained. A superficial examination is worse than useless. But since every excavation should have for its motive a definite line of inquiry, the extent of work on any site will vary according to the conditions. No hard and fast rule can be laid down, and indeed the point is one on which complete agreement is not to be expected. However this may be, it is at any rate evident that something like a general agreement on the direction of archaeological inquiry in Britain would be of the greatest possible value. By such means the energies of all the archaeological societies and institutions of the country might be concentrated on a definite programme of research, in which all might take part, avoiding side-issues and useless repetitions. The publication of results in a more or less uniform manner should not be impossible to achieve, and would not only be of signal advantage to ourselves, but could not fail to commend our British school of archaeology to the learned of other nations.

SIR CHARLES PEERS, *Antiquaries Journal*, 1929

LONG-BARROW FUNERALS

The excavation during the past summer of the Nutbane long-barrow in Hampshire has proved exceptionally important for the understanding of a distinctively British type of prehistoric monument (writes Jacquetta Hawkes).

These burial mounds, in shape resembling a calabash pear halved longitudinally, were the characteristic form of sepulchre for the first Neolithic farming people of southern England. Most of them must have been raised round about 4,000 years ago.

Although a less familiar part of our landscape than the later round barrows, there are plenty of them to be seen on the southern downlands. It had already been suspected that the piling of the last mound of chalk and soil was often only the last stage in a complicated funerary procedure, and this is what the brilliant digging at Nutbane has proved.

Set on Fire

The tribesmen seem first to have erected some kind of wooden ritual enclosure at what was the broad eastern end of the mound, and then, behind it, an embanked mortuary chamber where they laid the bodies of two middle-aged men and a child on a brushwood bed.

It is impossible to tell how long the burials were left in this condition before the ritual enclosure was succeeded by a larger and probably roofed, wooden building (where presumably relatives met to celebrate the funeral) and the mortuary chamber itself fenced in with sizeable posts.

The fourth body, that of another middle-aged man, was added with some disturbance of the other corpses. The time had now evidently come to seal the whole grave off; the entrance to the mortuary was blocked before it was piled with earth and chalk dug from deep flanking ditches.

The wooden building was then set on fire, and masses of chalk thrown into it while the flames were still leaping. So clear are the marks of burning that it is possible to tell that the wind was blowing from the north-west while this dramatic phase of the interment was being carried out.

Finally, the side ditches were extended westward to complete the tail of the mound and bring it to a total length of about 170 ft. The excavation was carried out by Mrs. F. de M. Vacher on behalf of the Ministry of Works. *The Observer*, October 19, 1958

SELECTIVE OR TOTAL?

The destructiveness of excavation imposes limitations on the activities of the beginner and the expert alike. Not even the most experienced excavator can extract *everything* from a site; something must always escape him. Yet archaeological technique is constantly improving, and it may well be that the excavators of the future will think our present methods as inadequate as we think the methods of the 'barrow-diggers' a century ago. They may be able to recover what we to-day lose. For this reason, therefore, we should hesitate to excavate unless we can be reasonably certain of gaining thereby new knowledge. We should in fact follow in general the advice of the late Professor R. G. Collingwood, to dig only in order to find the answer to a specific question.

The type of excavation advocated by Professor Collingwood is *selective*; it serves, that is, to give the main facts about the culture and chronology of a community, without going into details. It needs relatively little work, time, and money to excavate a site in this fashion, and for these reasons it is the most common type of excavation practised in this country.

Selective excavation, however, is not enough, for it provides only a skeleton of knowledge. From time to time something more is needed, to enable us to see the life and history of a typical community in all its details. For this purpose, therefore, there must be *total* excavation, the stripping of an entire site, layer by layer, down to bed-rock. This operation, unlike selective excavation, does not seek to answer any specific questions about the site; rather, it seeks to answer all the possible questions.

R. J. C. ATKINSON, *Field Archaeology*, 1946, Methuen and Co. Ltd.

THEY SEE WHEN HYPNOTISED

Two men and two women will dig to-day for treasure which they 'saw' when hypnotised.

By to-night they expect to have found a metal-bound casket filled with silver coins which was buried by refugee monks during the Reformation in the 16th century.

If the casket is unearthed it will bring success to a fantastic experiment.

For the site of the treasure, the burial of the casket and the Benedictine monks in their flowing robes were all 'seen' by the four assistants of an archaeologist who had put them into a 'deep relaxation' hypnotic state.

The archaeologist said yesterday: 'It seems fantastic and incredible but by putting my assistants into a form of trance on these historic sites I have been able to send their minds back into the past. They have been able to describe and make sketches of things which happened during the Norman Conquest'.

The archaeologist and his team are working on two sites near the ruins of a supposed haunted hunting lodge. Four of the assistants— a married couple, a young man and a young girl—have all been hypnotised there. They were able to describe the lodge as it was in the 16th century.

'There is no mental telepathy in this,' said the archaeologist. 'I leave my assistants to gather their impressions from the past and then I apply them to my own knowledge of these historic sites. In this way I know exactly where to excavate'.

Daily Sketch, August 18, 1953

USING THE VIRGULA DIVINA

As soon as the person's foremost foot comes near the attracting body, the end of the rod is repelled towards the face; then open the hands a little, replace the rod, and approach nearer, and the repulsion will be continued until the foot is on or over the attracting body.

When this is the case the rod will first be repelled a little, viz., 2 or 3 inches, and then be attracted towards the metallic body, i.e., its end will be drawn down towards it.

When it hath been drawn down, it must not be thrown back without opening the hands, a fresh grasp being necessary to every attraction, but then the least opening of the hand is sufficient.

As long as the person stands over the attracting body the rod continues to be attracted, but as soon as the forefoot is beyond it, then the rod is drawn backward to the face.

Metals have different degrees of attraction; gold is the strongest, next copper, then iron, silver, tin, lead, bones, coals, springs of water, and limestone.

The Gentleman's Magazine, November, 1751

THE MAGIC BOX

In a rain-sodden field beside the Great North Road near Water Newton, Hunts, a dowser pitted his ancient art on Saturday against the new science of electronics. And, be it lamented, it was yet another case of man being beaten by the machine.

The contest was the outcome of a description, in THE DAILY TELEGRAPH of Sept. 15, of a 'magic box' produced in the Laboratory for Archaeology and the History of Art, Oxford. The box detects buried objects by magnetic readings.

Mr. Philip Raine, chief chemist to a London firm of cable manufacturers and electrical engineers, discovered a few years ago that he has the power of divining. He promptly issued a challenge to a contest.

He has used his power frequently to find lost cables and other objects. He claimed that, with nothing more elaborate than two metal rods, he could do all that the machine could do.

Dr. Edward Hall, Director of the laboratory, and Dr. Martin Aitken, his deputy, who recently successfully used the new instrument on an archaeological site in Cyprus, were sceptical about dowsing. But they were sufficiently impressed by Mr. Raine's claims, sincerity and scientific background to consent to a trial.

The site chosen was on the outskirts of the Roman city, Durobrivae. Earlier this year the 'box', a transistorised proton resonance magnetometer, located a pottery kiln there $3\frac{1}{2}$ ft. below the ground. The spot was dug, the kiln was found, and later the excavation was filled. The ground was restored.

Reaction Marked—Pattern of Pegs

Two areas, 100 ft. by 50 ft., had been marked. One contained the kiln, the other was unexplored and only the scientists knew in which the kiln lay. Mr. Raine produced two pieces of thin brass rod, each with an end bent so that it could swivel.

He had not taken more than six paces before the rods, held horizontally, folded in towards his chest. He stopped. The spot was pegged. A minute later there was another reaction. Again the spot was marked.

Then it was seen that some of the marking pegs were beginning to assume a kind of pattern. By the time his survey of this section was complete, there were a score of pegs, eight of which formed a rectangular outline with one end curved.

He moved to the section containing the kiln. Several times the rods reacted. But over the kiln there was no reaction.

Then the 'box' was brought into action. The flickering of pointers on dials and the recording of readings on the 'plot' may not have been so spectacular as the rods. But the result was decisive.

Dr. Aitken broke to Mr. Raine the news that he had missed the kiln, and that there was no relation between readings and pegs. Mr. Raine took his defeat like a sportsman. 'I accept that,' he said. 'I am very disappointed.'

Daily Telegraph, November 17, 1958

EXCAVATION

Breaking up Roman concrete, hoping to date
A corridor by what the workmen dropped,
A rubbed coin or a broken pot illuminate
The hours before an era stopped.

Foundations remain, whatever disaster
Crushed this commercial city. Squatting
With a trowel and shovel, poking at plaster,
I find the Empire still rotting.

And what of us, I think, will our old saucepans
Pass through the hands of learned professors?
Will our halfpennies rolled under floorboards, brass pins
And buttons, please new possessors?

An aeroplane slides through the clouds across the sky,
Supposing, I think, men go on building,
Supposing new cities rise where old ones die.
But that supposes everything.

JULIAN MITCHELL, *The Times Literary Supplement*,
February 20, 1959

A PIECE OF WIRE

A three-strand gold bracelet made in the Bronze Age has been hanging in a farm shed at Great Bromley, near Colchester, for five years because it was thought to be a piece of wire.

A farm-worker found the bracelet on a tooth of his harrow and kept it in case he needed the wire. Recently, because of its shine, he took it to a Colchester jeweller . . .

Daily Telegraph, August 14, 1969

COIN IN THE CHICKEN

A gold coin dating from 14 to 20 B.C. was found in the crop of a chicken at Sudbury, Suffolk.

Daily Telegraph, April 3, 1969

4—*ANTIQUARY IN CHURCH*

A little lowly hermitage
Gothic and the fresh New Birth
Heartily Sick of Gothic
Gothic Vastly Great
All English to be Gothish
Other than of Gothic Grace
The Sisters
Regulbium
Camden at Lewes—
    —at Peterborough
The Noviomagians
Cambrians at Strata Florida
Kentish Tracery
A new church in Newcastle
Sacrilege and Robbery
Walpole on Westminster—
    —on Salisbury
Walpole and Painted Glass
Those Puseyites
Praise in Epitaphs
Kill'd by Icicle
Sir Dudly Digges, Knight
His sister Margaret, 1619
The Spiritual Railway
St Dunstan's Tongues
A faultless ruin
Grave-stones of Married Persons
Fourteenth Century in Kent
The Moonlight Cross
Winifred's Dukkeripen
That calm wee door
Clayton Village
An Archaeological Picnic
A free Belfry
Bell-swarmèd
For the Queene of Skotts
For the Dealers in Tobacco
Wrackes of Walsingam
Regency Pride
Taking Part in History

A LITTLE LOWLY HERMITAGE

A little lowly Hermitage it was,
Downe in a dale, hard by a forests side,
Far from resort of people, that did pas
In trauell to and froe: a little wyde
There was an holy Chappell edifyde,
Wherein the Hermite dewly wont to say
His holy things each morne and euentyde:
Thereby a Christall streame did gently play,
Which from a sacred fountaine welled forth alway.

Arriued there, the little house they fill,
Ne looke for entertainement, where none was:
Rest is their feast, and all things at their will;
The noblest mind the best contentment has.
With faire discourse the euening so they pas:
For that old man of pleasing wordes had store,
And well could file his tongue as smooth as glas;
He told of Saintes and Popes, and euermore
He strowd an Aue-Mary after and before.

EDMUND SPENSER, *The Faerie Queene*, 1596

GOTHIC AND THE FRESH NEW BIRTH

And meanwhile of the world demanding architecture, what are we to do? Meanwhile? After all, is there any meanwhile? Are we not now demanding Gothic Architecture and crying for the fresh New Birth? To me it seems so. It is true that the world is uglier now than it was fifty years ago; but then people thought that ugliness a desirable thing, and looked at it with complacency as a sign of civilisation, which no doubt it is. Now we are no longer complacent, but are grumbling in a dim unorganised manner. We feel a loss, and unless we are very unreal and helpless we shall presently begin to try to supply that loss. Art cannot be dead so long as we feel the lack of it, I say: and though we shall probably try many roundabout ways for filling up the lack; yet we shall at last be driven into the one right way of concluding that in spite of all risks, and all losses, unhappy and slavish work must come to an end. In that day we shall take Gothic architecture by the hand, and know it for what it was and what it is.

WILLIAM MORRIS, *Lecture on Gothic Architecture*,
Longmans, Green and Co. Ltd.

HEARTILY SICK OF GOTHIC

. . . between us I am heartily sick of Gothic;—indeed I have resolved that I *won't* contribute a single penny towards any new church unless designed in the Palladian style, & having a dome. Broach spires are an abomination to me,—I take no delight in Decorated windows,—yes, even deep & reverend chancels are works in which I have no pleasure,—it is all humbug every bit of it . . . *Distinctness* . . . I maintain is a beauty even on a glass painting,—Pugin, Wailes, Warnington, & ye defunkt Camden Societie non obstantibus. . . .

C. WHISTOW to ALBERT WAY, October 15, 1847. *Society of Antiquaries Correspondence*, 1844–8

GOTHIC VASTLY GREAT

Here also I beg leave to add a few remarks upon churches in general. The architecture of most of our old churches is Gothic; yet notwithstanding all the barbarousness of them to whom the order owes its name, and the many rudenesses it is itself charged with, this I think may be said for some Gothic buildings, that they abound with as much variety, and sometimes strike the eye as agreeably, as the finest pieces of the more regular orders. Thus, if we consider the best buildings we have of this kind in England, there is something vastly great and magnificent, and something also vastly beautiful in the composure. For instance, if we look upon an inside for a neat structure with pillars, where do we see any finer turned than those of the Temple Church, or Westminster Abbey, or the Cathedral of Lincoln? Some think their beautiful taper pillars far exceed the more modern bulky supporters of St Paul's, which, they say, have little else but the flutings and capitals of the Corinthian order to recommend them. For a structure without pillars, nothing hardly equals King's College Chapel, in Cambridge. If we look upon an outside, Peterborough Cathedral, as it now is, will scarce yield to any that I know of; but were it finished according to the model which we see in that part that is so, almost all, I think, must submit to it. This I speak of the west end, which, if it and the lantern were finished, would show five steeples in front. From the east this church likewise presents us with a view surprisingly entertaining. . . . Our old parish churches, indeed, do not often present us with anything so vastly fine, but sometimes we meet with a steeple among them remarkably elegant. . . . Possibly, then, by a nice examination of the different modes in the fabric of parish churches, the different ages when they were in use may be nearly ascertained.

THOMAS ASTLE, F.S.A., to *The Antiquarian Repertory*, 1808

ALL ENGLISH TO BE GOTHISH

Next we take notice of the signal structures which each County doth afford. Indeed the *Italians* do account all *English* to be *Gothish Buildings*, onely vast . . . however abating to their advantage above us in *Materials*, *Marble*, *Pophery*, etc. their pallaces may admire the art in some *English fabricks*; and in our *Churches* especially. . . . But well may we weep when looking back on our late *Civil War*, remembring how many beautiful *Buildings* were ruined thereby. . . .

THOMAS FULLER, *The History of the Worthies of England*, 1662

OTHER THAN OF GOTHIC GRACE

Verses written among the ruins of Saint Augustine's Monastery, Canterbury; part of whose scite is converted into a Bowling Green, and a Cockpit.

> *As through old Austin's fane I stray,*
> *And through his ravag'd groves;*
> *Companion of my pensive way,*
> *The fairy Fancy roves.*
>
> *She waves her magic wand, again*
> *His ancient pomp recalls;*
> *And rears again his lofty fane,*
> *And builds his lordly walls:*
>
> *His cope-clad priests, with chaunt divine,*
> *The sacred host upraise;*
> *And girt with taper's holy shine*
> *His gorgeous altars blaze.*
>
> *Entranc'd in more than mortal joys*
> *My ravish'd senses dwell;*
> *Oh curse on yon unhallow'd noise*
> *That breaks the fairly spell!*
>
> *Sounds as of ruffians drunk with wine*
> *Offend my sober ear;*
> *And other than of chaunt divine,*
> *Or holy hymn I hear.*

93

Sights other than of Gothic grace
  I see, or fretted roof;
And others than of storied glass,
  Or pillar massy proof.

Alas! no more the well arch'd aisle
  Extends its lengthen'd walks;
But o'er the desolated pile
  The giant ruin stalks.

And mid rich sculpture's proudest charms
  The gadding ivy crawls,
And scarce with all its hundred arms
  Upholds the tott'ring walls.

Thus robb'd of fancy's elfin joys,
  I bade the fane farewell:—
And curs'd again the unhallow'd noise
  That broke the fairly spell.

WILLIAM JACKSON, 1757–89

THE SISTERS
Written at Reculver

By the white margin of the tide,
  Lone wand'rer as I stray,
How free from care, how tranquil glide
  My morning hours away!

Yet here my not inactive mind,
  What various scenes employ;
For in this solitude I find
  Variety of joy.

Whether amidst these sons of toil
  That plough the swelling sea,
On yonder bench I rest awhile,
  And join their jocund glee:

And briskly whilst from guest to guest
  Goes round the nut-brown ale,
I listen to the sailor's jest,
  Or hear the woodman's tale:

94

Or whether on the pebbly beach,—
  Engenio by my side,—
At length my listless limbs I stretch,
  And watch th'approaching tide:

And sometimes by the winding shore
  I wander all alone;
And listen to old ocean's roar,
  And hear the seagull's moan.

And oft as by the rolling sea
  In thoughtful mood I stray,
The favouring Muse will deign to be
  Companion of my way:

And, oft regardless of the shore,
  She turns my wand'ring eyes,
To where, yon brown cliff peering o'er
  The Sister spires arise.

Ye Sisters then, alas the while!
  A pitying tear I pay;
To weep your venerable pile
  Now hast'ning to decay:

For ruin,—ill betide the deed,—
  Usurps each mould'ring stone;
And hastes, with unobstructed speed,
  To claim ye for his own.

But oh!—nor let me plead in vain,—
  Th'unhallow'd deed forbear;
Ye winds respect the holy fane,
  And you, ye wild waves spare!

But yet if neither wind nor wave
  Respect the tott'ring wall;
O son of commerce haste and save
  The sea-mark from its fall!

Lest, homeward bound, thy luckless crew
  Attempt this dang'rous shore;
And all in vain with anxious view
  The Sister spires explore.

And thou with fruitless grief behold
　　Thy good ship dock'd in sand;
And all thy stores of future gold
　　Bestrew the length'ning strand.

But, oh! to winds untaught to hear
　　I pour the fruitless lay,
To waves unheedful of my pray'r,
　　And men more rude than they.

Ye Sister spires! though,—lasting shame!—
　　Your ruins strew the plain;
To blot the memory of your fame
　　Oblivion strives in vain.

For that to latest time consign'd,
　　Shall live, shall flourish long;
Your fame in Keate's soft tale enshrin'd,
　　And Stella's moral song.

And aye perhaps, if right I ween,
　　This little lay shall tell
To future times, ye once have been:—
　　So Sisters fare ye well!

WILLIAM JACKSON, 1757–89

(*The twin towers of Reculver church, a far-seen monument on the north-east coast of Kent, were, in the terms of a popular legend, built by an Abbess of Davington Priory as a memorial to her twin sister who died in a shipwreck off the coast. For many years they were preserved solely as a ship-mark.*)

REGULBIUM

Once more ye mould'ring walls with ivy clad,
Ye crumb'ling relicks of antiquity,
I greet ye with a verse; once more I tread
With mournful reverence your sacred bounds,
And view your scatter'd fragments strew'd around!
And thou fair monument of piety,
Rear'd in a distant and more pious age,
Whose sister spires raise high their stately forms
To guide the seaman, and to grace the view,

Thee too I hail!—long hast thou born the rage
Of elements combin'd to work thy fall;
Long have the raving winds and dashing tides,
The iron-armed frost, and driving rain,
With all their dread artillery essay'd
To lay thee in the dust; they strove in vain!
Still firm thou stand'st, tho' torn with many a rent
Deform, and many an honour swept away.

But though no local monuments remain,
And ocean occupies thy former site;
Yet shall some tokens of thy ancient state,
Descend to future ages, and be shewn,
In cabinets of antiquarian wealth;
For lo, yon group slow moving on the beach,
With tatter'd garments, floating in the wind,
Congenial with the scene, whose searching eyes
Intently fixed upon the yellow sand,
There frequent find, wash'd by the briny wave,
Relicks of ancient Rome, and ancient days,—
For rich in buried treasure is the soil
By winds and tides o'erthrown;—full many a coin
Impress'd with Caesar's image, gold or brass,
Or silver, or electrum, swells their store;
Full many an implement of little worth
Original, but precious made by time,
And rich with verdant rust, repay the search.
These when the curious traveller arrives
Their rude possessors bring, well pleas'd to change
Relicks of ancient Rome, for British pence,
Caesar for George, or silver roundels smooth
Without impress, current, though never coin'd.

R. FREEMAN, *Regulbium, a poem with an Historical and Descriptive Account of the Roman Station at Reculver, in Kent,* 1810

(*Here again is reference to the twin towers, but more particularly to the many discoveries of antiquities in the area of the Roman fortress within which the medieval church stood and still stands.*)

CAMDEN AT LEWES—

Yet there are 6 Churches still remaining in the town, amongst which, not far from the Castle, there stands beneath it a little one quite desolate, and overgrown with bramble, in the walls whereof are engraven in arched work certain rude verses in an obsolete Character; which imply, that one *Magnus*, descended of the Blood Royal of the Danes, embracing a solitary life, was there buried. But here take the verses themselves, tho' imperfect, and *gaping*, if I may so say, with the *yawning* joynts of the stones.

Clauditur hic miles Danorum regia protes,
Magnus nomen ei, magnae nota progeniei,
Deponens Magnum, prudentior induit agnum:
Praepete pro vita fit parvulus Anachorita.

Here lies a Knight of Denmark's royal blood,
Magnus his name, whence his great race is show'd.
Resigning all his grandeur he became
Hermit from soldier, and from wolf a lamb.

WILLIAM CAMDEN, Britannia, 1586, ed. Gibson, 1695

—AT PETERBOROUGH

So that of a Monastery it became a Cathedral Church, which, if you survey its building, is very fine, even in respect of its antiquity; its Front is noble and majestic, its Cloisters fine and large; in the Glass windows there is represented the history of *Wolpher*, the founder, with the succession of its Abbots. *St Mary's* Chapel is a large piece of building, and full of curious workmanship: and the Choir is very fine; wherein two Queens, as unfortunate as could be, *Catherine* of Spain, and *Mary* Queen of Scots, lye interr'd, finding rest here from all their miseries.

WILLIAM CAMDEN, Britannia, 1586, ed. Gibson, 1695

THE NOVIOMAGIANS

To write all that was seen and said on this day would be to produce a much better guide-book than at present exists. They examined the Abbey from its commencement in the East, to its extreme extremity in the west, and found in every inch of its long length matter to interest and delight them. Apart from the variety of styles which it presents, and its general effect, there are numerous minute points in the Abbey to occupy the attention of those who know 'how to observe'. The carving in some of the chapels is exquisite, (infinitely better, by the way, than that afterwards exhibited by our Chairman at dinner) and cannot be too highly praised. Part of the cloisters which remain, (attached to the south transept), contain some very curious intersecting semicircular arches. The power of this building to induce poetical feelings in the spectator is strikingly exemplified by the numerous verses to be found within its walls. They have been mostly lithographed by their inspired authors, that is, drawn on stone,—and will probably be published for the benefit of posterity. The following is a specimen of their elevated, not to say sublime, character—

> *Thou relict of a by-gorn day,*
> *Where is the man that would dear to say,*
> *He cears not, thou mayst pass away.*

The bold attempt made in the first line to shadow forth the widowed state of the building by a single word, is perhaps, not to be equalled in the English language.

After viewing the Abbey, the members proceeded to St. Michael's Church to see the monument of the great Lord Bacon. Bacon, as every-one knows, was a man who 'went the whole hog', and in the statue of him there set up, (to apply the observation of another), he certainly 'looks the hog he went'. The Reading desk here, displays a stand for the hour glass by which preachers formerly regulated their discourse. It is not exactly known if when they gave up the glass they abandoned the bottle.

Minutes of the 16th Anniversary Meeting of the Noviomagian Club,
St Albans, 1st July, 1844

CAMBRIANS AT STRATA FLORIDA

The scene at the Abbey was at one time a most interesting one, several ladies having joined the party. Architects and draughtsmen were measuring and sketching portions of old buildings, one dignitary of the Church was transferring the resemblance of the gateway to his sketch-book, whilst another dignitary lent an attentive ear to some amusing anecdote of by-gone days. Some were loud in their condemnation of the ruthless vandalism that had consigned so beautiful a specimen of architecture to wanton destruction, and fervently hoping that the present proprietor would cause the ruins to be carefully cleaned out and properly fenced in to prevent any further depredation by relic-seeking tourists. All seemed to vie with each other who should do most towards the advancement of the object of the excursion; and whilst intelligent commoners were measuring the building, an enthusiastic nobleman might be seen busily washing the tiles and ornaments for removal and preservation.

The Welshman, September 17, 1847

KENTISH TRACERY

The very interesting Church of *Chartham*, about half way between Chilham and Canterbury, and seen rt. from the rail, must be visited from the latter city, 3½ m., since there is no station here.

The nave is partly E.E., the chancel Dec. (toward the end of Edward II's reign), and has 4 windows on either side, the tracery of which is very beautiful and unusual. The E. window is the double of one of the side windows. Examples of this peculiar tracery, which has been called 'the Kentish,' occur in the hall windows at Penshurst, in the chapel windows at Leeds Castle, and in the windows of the hall at Mayfield, Sussex. Observe the trefoil moulding which connects the windows within. Some of the original stained glass remains, and deserves careful notice; the red and green vine-leaf pattern bordering the lights is especially graceful. On the N. side is an unknown tomb, probably that of the builder of the chancel, and on the floor the very fine brass of a knight of the Septvans family, an excellent example of armour, temp. Edw. II: on his shield, surcoat, and aillettes or shoulder-pieces, are 3 wheat screens or *fans*, the arms of the Septvans. The mailed coif is thrown back from the head. The 'hauketon' of leather, appears at the wrists, and again below the ringed hauberck. The 'poleyns' or knee-pieces are highly ornamented. There are 3 smaller 15th cent. *Brasses* for rectors of Chartham.

Between the nave and chancel are trefoil-headed hagioscopes.

In the S. transept is an elaborate monument by Rysbrach for Sir William Young and his wife Sarah Fagg; and adjoining are other records of the Faggs of Mystole, all of whom it appears 'exemplarily satisfied the ends for which they were born'. The N. transept contains the monument of Dr. Delangle, 1724, a French refugee, who became canon of Westminster and rector here. The whole of this ch., but especially the chancel, deserves the most careful examination.

The village of Chartham is built round a green, on one side of which is the 'Delangle House,' built by the Doctor, and marked by a bust of Charles II, with sceptre and cushion, in a niche over the entrance. At the back of the village is a large paper-mill, the smoke from which is conspicuous throughout the whole valley.

In 1668 one of the first discoveries of enormous fossil bones which attracted the attention of the learned was made at Chartham in sinking a well, and gave rise to various speculations.

On the Downs above the village, W., are some relics of a number of tumuli called *Danes' Banks*, the greater part of which were examined by Mr. Faussett. S. of the tumuli the Downs are marked by entrenchment lines which cross them from E. to W.

MURRAY'S *Handbook for Travellers in Kent and Sussex*, 1858

A NEW CHURCH IN NEWCASTLE

Two stained glass windows have been recently placed in the new church of St Peter, Newcastle, the work of Mr Wailes of that town. One is in the chancel, and contains the figures of the Apostles St John and St James the Greater. As this part of the church contains six windows, of two lights each, the opportunity is presented of depicting the Twelve Apostles. . . . The other specimen of Mr Wailes's art is an *obituary window*, to the memory of the late Vicar of Newcastle, the first of the kind, it is believed, in the diocese. The Archdeacon of Northumberland, at his late visitation, very judiciously recommended this specimen of memorial, which forms at once a pious testimony to the departed, and a rich and appropriate ornament to the building where it is placed, and thus makes the indulgence of affectionate regret on the part of the survivors subservient to the permanent decoration of the house of God. The window is about seventeen feet in height, by nearly six feet in breadth, of the decorated style of the early part of the fourteenth century, and consists of three *lights*, surmounted by three *quatrefoils*. . . . The window is placed at the extremity of the south aisle, and whilst it is most creditable to the skill and ability of Mr Wailes, it forms, at the same time, a remarkably interesting feature of the internal decoration of the building. The Church is just completed, and there is but one opinion concerning it, that, for beauty and correctness of architecture, it is not surpassed by any church of the same dimensions in the North of England. Nearly one-half of the whole accommodation, which is adapted for 1,200 persons, is to be devoted to the gratuitous use of the poor.

The Gentleman's Magazine, March, 1843

SACRILEGE AND ROBBERY
Ten Pounds Reward

WHEREAS, on the Night of Wednesday or Thursday last, several
Pieces of
STAINED GLASS,
Containing ancient Heads and Figures were feloniously stolen and
Removed from the South-East Window of the

*Parish Church of
All Saints, Northstreet
in this City*

A Reward of TEN POUNDS will be paid by the Churchwardens

of the said Parish to any Person or Persons who shall give such Information as will lead to the Conviction of the Offenders

York, October 14, 1842

P. J. SHAW, *An Old York Church: All Hallows in North Street*, 1908

WALPOLE ON WESTMINSTER—

Berkeley Square, January 5, 1780

. . . The picture found near the altar in Westminster Abbey, about three years ago, was of King Sebert. I saw it, and it was well preserved, with some others worse; but they have foolishly buried it again behind their new altar-piece; and so they have a very fine tomb of Anne of Cleves, close to the altar, which they did not know till I told them whose it was, though her arms are upon it, and though there is an exact plate of it in Sandford. They might at least have cut out the portraits and removed the tomb to a conspicuous situation; but though this age is grown so antiquarian, it has not gained a grain more of sense in that walk: witness as you instance in Mr Grose's 'Legends', and in the Dean and Chapter reburying the crown, robes, and sceptre of Edward I. There would surely have been as much piety in preserving them in their treasury, as in consigning them again to decay. I did not know that the salvation of robes and crowns depended on receiving Christian burial. At the same time, the Chapter transgress that Prince's will, like all their antecessors; for he ordered his tomb to be opened every year or two years, and receive a new cere-cloth or pall; but they boast now of having enclosed him so substantially, that his ashes cannot be violated again.

It was the present Bishop-Dean who showed me the pictures and Anne's tomb, and consulted me on the new altar-piece. I advised him to have a light octangular canopy, like the cross at Chichester, placed over the table or altar itself, which would have given dignity to it, especially if elevated by a flight of steps; and from the side arches of the octagon, I would have had a semicircle of open arches that should have advanced quite to the seats of the prebends, which would have discovered the pictures; and through the octagon itself you would have perceived the shrine of Edward the Confessor, which is much higher than the level of the choir—but men who ask advice seldom follow it, if you do not happen to light on the same ideas with themselves.

P.S. The Houghton pictures are not lost—but to Houghton and England!

Letters of Horace Walpole, XCII. To THE REVD WILLIAM COLE.
Everyman edition, 1948, J. M. Dent and Sons Ltd.

102

—ON SALISBURY

Strawberry Hill, August 24, 1789

I shall heartily lament with you, Sir, the demolition of those beautiful chapels at Salisbury. I was scandalised long ago at the ruinous state in which they were indecently suffered to remain. It appears as strange, that, when a spirit of restoration and decoration has taken place, it should be mixed with barbarous innovation. As much as taste has improved, I do not believe that modern execution will equal our models. I am sorry that I can only regret, not prevent. I do not know the Bishop of Salisbury even by sight, and certainly have no credit to obstruct any of his plans. Should I get sight of Mr Wyatt, which it is not easy to do, I will remonstrate against the intended alteration; but, probably, without success, as I do not suppose he has authority enough to interpose effectually: still, I will try.

It is an old complaint with me, Sir, that when families are extinct, Chapters take the freedom of removing ancient monuments, and even of selling over again the sites of such tombs. A scandalous, nay, dishonest abuse, and very unbecoming clergymen! Is it creditable for divines to traffic for consecrated ground, and which the church had already sold? I do not wonder that magnificent monuments are out of fashion when they are treated so disrespectfully. You, Sir, alone, have placed several out of the reach of such a kind of simoniacal abuse; for to buy into the church, or to sell the church's land twice over, breathes a similar kind of spirit. Perhaps, as the subscription indicates taste, if some of the subscribers could be persuaded to object to the removal of the two beautiful chapels, as contrary to their view of beautifying, it might have good effect; or, if some letter were published in the papers against the destruction, as barbarous and the result of bad taste, it might divert the design. I zealously wish it were stopped, but I know none of the Chapter or subscribers.

Letters of Horace Walpole, XCIV. To RICHARD GOUGH. Everyman edition, 1948, J. M. Dent and Sons Ltd.

WALPOLE AND PAINTED GLASS

Strawberry Hill, July 20, 1749

I am returned to my Strawberry, and find it in such beauty, that I shall be impatient till I see you and your sisters here. They must excuse me if I don't marry for their reception; for it is said the Drax's have impeached fifteen more damsels, and till all the juries of matrons have finished their inquest, one shall not care to make one's choice: I was

103

going to say, 'throw one's handkerchief,' but at present that term would be a little equivocal.

As I came to town (from Mistley) I was extremely entertained with some excursions I made out of the road in search of antiquities. At Layer Marney is a noble old remnant of the palace of the Lords of Marney, with three very good tombs in the church well preserved. At Messing I saw an extreme fine window of painted glass in the church: it is the duties prescribed in the Gospel, of visiting the sick and prisoners, &c. I mistook, and called it the seven deadly sins. There is a very old tomb of Sir Robert Messing, that built the church. The hall-place is a fragment of an old house belonging to Lord Grimston; Lady Luckyn his mother, of fourscore and six, lives in it with an old son and daughter. The servant who showed it told us much history of another brother that had been parson there; this history was entirely composed of the anecdotes of the doctor's drinking, who, as the man told us, had been *a blood*. There are some Scotch arms taken from the rebels in the '15, and many old coats of arms on glass brought from Newhall, which now belongs to Olmius. Mr Conyers bought a window there for only a hundred pounds, on which was painted Harry the Eighth and one of his queens at full length: he has put it up at Copthall, a seat which he has bought that belonged to Lord North and Grey. You see I persevere in my heraldry. T'other day the parson of Rigby's parish dined with us; he has conceived as high an opinion of my skill in genealogies, as if I could say the first chapter of Matthew by heart. Rigby drank my health to him, and that I might come to be garter king at arms: the poor man replied with great zeal, 'I wish he may with all my heart'. Certainly, I am born to preferment; I gave an old woman a penny once, who prayed that I might live to be Lord Mayor of London! What pleased me most in my travels was Dr Sayer's parsonage at Witham, which, with Southcote's help, whose old Roman Catholic father lives just by him, he has made one of the most charming villas in England. There are sweet meadows falling down a hill, and rising again on t'other side of the prettiest little winding stream you ever saw.

Letters of Horace Walpole, LXXVIII. To GEORGE MONTAGU. Everyman edition, 1948, J. M. Dent and Sons Ltd.

THOSE PUSEYITES

Oh those Puseyites, the mischief they have done! It will take 50 years to undo it; & this when things were going so nicely! It is an old saying that God Almighty sends *vittles* but the Devil sends Cooks:

& so here, people were naturally taking up church views, when these fools, by beginning at the wrong end, come in & *bitch* their case. I really have no patience with them.

C. WHISTOW to ALBERT WAY, June 20,?1844. *Society of Antiquaries Correspondence*, 1844–8

PRAISE IN EPITAPHS

It is too much the habit to under-estimate the praise which is couched in an epitaph; yet the epitaphs, in England at least, are few in which the encomiums bestowed in them would not be borne out by the testimony of those who were acquainted with the persons who are the subjects of them.

THE REVD JOSHUA HUNTER, F.S.A., *Lupset, the Heath and Charlton*, 1868

KILL'D BY ICICLE

Here he lies
Bless my iiiiii
In a sad pickle
Kill'd by icicle
In the year 1776

Epitaph, Bampton, Devon

SIR DUDLY DIGGES, KNIGHT

Whose death the wisest men doe reckon amongst the publique calamities of these times, On the 18 day of March, the year from the Virgin Mother 1638, he resigned his spirit into the hands of his Maker, his body to the peacefull shades below, in humble confidence he shall awake, rise up, be clothed with immortality, in the dawne of that glorious day which shall know noe night. Thou mayest behold the grave of his person, not of his memory, what was earthly is sunke downe into the land where all things are forgotten. But the remembrance of his great example wil live, though through age, the disease of stones as well as men, the witness of his death this tombe itselfe should dye. The story of his life may be the rule of ours, His understanding few can equall, his vertues fewer will. Hee was a pious Sonne, a carefull Father, a loving Husband, a fatherly Brother, a courteous neighbour, a mercifull landlord, a liberal master, a noble friend. When after much experience gained by traveil and an exact survey of the lawes and people of forraigne Kingdomes, hee had inabled himself for the service of his country, observing too many justle for place, and crosse the publique interest if not joined with their private gain, hindering the motion of the great body of the Commonwealth unless the inferior orb of their estates was advanced thereby, Hee was satisfied with the conscience of meritt, knowing, good men only can deserve honours, though the worst may attaine them. His noble soule could not stoop to Ambition nor be beholding to that (though the most generus) vice, for an occation to exercise his vertues. Out of such apprehensions his moderate desires confined his thoughts to the innocency of a retired life, when the most knowing of princes King James who ever made choice of the most able ministers judgeing none more equall to imployments than those who would not unworthily court them sent him Embassador to the Emperor of Russia, after his return and some years conscionably spent in the service of the State, being unbyast by popular applause or court hopes, he was made Master of the Rolles this did crown his former actions, and though it could not increase his integrity, it made it more conspicuous, and, whom his aquaintance before, now the Kingdome honoured, if the example of his justice had powerful influence on all Magistrates, the people who are governed would be happy on earth, and the rulers in Heaven with Him, who counted it an unworthy thing to be tempted to vice by the reward of Vertue.

Chilham Church, Kent

SIR ANTHONY PALMER KNIGHT OF THE BATH ERECTED THIS MONUMENT IN MEMORIALL

of D.Margaret, Sister of Sir Dudly Diggs of Chilham Castle Knight His late loving loved wife whose goodnesse where shee lived and died [1619] since it cannot be buryed in Putney needs noe

Epitaph

Shee was fayrer then most women wiser then most men neither in her owne opinion longer then shee pleased her husband whose onely daughter by a former wife shee more loved and cherisht then most mothers doe ther owne Fewe wives were so respectfull of their husband as shee was Of her brother few sisters so affectionately kinde unto their brothers as shee was To her frinds few friends (if any) so cheerefully ready to give councell comforte or releife as shee was to the poore upon whose sicknesse lamenesse blindnesse her charitable hands

wrought dayly cures like miracles for which (no doubt) God blessed
her with a threefould yssue (John, Dudly, Anthony, like her thoughts
words workes all perfecte masciline of which although the blessed
first (like to her pious meditations) stayed little in this world the other
two yett live like those fruites of her virtuous knowledge her speeches
and her actions still calling to remembrance the modest awfull and yett
ever witty pleasing conversation of her whole lyfe that never knew
mans ill affection womans envye

Chilham Church, Kent

THE SPIRITUAL RAILWAY

In Memory of Wm Pickering who died Dec. 24 1845
Aged 30 years
Also Richard Edgar who died Dec. 24 1845
Aged 24 years

The line to Heaven by Christ was made
With heavenly truth. The rails are laid,
From Earth to Heaven the line extends
To Life Eternal where it ends.

Repentance is the Station then
Where Passengers are taken in,
No Fee for them is there to pay
For Jesus is himself the way.
God's Word is the first Engineer
It points the way to Heaven so clear,
Through tunnels dark and dreary here
It does the way to Glory steer.
God's Love the Fire, his Truth the Steam
Which drives the Engine and the Train,
All you who would to Glory ride
Must come to Christ, in him abide
In First, and Second, and Third Class,
Repentance, Faith and Holiness,
You must the way to Glory gain
Or you with Christ will not remain.

Come then poor sinners now's the time
At any Station on the Line,
If you'll repent and turn from sin
The Train will stop and take you in.

Lincoln Cathedral

ST DUNSTAN'S TONGUES

He was a great chymist. The storie of his pulling the devill by the nose with his tongues as he was in his laboratorie, was famous in church-windowes, *Vide* Gazaei *Pia Hilaria*, (where it is) delicately described. . . .

Of St Dunstan: JOHN AUBREY's *Brief Lives*, *circa* 1680

A FAULTLESS RUIN

The treatment has been absolutely judicious; it has not been furbished up into smug neatness, as has been the case with Tintern and Kirkstall; it is not abandoned to cumulative decay, like Rievaulx. The trees and luxuriant ivy are kept well within bounds, the dèbris has been removed, the disintegration stopped. As a result, Netley is a faultless ruin, a thing of almost unimaginable beauty . . . a living poem . . . it is perhaps the most wholly lovely thing amongst all the abbeys of Great Britain.

R. A. CRAM, *The Ruined Abbeys of Great Britain*, 1906, Gay and Hancock

GRAVE-STONES OF MARRIED PERSONS

The study of the Antiquities of this country has long been my favourite amusement, and I seldom pass a summer in the country without visiting every place of note in the neighbourhood, and particularly the Churches, in search of Inscriptions, ancient Monuments, and other curiosities.

In the course of these pursuits I have observed, that on most of the engraved brass plates laid over grave-stones, where they represent a man and his wife, among the ancient ones the lady takes the right hand of her husband, but in those of more modern date, the husband lies on the right of his wife.

I have some doubt whether this is universally the case; if it is, it may be accounted for, from the high honours paid to the fair sex in the days of chivalry; but when those romantic notions began to go out of fashion, the husbands seized the opportunity to assert their superiority, and their wives were removed from the place of honour, which the male sex for many years maintained. All public addresses to a mixed assembly of both sexes, till sixty years ago, commenced Gentlemen and Ladies; at present it is Ladies and Gentlemen.

As the field of my observations is extremely limited, I should be much obliged to any of your correspondents whose knowledge on this

head is more extensive, if they would favour me with answers to the
following questions.

First, Whether they have observed any particular mode or position
respecting the right or left hand in those grave places representing a
married couple which have fallen under their inspection?

Secondly, At what particular periods were they used?

And lastly, Whether there can be any reason given for thus placing
them?

I am, Sir, your's, &c.,

A Lover of Antiquities.

Letter to FRANCIS GROSE, F.S.A., ? 1807

FOURTEENTH CENTURY IN KENT

The nave was not very large, but it looked spacious too; it was
somewhat old, but well-built and handsome; the roof of curved wooden
rafters with great tie-beams going from wall to wall. There was no
light in it but that of the moon streaming through the windows, which
were by no means large, and were glazed with white fretwork, with
here and there a little figure in very rich deep colours. Two larger
windows near the east end of each aisle had just been made so that the
church grew lighter toward the east, and I could see all the work and
great screen between the nave and chancel which glittered white in
new paint and gilding; a candle glimmered in the loft above it, before
the huge rood that filled up the whole space between the loft and the
chancel arch. There was an altar at the east end of each aisle, the one
on the south side standing against the outside wall, the one on the
north against a traceried gaily-painted screen, for that aisle ran on
along the chancel. There were a few oak benches near this second
altar, seemingly just made, and well carved and moulded; otherwise
the floor of the nave, which was paved with a quaint pavement of
glazed tiles like the crocks I had seen outside as to ware, was quite clear,
and the shafts of the arches rose out of it white and beautiful under the
moon as though out of a sea, dark but with gleams struck over it.

The priest let me linger and look round, when he had crossed himself and given me the holy water; and then I saw that the walls were
figured all over with stories, a huge St. Christopher with his black
beard looking like Will Green, being close to the porch by which we
entered, and above the chancel arch the Doom of the Last Day, in which
the painter had not spared either kings or bishops, and in which a lawyer
with his blue coif was one of the chief figures in the group which the
Devil was hauling off to Hell.

109

'Yea,' said John Ball, "'tis a goodly church and fair as you may see 'twixt Canterbury and London as for its kind.'

WILLIAM MORRIS, *A Dream of John Ball*, 1888, Longmans, Green and Co. Ltd.

THE MOONLIGHT CROSS

And then he wept, and his tears fell thick upon his bosom and upon the amulet. The truth was clear enough now. The appalling death of his first wife, his love for her, and his remorse for not having jumped down the cliff and died with her, had affected his brain. He was a monomaniac, and all his thoughts were in some way clustered round the dominant one. He had studied amulets because the 'Moonlight Cross' had been cherished by her; he came to Switzerland every year because it was associated with her; he had joined the spiritualist body in the mad hope that *perhaps* there might be something in it, perhaps there might be a power that could call her back to earth. Even the favourite occupation of his life, visiting cathedrals and churches and taking rubbings from monumental brasses, had begun after her death; it had come from the fact (as I soon learnèd) that *she* had taken interest in monumental brasses, and had begun the collection of rubbings.

'Really, child, you are puzzling me. But I have observed you now for some weeks, and I quite believe you would make one of the best rubbers who has ever held a ball. I am going to Salisbury next week, and you shall then make your *debût*.'

This was in the midst of a very severe winter we had some years ago, when all Europe was under a coating of ice.

'But, father,' I said, 'shan't we find it rather cold?'

'Well,' said my father, with a bland smile, 'I will not pretend that Salisbury Cathedral is particularly warm in this weather, but in winter I always rub in knee-caps and mittens. I will tell Hodder to knit you a full set at once.'

'But, father,' I said, 'Tom Wynne tells me that rubbing is the most painful of all occupations. He even goes so far sometimes as to say that it was the exhaustion of rubbing for you which turned him to drink.'

'Nothing of the kind,' said my father. 'All that Tom needed to make him a good rubber was enthusiasm. I am strongly of opinion that without enthusiasm rubbing is of all occupations the most irksome, except perhaps for the quadrumana (who seem more adapted for this exercise), the most painful for the spine, the most cramping for the thighs, the most numbing for the fingers. It is a profession, Henry, demanding, above every other, enthusiasm in the operator. Now Tom's enthusiasm for rubbing as an art was from the first exceedingly feeble.'

'And in the spring,' continued my father, 'we are going into Wales to rub.'

WINIFRED'S DUKKERIPEN

I need not describe my journey to North Wales. . . . Before the dinner was over another tourist entered—a fresh-complexioned young Englishman in spectacles, who, sitting next to me, did at length, by force of sheer good humour, contrive to get into a desultory kind of conversation with me, and, as far as I remember, he talked well. He was not an artist, I found, but an amateur geologist and antiquary. His hobby was not like that fatal antiquarianism of my father's, which had worked so much mischief, but the harmless quest of flint implements. His talk about his collection of flints, however, sent my mind off to Flinty Point and the never-to-be-forgotten flint-built walls of Raxton church. . . .

THEODORE WATTS-DUNTON, *Aylwin*, Third ed., 1899, Hutchinson and Co. Ltd.

THAT CALM WEE DOOR

'What are those wonderfully white roses?' Mrs Shamefoot inquired of the Bishop, as she trailed with him away.

In a *costume de cathédrale*, at once massive and elusive, there was nostalgia in every line.

'They bear the same name as the Cathedral,' the Bishop replied: 'St Dorothy.'

Mrs Shamefoot touched the episcopal sleeve.

'And that calm wee door?' she asked.

'It's the side way in.'

'Tell me, Doctor Pantry, is there a ray of hope?'

'Without seeming uncharitable, or unsympathetic, or inhuman, what am I to say? With a little squeezing we might bury you in the precincts of the Cathedral.'

'But I don't want to be trodden on.'

'You might do a great deal worse than lay down a brass.'

'With my head on a cushion and my feet upon flowers. Oh!'

111

'Or a nice shroud one. Nothing looks better. And they are quite simple to keep clean.'
'But a brass,' she said, 'would lead to rubbings. I know so well! Persons on all fours, perpetually bending over me.'

RONALD FIRBANK, *Vainglory*, 1915, Gerald Duckworth and Co. Ltd.

CLAYTON VILLAGE

This white lane running like a parting
Through falling curves of blond Down—
Flax swerved off from corn by flint walls
And the church, hennish and squat, cooling murals
Faded pink, lapis lazuli, St. John's white—
The patient Last Judgment of Cluniac monks
Tramping past priory and farm, heat
Resting on the dust, air smarting with light.

Eight centuries older, we admire the firm
Drawing of fingers and feet, the gravity
Of Byzantine faces, of Christ's face, flanked
By trumpeting angels, freed of self-pity—
Murmuring over romanesque washwork, to visitors
Indicate Satan riding his hell-horse, nod
To bishops in pallium and chasuble—on terms now
With ochre processions of gloomy laity,

Pause, too, to point, in French-mannered Sussex,
To Saxon relics—this chancel arch, foliage
Sprayed over gleaming capitals, beautiful
As any French Christ in his oval aureole.
Outside among tombstones aimed at the South,
Yews drain up the sunlight, cattle, as if
Cut out of chalk, flat on the free curve
Of steep slopes where, low over dew ponds,
Gulls cruise the windmills to Wolstonbury and beyond.

Grown used to it, no longer surprised
When returning by its contours, the sudden intake
Of light as the Downs back away and the fields
Spill up to the lane, buttery and golden—
But at the pleasure of finding it the same,

112

Our pleasure the same—arranged
As in marriage—no more fear in the night,
Nor the first shock of delight—
Only anticipated prospects, only seasonal change.
ALAN ROSS, *To Whom it May Concern*, 1958, Hamish
Hamilton Ltd.

AN ARCHAEOLOGICAL PICNIC

In this high pasturage, the Blunden time,
  With Lady's Finger, Smokewort, Lovers' Loss,
And lin-lan-lone a Tennysonian chime
  Stirring the sorrel and the gold-starred moss.
  Cool is the chancel, bright the Altar cross.

Drink, Mary, drink your fizzy lemonade
  And leave the king-cups. Take your grey felt hat;
Here where the low side window lends a shade,
  There, where the key lies underneath the mat
  The rude forefathers of the hamlet sat.

Sweet smell of cerements and cold wet stones,
  Hassock and cassock, paraffin and pew,
Green in a light which that sublime Burne-Jones
  White-hot and wondering from the glass kiln drew
  Gleams and re-gleams the Trans arcade anew.

So stand you waiting, freckled innocence!
  For me the squinch and squint and Trans arcade:
For you, where meadow grass is evidence
  With flattened pattern by our picnic made,
  One bottle more of fizzy lemonade.

JOHN BETJEMAN, *New Bats in Old Belfries*, 1945. From *Collected*
Poems, 1958, John Murray Ltd.

A FREE BELFRY

  This is a belfry that is free
    for all those that civil be
    and if you please to chime or ring
    it is a very pleasant thing

113

There is no music play'd or sung
like unto bells when they're well rung
then ring your bells well if you can
Silence is best for every man.

But if you ring in spur or hat
sixpence you pay—be sure of that
and if a bell you overthrow
Pray pay a groat before you go.

All Saints, Hastings, 1756

BELL-SWARMÈD

In sweetest sounds let each its note reveal
Mine shall be the first to lead the peal

The public raised with a liberal hand
We come with harmony to cheer the land

Stroud, 1815

Fear God, Honour the King.
Peace and Good Neighbourhood.
I to the church the living call and
to the grave do summon all

St Nicholas, Brighton, 1777

When you me ring I'll sweetly sing.
Prosperity to all our benefactors.
Prosperity to this town and parish.

Painswick, 1731

Our voices shall with joyful sound
Make hills and valleys echo round

In Wedlock bands all ye who join
With hands your hearts unite
So shall our tuneful tongues combine
To laud the nuptial rite

St Mary, New Shoreham, 1767

FOR THE QUEENE OF SKOTTS

Memd that we did ringe at oure parish churche the ix day of Feb-
rarie in ano 1586 and was for joye that the Queene of Skotts that

ennemy to oure most noble Queens Matie and ower contrie was beheaded for the wch the Lorde God be praysed and I wold to God that all her confederates weare knowne and cut of by the lyke means.

Registers of St. Botolph, Aldgate

FOR THE DEALERS IN TOBACCO

The dealers in tobacco caused all the bells, in each of the churches at Derby, to be rung on the arrival of the news of the duty on that article being taken of.

Registers of All Saints, Derby, April 19, 1733

WRACKES OF WALSINGAM

In the wrackes of Walsingam
Whom should I chuse
But the Queen of Walsingam
to be guide to my muse;
Then thou Prince of Walsingam
Gaunt me to frame
Bitter plaintes to rewe thy wronge
bitter wo for thy name,
Bitter was it so to see
The seely sheepe
Murdred by the ravening wolves
While the sheephardes did sleep,
Bitter was it oh to vewe
The sacred vyne,
While the gardiners plaied all close,
rooted up by the swine,
Bitter bitter oh to behould
the grasse to growe
Where the walles of Walsingam
So stately did shewe,
Such were the workes of Walsingam
While shee did stand,
Such are the wrackes as now do shewe
of that holy land.
Levell levell with the ground
the towres do lye,
Which with their golden glitteringe tops,
Pearsed once with the skye,

115

Wher were gates no gates are now,
the waies unknowen
Where the presse of peares did passe
While her fame was blowen.
Oules do skrike wher the sweetest himnes
lately weer songe,
Toades and serpentes hold ther dennes
Wher the Palmers did thronge.
Weepe weepe o Walsingam
Whose dayes ar nightes,
Blessinges turned to blasphemies
Holy deedes do dispites,
Sinne is wher our Ladie sate,
Heaven turned is to Hell.
Sathan sittes wher our Lord did swaye;
Walsingam oh Farewell.

Anon.

REGENCY PRIDE

The new parish church of St Mary la Bonne . . . now completed, and opened for divine service, is beyond all doubt one of the handsomest structures of the kind. The north front is extremely rich and elegant, and consists of a noble portico of the Composite order, supported by eight rich pillars, and two pilasters, with a handsome balustrade, extending round the whole of the church. The steeple is of exquisite workmanship; a square rustic tower supports a beautiful cupola, raised on Corinthian pillars, on the capitals of which are eight angels, supporting another cupola: on its summit is a small openwork tower and vane. The inside of this edifice is superb. The roof of the church is just visible above the balustrade: the body is brick, covered with Roman cement; the steeple and portico of stone. The north-east and west corners have each two composite columns and pilasters; between these pilasters are niches, and above them an architrave and cornice.

Mary la Bonne Church was consecrated, in the year 1817, by the Bishop of London, in the presence of a great number of persons of distinction. The organ is placed at the back of the altar, and in the centre of the organ is an open arch, in which is placed a very fine picture, painted by Benjamin West, Esq., President of the Royal Academy: the subject is, the Angel of the Lord appearing to the Shepherds. . . .

In Broad-street, vulgarly Broad St. Giles's . . . stands the parish church of St Giles in the Fields. The outside of the church has a rustic basement, and the windows of the galleries have semi-circular heads, and over them, a modillion cornice. The steeple is one hundred and sixty-five feet high, and consists of a rustic pedestal, supporting a Doric order of pilasters; and over the clock is an octangular tower, with three quarter Ionic columns, supporting a balustrade, with vases, on which stands the spire, which is also octangular and belted. The interior is chaste and beautiful; the ornamental ceiling being one of the best in the metropolis. . . .

Nothing, it must be acknowledged, can more sensibly evince the present state of improvement than the contrast which may still be made between our ancient and the more modern structures in various parts of this metropolis. To pass over the exceeding rude dwellings of our early forefathers, the buildings of the middle ages, with stories projecting beyond each other as they ascended, still remind us of the slow march of improvement during several ages. A few of them which exhibit a specimen of old London, remain about Bishopsgate and Leadenhall Streets, and particularly in Holywell-Street, in the Strand. However, it is probable that another half century will obliterate the remembrance of them from almost every testimony but the works of those artists whose taste, skill, and indefatigable research have preserved many rare and valuable representations of the remains of antiquity, no longer visible.

DAVID HUGHSON, *Walks Through London*, 1817

TAKING PART IN HISTORY

A grant made by King Henry II as part of his penance for the assassination of Archbishop Thomas Becket is still being paid 800 years later, Dr. W. Urry, archivist to the Dean and Chapter Library at Canterbury, disclosed at Hastings yesterday.

Dr. Urry, who was addressing a meeting of the Sussex Archaeological Society, said that when Henry II went to Canterbury on July 12, 1174, to do penance at the tomb of the Archbishop, his first act was to make a grant in perpetuity to the almshouses at Harbledown, Canterbury, worth £13 6s. 8d.

He said he had been trying to trace the history of this grant, and he had followed it down through the centuries to the year 1881.

Origin Forgotten

He then thought he would see what was happening about it to-day because the almshouses were still there, so he rang up the Canterbury

City Treasurer and learned that the grant was still being paid to the almshouses, although its origin and why it was being done had been completely forgotten.

The City Treasurer told him that he had no idea why the payment was being made except that it had always been made. He was able to tell the City Treasurer that the payment was 'an astonishing survival of a Royal grant founded eight centuries ago'.

Dr. Urry commented: 'Every time anyone living in the city of Canterbury to-day pays his or her rates he or she is contributing towards the penance made by King Henry II for the assassination of Archbishop à Becket. It is like taking part in a piece of history'.

The Observer, November 2, 1958

REMARKS FROM THE VISITORS' BOOK AT A CERTAIN ANCIENT MONUMENT

First visiters book I've signed
A bit creepy
Long live the King
Much older than I first thought
Crusaders are interesting
God Bless Soviet Russia
Very unsafe by the looks of it
Wish I knew more about it
Not bad for a chapel
Nice place for nice people
Beautiful climax to a very happy honeymoon
Latin, reverent

Copied by R.J.

5—CREDULOUS INNOCENCE OR, FAKES AND LOST CAUSES

CREDULOUS INNOCENCE
OR, FAKES AND LOST CAUSES

The Vulgar Cockatrices
Why They Do It
Thisis forc attleto Rubon
Laelia Rufina
Bill Stumps again
Billy and Charley—
   —the notorious scamps
Eighteen a Shilling
Every Result was Bad
Shirtless Jack
A Person from Brandon
The Castle Hedingham Potter
A moral to be drawn?
And what is the moral?
The Ghost of Piltdown
Stonehenge-in-Uredale
A good spirit, or bad?
Deep anxiety at Kilbarry
A use for holy water—
   —and for a toe

THE VULGAR COCKATRICES

I cannot without laughing remember the old Wives tales of the Vulgar Cockatrices that have been in *England*, for I have oftentimes heard it related confidently, that once our Nation was full of Cockatrices, and that a certain man did destroy them by going up and down in Glasse, whereby their own shapes were reflected upon their own faces, and so they dyed.

EDWARD TOPSELL, *History of Four-footed Beasts and Serpents*, 1607

WHY THEY DO IT

The first [reason], which takes the lead of all others, is the desire of gain; to sell objects, to sell collections, and to secure for them a money consideration in proportion to the completeness and rarity of the pretended discoveries.

The second—self-conceit (*l'amour propre*); to discover and possess that which no other person has discovered or possesses, and above all to publish a sensational report.

The third—a foolish national pride, which leads one to find in his own country everything that has been found elsewhere, and even something more.

The fourth—philosophical and religious prejudices, which, fearing the light of truth, lead one to oppose certain studies by exposing them to ridicule.

The fifth—jealousy (*la vendetta*) of some person whose reputation an opponent wishes to undermine.

Lastly—what may be called the love of mystification (*l'amour de la fumisterie*), the mere pleasure of playing a mischievous joke.

GABRIEL DE MORTILLET, *L'Homme*, 1885, Reproduced in ROBERT MUNRO, *Archaeology and False Antiquities*, 1905

THISIS FORC ATTLETO RUBON

Last October the *Dundee Courier* published the first news of an 'important discovery at Glamis' purporting to be a 'Runic record of a 7th century battle'.

It was carved on a flat stone dug up in a garden in the village of Charleston, and a photograph of it was submitted to Lt-Colonel L. A. Waddell, the author of various books which have not been reviewed in *Antiquity*. 'The first glance showed', he says, 'that it was an inscription in the old Runic writing, and the record disclosed that

it was written, not in Scandinavian, like so many of the Runic inscriptions hitherto found in Britain, but in the British language, and chronicled a battle on the spot'. The date assigned was the 7th century. Colonel Waddell transliterated the inscription as follows:—
STALE: KISTS: KAULT: HERE: JARLS: ALSA: J: LITTLE: TA: THE: LA: TWA: AH: (I: M:);
and his translation was:—
'The army cists [stone coffins] (of the) killed here; of Earl Alsa (and) Earl Little. This is the lair (tomb) of the twain. Ah! (Alas!). (I: made [this])'.

Mindful of Glozel we sent the cutting to Professor R. A. S. Macalister, who occupies the Chair of Celtic Philology in the University of Dublin. His transcription was as follows:
STONE CISTS FOUND HERE AS ALSO A LITTLE TO THE NORTH. I.M.

A precisely similar transcription reached us at the same time and independently from a correspondent in Scotland, with some amusing comments on the inaccuracies of the one first published and of the deductions drawn from it. It is plain that it belongs to the same class as another which acquired a brief celebrity—THISIS FORC ATTLETO RUBON THE YAREAS SESASSAY ITAINT; and the rock-inscription of Barnspike in Cumberland, which is solemnly discussed in Stephens' *Northern Runic Monuments*, pt. 2, pp. 648-54, but which is now known to have been a practical joke—as indeed the shape of the letters might have shown (see W. G. Collingwood's *Northumbrian Crosses of the pre-Norman Age*, 1927, p. 66).

The Glamis inscription was evidently the work of an antiquary, and there are reasons to suspect a certain individual who died towards the end of the last century. The initials I.M. (or J.M.?) would probably suffice for his identification if anyone should think it worth while to follow up the matter—which we do not! We publish these facts because they were suppressed by the Editor of the *Dundee Courier*.

O. G. S. C[rawford]
Antiquity, March, 1930

LAELIA RUFINA

*D(is) M(anibus) Laeliae Rufinae vixit a(nnos) xiii
m(enses) iii d(ies) vi*

[To the memory of Laelia Rufina who lived 13 years,
3 months and six days]

We may fairly look on the inscribed urn with suspicion. For in the first place its origin is obscure. In the second place, its ceramic character is unquestionably post-Roman. And thirdly, the inscription itself is of a somewhat unexpected kind . . . the lettering is by no means above suspicion, and it becomes impossible to avoid the fear that the inscription may have been added to the urn by a modern hand; it may indeed be a copy of a genuine inscription actually found in Rome.

CHARLES ROACH SMITH, *Collectanea Antiqua*, V, 1861. *Victoria County History of Norfolk*, I, 1901

BILL STUMPS AGAIN

Our old friend Bill Stumps has been busy again in Scotland, this time in Fife, where he has successfully planted a nondescript stone object on a local paper, having previously carved on it the date (A.D. 1016) in Arabic numerals! (*Bulletin and Scots Pictorial*, 24 January, 1936.)

[O. G. S. Crawford]
Antiquity, March, 1936

BILLY AND CHARLEY—

The whole value and interest of an antiquity sometimes consists in the knowledge of how and where it was found, and this system of fictitious finding, in which the terms finding and invention are strictly synonymous, has often been turned to profitable account.

Some thirty years ago an action was brought by a London dealer against the *Athenaeum* newspaper for libel in asserting that a series of objects in his possession were forged. The dealer, like many others, had probably been taken in. He had purchased for a considerable sum a large collection of objects in lead or pewter, which were said to have been found during the formation of a new dock at Shadwell. Many of them were supposed to be what are known as pilgrims' signs, and all were said, on no mean authority, to be evidently connected with some religious proceedings, though it was admitted that there was a considerable inconsistency between many of the articles, which, however, was to be accounted for by their belonging to different ages.

There were crowned monarchs in ecclesiastical vestments, knights in various kinds of armour, archbishops, bishops, priests with mitres, croziers, and different emblems, incense-cups, patens, ewers, reliquaries, and vessels of all shapes, besides numerous medallions and plaques with loops for suspension. The great variety of form and the strangeness of some of the devices seemed to raise a presumption that such a fertility of imagination and such dexterity of workmanship could hardly be possessed by any single forger, and therefore that, though exceptional, these objects were to be accepted as genuine.

Unfortunately for such a view, the late Mr Charles Reed succeeded in discovering the place of manufacture, and even exhibited to the Society of Antiquaries some of the moulds in which the relics were cast. . . .

The fact is that the whole fraud was perpetrated by a couple of illiterate mud-rakers, who prepared their moulds in plaster of Paris, cast their pseudo-antiques in a mixture of lead and pewter, immersed them for a short time in a bath of nitric acid, and finally, having daubed them with a coating of river mud, offered them for sale to enquiring antiquaries.

Sir John Evans in a lecture to the Royal Institution published in *Longman's Magazine*, December, 1893

—THE NOTORIOUS SCAMPS

Such tricks as the foregoing unfold to us a system of chicanery deserving heavy punishment; but still worse frauds are practiced by the firm in Rosemary Lane, Tower Hill. Ancient stone, bone, and terracotta materials, are re-wrought in strange forms by Messrs 'Billey and Charley'. Fragments of Samian vessels are made to assume the contours of beads, spindle-whorls, stars and crescents, and of fish and flowers such as seldom swim in the water or blossom on the earth.

Among other of the doings of these impostors is the incising of figures and carving of legends on genuine Roman *tegulae*. . . .

H. Syer Cuming, A Few Words on Forgeries, *Journal of the British Archaeological Association*, XXV, 1869

EIGHTEEN A SHILLING

About a fortnight ago a respectable jeweller in this city, who purchases for me such coins and other articles of archaeological interest as may come in his way, informed me that a poor labouring man had left with him several fine specimens of flint arrow-heads, which he said had been found in a barrow about 8 miles from Winchester. On seeing them, although great care had evidently been taken to soil them and make them look old, I at once said they were modern. As the price for the whole was only 1s., I purchased them, and told my friend the jeweller that he was to let me know if any more were offered to him.

In a few days the man called again with more specimens, and was at once sent up to me. He showed me about eighteen of them, and pressed me to purchase the whole, offering them at 1s. I at once challenged him with the disgraceful act of selling for antiques what he knew to be of modern manufacture. For a time the man denied the charge stoutly, and said, 'Why, sir, you can see for yourself what they are'. 'But surely,' said I, 'you cannot suppose that I can purchase these for genuine old arrow-heads? You are evidently acting dishonestly, or have been imposed upon yourself.'

After a little more pressure he said, 'A poor man must live, and nobody with any knowledge of the real flint weapon can be taken in with these.' 'Why, then,' said I, 'did you offer them to me?' 'If you remember,' he said, 'I did not say what they were, I simply asked you to buy them:' and such was the case; he had offered them at the jeweller's shop as antiques, and told the story of the barrow by way of proof, but with me he was more wary.

I now pressed him to tell me all about them. 'Where did you get them. They are certainly fine specimens,' said I. 'Did you make them?' The man at length confessed that he made them himself, and said that for a small consideration he would show me the 'art and mystery.' Pulling out of his pocket a small dirty bag, he took from it a common carpenter's awl, and the hasp which goes over the staple of a padlock, and then taking from another pocket some pieces of flint, he sat down, and holding the flint dexterously between his thumb and finger, and resting his hand upon his knee, he soon formed a beautiful specimen. . . . The awl he used for making the angles at the base, and rounding the barbs. The man's skill and quickness were remarkable, being, as he informed me, the effect of several years' practice in this art. I ought to say that the long portion of the hasp formed the handle, and the circular part the hammer with which he broke the flints. The man was evidently in great poverty, and probably an idle vagabond, and was making his way to London, and I have no doubt that on his route he has left many specimens of his ingenuity. Probably this notice and the sketch subjoined illustrative of the man's art, may save many of your readers from a gross imposition.

CHARLES COLLIER, *The Gentleman's Magazine*, July, 1863

EVERY RESULT WAS BAD

When I first lighted on the North London Palaeolithic floor, I was most careful to keep the workmen entirely in the dark as to the real nature of my quest. Under these circumstances, I was able to secure such antiquities as were brought to light in an easy and pleasant manner, without any extravagant expenditure of time or money. After my first paper was laid before the *Anthropological Institute*, it became general knowledge that Palaeolithic implements could be found in the gravels and sands of north-east London, and this knowledge was used in an improper way by curio collectors, who neither knew or cared anything for the knowledge which might be obtained from a careful examination of the sections and relics, but whose sole object was to secure implements at any price and by any means.

The result of this was, that the men, who were at first friendly and obliging, became very unfriendly, and I was even exposed to personal violence, because the workmen could easily get from strangers five or ten times the sum I had been in the habit of giving. Some of the men pawned implements and sold the tickets, others took implements to public-houses and got beer and gin advanced on them: purchasers sometimes went to these public-houses, paid the score, and secured the tools. In another instance a landlady took several tools as security for unpaid rent. The men were no better for extra pay, as nearly all the money went into the public-houses, and when drunk the men got discharged, and then violent scenes often occurred at their homes. Every result was bad.

WORTHINGTON G. SMITH, *Man, the Primeval Savage*, 1894

SHIRTLESS JACK

... Card 12 contained one *admitted*, and several other palpable, forgeries; No. 13, adjoining, has two arrows, found by Mr Tindall and Mr Barugh, good,—most, if not all the rest, were spurious. Card 34 had one arrow by 'Bones,' as this knave is called by Whitby. In the East Riding he is known as 'Jack Flint,' and in North-West Yorkshire he is known as 'Shirtless.' He has wonderfully improved since he took to the trade, as might be seen by examining the curious specimens of forgeries gathered together here from various parts of the country, by Mr Ruddock, for the purpose of exposing the nefarious traffic. There was a card dated 1852, rude, compared to his latter work; yet the style is the same, if not so finished. There was a stone hammer or hatchet in Mr Tindall's lot, and there was the sister to it among the forgeries, the precise form, size—even the material is the same. The latter, and another of the like kind, were lent by a gentleman of York, who had been *done*. Mr Tindall had fourteen celts; several were described as Irish. No. 6 looked suspicious; if we compared it with the forgeries, our doubts would increase. The large blue celt was made for

2s. 6d., beautiful hammers for 5s. each, and some arrows and spears, whose history and place of manufacture are well known, have been sold for 1s. each. Some of those, except to an experienced eye, were difficult to detect, and were of greater likelihood than the Bridlington collection. Mr Barugh, an extensive occupier of land near the above place, has searched for days together, and has instructed his servants to look over his fields, 100 acres in extent; and although he had at one time sixty flints, mostly of the undefined kind, yet he met in all his explorations very few arrows or spears, and only *one* barbed arrow. All Mr Barugh found went into Mr Tindall's collection some time ago. Several of them were pointed out to us by that gentleman, who afterwards presented to the York museum thirty, which he had purchased before he knew the difficulty of obtaining genuine specimens.

The Gentleman's Magazine, October, 1857

A PERSON FROM BRANDON

A correspondent at Ipswich mentions the fact of flint arrows and spear-heads being manufactured at the present day at Brandon; and states that a person has been travelling with specimens, many of which he has succeeded in selling. The truth is, these rogues are encouraged and emboldened by the avidity with which collectors of antiquities buy objects, which most of them want the knowledge to understand and the experience to discriminate.

The Gentleman's Magazine, October, 1857

THE CASTLE HEDINGHAM POTTER

Even if the British Museum had been next door to the potter and Bingham had been commissioned to reproduce some of the rare specimens of early ceramics, it is doubtful whether he could have achieved better results than he did in his remote Essex village, far away from all advantages. He copied probably between three and four hundred ancient pieces, and the source or sources from which he obtained his models is yet to be discovered. . . .

Bingham made one of his rooms into a museum, and the contents of his catalogue prove him to have been a keen collector of old china and pottery, spear and arrow flint heads, fossils, prints, books, old deeds, coins and curios.

HENRY CLAY, 'Edward Bingham, potter of Castle Hedingham,'
The Connoisseur, XCIV, 1934

A MORAL TO BE DRAWN?

No workman ever received a single word of information from me as to tools, or their marks of authenticity; others, however, were not so cautious, but told the men everything they knew, and explained the various characteristic points of form, mineral condition, and abrasion of implements.

The consequence was that carpenters and plasterers, men who knew how to use different forms of hammer and punch, speedily produced forgeries. The forgeries were never made by the labourers, as they were without the necessary skill of hand. The carpenters and plasterers sold the forgeries to the labourers for small sums, and the labourers resold the stones, often for very large sums, to collectors of curios. A sovereign has many times been received for a good forgery, and I know of an instance where five pounds was foolishly paid for an example of surpassing size, weight, and finish.

Collectors at one time lent the men their best genuine tools as aids to discovery . . . the genuine Stoke Newington implements are often keen-edged, and as often highly lustrous. At first the forgeries were all dull and lustreless. On this fact being made known to the forgers they vigorously brushed their forgeries all over with a very hard brush; the result was an excellent and natural-looking lustre or polish.

Next, the collectors wanted slightly abraded edges, some genuine tools being slightly abraded. To meet this demand the men put the tools into a twisted sack, and shook the sack with its contained implements together with natural stones and sand, till the tools exhibited a proper amount of abrasion.

Some wise person next showed the men that many genuine tools were stained with ochre, caused by the presence of iron in the soil. To provide this colour the men kept large iron saucepans constantly boiling on their fires—saucepans filled with forged implements, old rusty nails, and other iron fragments; this gave the required tint, but some of the purchasers suspected the tools, and put them again into boiling water, with the result that the ochreous colour soon came off and left the tools grey. Potash removed the colour. This was because the men at first boiled the tools after they had brushed them up to produce a lustre.

The forgers now boiled their unpolished grey tools in their saucepans and polished them up afterwards. When this was done, re-boiling would not remove the ochreous colour derived from the iron, and the longer the tools were boiled the more permanently ochreous they became. . . .

The moral to be drawn from the facts narrated is—be very careful in dealing with workmen, especially London workmen. It is a different state of things in the country, where fewer persons are on the look-out for antiquities. But even in the country it is in the highest degree inadvisable to inform workmen of the nature and points of authenticity of stone tools; the whole mischief is brought about by collectors of curios airing their superficial knowledge before groups of workmen. . . .

It is a curious fact in regard to the Stoke Newington forgeries, that some of the collectors who informed the workmen of the points of authenticity in stone tools were themselves severely bitten by the forgers. This fact should delight the hearts of all antiquaries.

WORTHINGTON G. SMITH, *Man, the Primeval Savage*, 1894

AND WHAT IS THE MORAL?

It is, however, time to conclude this long history of ingenious frauds perpetrated in every branch of archaeology. And what is the moral? Are collectors to confess to an absolute inability to protect themselves from fraud, and cease collecting in despair, or are there still grounds for hoping that collections immaculate from forgeries may still be formed? The case, after all, is not so bad as it appears, for, great as may be the forger's skill, not one of his frauds in a thousand eventually escapes detection. By those long versed in any particular branch of archaeology a kind of intuitive perception is gained which enables them almost at a glance to distinguish between the true and the false. While attaining to this happy stage, the fact of being occasionally taken in helps to sharpen the powers of observation, so that the existence of forgeries can hardly be regarded as an unmixed evil. The knowledge of their existence tends, moreover, to encourage a more minute and scholarly investigation of every detail in genuine objects of antiquity, and assists in creating that judicial frame of mind which avoids too sudden conclusions. In the advance of science it is hard to say which is the more mischievous—to believe too little or to believe too much; and the true moral of what we have been considering seems to be that which two thousand years ago was enunciated by Epicharmus—'that

129

the very nerves and sinews of knowledge consist in believing nothing rashly'.

Sir John Evans in a lecture to the Royal Institution, published in *Longman's Magazine*, December, 1893

THE GHOST OF PILTDOWN

Since November 1953, further investigations have been made on the specimens reported from the Piltdown gravel.

These studies, making use of several new techniques, have not only confirmed that the Piltdown jawbone is that of a modern ape which has been faked to resemble a fossil, but they have shown that the thick bones of the brain-case, although fairly recent, were fraudulently stained and placed in the gravel.

Furthermore, there is evidence that none of the fossil animal bones or teeth, nor the bone and flint implements found with the skull, occurred in the gravel genuinely. Evidently they had all been 'planted' at the site to suggest that the Piltdown skull belonged to a very early period.

From a case label in the British Museum (Natural History)

We have laid the ghost of Piltdown Man, who, as it happens, never fitted very happily into any scheme of man's evolution. Indeed we have gained, because half a dozen new experimental methods have been developed which will not only make any repetition of such a hoax impossible in the future, but will materially assist the scientific study of fossils.

From a broadcast by Sir Gavin de Beer, Director of the British Museum (Natural History), June, 1954

STONEHENGE-IN-UREDALE

The moon was up now and the bracken in sharp relief against its own dense shadows, the death of the moon reflected on the landscape, all the cold terror that keeps one indoors at night. Monoliths, and another black wood on the right, and there is the stone circle in full moonlight on the hillside. All effort and owl-terrors fall away; once inside, past the heavy shadows of the entrance, the warm stones enclose a different moonlight, the lovely tranquillity of Palmer and the poets, a very rare moonlight indeed.

The stones hold back the bracken as well as terror, and preserve a fine springy turf that is for once the true dark green carpet of the similes, and on it stands the tightly-knit henge of trilithons and monoliths, not in a circle but a big ellipse, ten or twelve feet high, seventy-five feet long, still a little huddled against the awful winter weather. In the centre though, a tall monolith stands on three round steps as though no wind ever reached it; a slip, too, from druidical research into the Roman taste, for in a prehistoric circle or horseshoe the 'altar stone' is back from the centre, and so it is here, but the monolith dominates the scene like a commemorative column in a forum and the altar takes second place. Beyond it, through a screen of cobby trilithons is a second, smaller ellipse of stones, surrounding a slab like a tortoise, and ending in a last enclosure, a black cave in the hillside.

BARBARA JONES, *Follies and Grottoes*, 1953, Constable and Co. Ltd.

A GOOD SPIRIT, OR BAD?

Anno 1670, not far from *Cyrencester*, was an Apparition Being demanded, whether a good Spirit or a bad? returned no answer, but disappeared with a curious Perfume and a most melodious Twang. Mr. *W. Lilly* believes it was a Farie. So *Propertius*.

JOHN AUBREY, *Miscellanies*, 1696

DEEP ANXIETY AT KILBARRY

Last autumn a peasant named Thomas Power, who holds a few acres of ground in the townland of Kilbarry, immediately outside the deer-park wall of Castlecor, dreamed that there was a large quantity of gold and other treasure buried deep beneath the ruins of an old Danish fort, which lies on the ground. After he awoke, he lay musing for some time, until sleep overcame him again, when the same dream occurred to him a second time, as also a third time, on the same night. The last time he awoke the day dawned; he got up and called one of his sons, to whom he communicated his dreams; with eagerness they proceeded to the spot to which the dreams had accurately directed them; they surveyed the place with deep anxiety for some time, and at length perceived a scarcely perceptible hollow in the ground, as if a drain had once been there which time had filled up. The fort is situated on the top of a small glen, through which, or along which, a small stream runs. This stream divides the lands of Kilbarry from Drummin. The drain from the first went towards the rivulet, like the tail-race of a mill, and here it was they commenced operations. They first discovered a bed of rich manure, which they were raising and drawing away for a fortnight; they took out 300 horse-loads, making an opening towards the fort 30 feet in length, 11 feet deep, and wide enough for a horse and cart to turn in. Their work was at length impeded by a large piece of timber, from which they cleared the manure with great labour, and discovered a perfect tank, 12 feet square and 3 feet deep, made of black oak, each plank 4 inches thick, it resting upon four pillars or legs, 2 feet high and 1 foot square. Into the tank was a shoot, as if to convey water, made of the same timber, one foot wide at the mouth, the whole in almost perfect preservation. How it was joined could not be ascertained, as the labourers took it asunder when they found it; but there was no appearance of nails; the joints appeared decayed. The tank was buried 11 feet under the ground.

The Gentleman's Magazine, March, 1843

A USE FOR HOLY WATER—

As I was troubled with fits, she advised me to bathe in the loff, which was holy water; and so I went in the morning to a private place along with the housemaid, and we bathed in our birth-day soot, after the fashion of the country; and behold, whilst we daddled in the loff, Sir George Coon started up with a gun; but we clapt our hands to our faces, and passed by him to the place where we had left our smocks— A civil gentleman would have turned his head another way—My comfit is, he new not which was which, and, as the saying is, *All cats in the dark are grey.*

TOBIAS SMOLLETT, *Humphrey Clinker*, 1771

—AND FOR A TOE

'You used to say the toe, 'm, of the married sister of the Madonna, the one that was a restaurant proprietress (Look alive there with those devilled-kidneys, and what is keeping Fritz with that sweet omelette?), in any fracas was particularly potent.'

RONALD FIRBANK, *Valmouth: a Romantic Novel*, 1919, Gerald Duckworth and Co. Ltd.

6—FINDING AND KEEPING

FINDING AND KEEPING

Shank bone of a Horse
A mace from Cumberland
The children's beads
Dinders after Rain
Jennifer's Necklace
Sword for Topping
Choirboys' Hecate
A Priceless Toy
Use for Roman Coins
A rare Farthing
Dwarf Money
Places and Faces
Brampton Urns
Gamesmanship
Finding and Keeping
The unlucky Sergeant
A King's Ring
A Queen's Ring
A Bishop's Ring
Unskilled and Ignorant?
The American's Roman Eagle

SHANK BONE OF A HORSE

Cirecestre, corruptely for Churnecestre, peraventure of Ptoleme cawlled Coriminum, stondeth in a botom apon the ryver of Churne. . . . Among divers *numismata* fownd frequently there Dioclesian's be the most fairest, but I cannot adfirme the inscription to have bene dedicate onto hym. In the middes of the old town in a medow was found a flore *de tessellis versiocoloribus*, and by the town *nostris temporibus* was fownd a broken shank bone of a horse, the mouth closed with a pegge, the which taken owt a shepard founde yt fillid *nummis argenteis*. . . .

JOHN LELAND, *Itinerary*, circa 1536–9, Hearne's 2nd ed., 1744–5

A MACE FROM CUMBERLAND

Perhaps the following description of the stone will not be thought superfluous, in addition to the plate. The central part of it is, in figure, an imperfect oval; its two greatest diameters are $2\frac{1}{2}$ and $1\frac{3}{4}$ inches. It projects both ways, in respect to the thinner parts of the stone, and the two prominences are neither equal in height nor similar in form; the greater is terminated by an oval plane, which is $1\frac{3}{4}$ by $1\frac{1}{4}$ inches; the less is bounded by a surface somewhat convex, and both parts are marked with rings parallel to their common base; those of the former are oval, but those of the latter nearly circular; the two projections uniting in their common base form an acute angle, which inclines a little towards the higher side; and the whole is something more than $1\frac{1}{4}$ inches in thickness. The two thinner parts of the stone, which may be called the blades of the instrument, are alike in size and figure, projecting about an inch from the longer sides of the central part to which they are fixed; their ends appear to be arches of circles, and their diameters contract a little where they join the prominent part, forming two depressions on each blade; they are convex on both sides, but more so on one side than the other, and the angle which constitutes their edges resembles that mentioned above, surrounding the central part. . . .

It does not strike fire with steel; its weight in air is 6 oz. 18 dwts. 13 gr.; in water, 4 oz. 5 dwts. 8 gr.; therefore its specific gravity is expressed by 2.604. . . .

Being no antiquary myself, and supposing the curiosity worthy the attention of persons of this description, I have deposited it in the public museum of Mr. Crosthwaite, of Keswick, for the inspection of such as may have an opportunity and inclination to examine it.

D. G.

The Gentleman's Magazine, September, 1790

THE CHILDREN'S BEADS

Towards the year 1773, in passing through Ash, I observed some children looking with much eagerness among the sand in the pit: on enquiry, they told me they were picking up glass beads, several of which I received from them; and, by their direction, I found in the miller's house, situated close to the pit, many remains of iron arms taken from thence; which, I find, were since procured from the mill by the Rev. Mr Fausset.

JAMES DOUGLAS, *Nenia Britannica*, 1793

DINDERS AFTER RAIN

The Secretary spoke of a certain schoolmr at Wroxcester that usd to send his boys to gather dinders as they call roman moneys after a shower of rain, and he melted all the silver ones into a tankard. The lord of the manor of Wroxeter puts it into his leases that the tenants shall bring all Antiquitys found there on forfeiture of their lease. A vast quantity of coyns etc. found there brought to Mr Ashmole were burnt in the fire of London.

Society of Antiquaries Minute Books, May 12, 1725

JENNIFER'S NECKLACE

A Coroner's jury at Dorking yesterday decided that a gold coin of Philip II of Spain—found by Jennifer Holmes, aged 13, while she was weeding her father's garden at Great Bookham—was not treasure trove, and the Coroner, Dr Murray Robertson, handed it to Jennifer with the suggestion that she might wear it on a necklace.

Daily Telegraph, February 13, 1958

SWORD FOR TOPPING

A Bronze Age sword, believed to have been made between 1200 and 800 B.C., has been handed to Mr J. C. Parrott, a Norfolk collector.

A farm worker who found it nearly three years ago had been using it for topping sugar beet.

The Times, June 3, 1951

CHOIRBOYS' HECATE

A stone 'football' found by three choirboys at Sudbury, Middlesex, has been identified as a headpiece of a statue of Hecate, the goddess who was worshipped at cross-roads in the wilder parts of ancient Greece.

Evening Standard, April 26, 1957

A PRICELESS TOY

A farmer who dug up a plain band of metal and gave it to his children as a toy, yesterday learned that it was a priceless bracelet of pure gold which belonged to a Celtic princess 3,000 years ago.

An inquest will be held to decide if the bracelet, as Treasure Trove, is Crown property.

Daily Sketch, July 18, 1958

USE FOR ROMAN COINS

Not realising the value of 20 Roman coins, more than 1,500 years old, which they dug up while repairing a road at Brockwell, Derbyshire, labourers used them to buy cigarettes, beer, and cups of tea.

No one noticed the difference until a collector heard of the discovery. He traced the coins, and found that 19 were silver and one was bronze. Most of them bore the heads of Roman emperors who lived between 194 and 241.

Now the collection has been acquired by the Chesterfield borough librarian, Mr. G. R. Micklewright, and is to be exhibited in the town's library.

Nottingham Evening Post, October 30, 1953

A RARE FARTHING

Having been informed that you are one of the members & secretary of the Antiquarian Society in England where the greatest rarities are collected . . . has for sale a Queen Anne farthing, 1711, 1 of only 2 ever minted, the other is in Scotland.

From FRANCIS D'AUBERTIN, Armagh, January 28, 1796. *Society of Antiquaries Correspondence*, XVIII Century file

137

The Walche Poole a preati town having a castel, now set as part of the new shire of Montgomerike.

Yn what places of the shyre any mony of brasse or sylver of the Romanyne coyne hath be fownd yn pottes by plowgyng, diggyng, or otherwyse.

At Kenchester iii myles fro Heneforth westward a myle fro the bank of Wye was a palays of Offas, as sum say. The ruines yet remayne, and the vaultes also. Here hath bene and is fownd *a fossoribus et aratoribus* Romayn mony, *tessellata pavimenta*, a litle crosse of gold to were abowte ons nekke, and ther they cawle them Dwery, or Dwerfich, half pens or mony.

JOHN LELAND, *Itinerary*, *circa* 1536–9, Hearne's 2nd ed., 1744–5

'A PEDESTRIAN'S IMPRESSIONS OF PLACES AND FACES'

Looking through a gap in the wall I saw, close by on the other side, a dozen men at work with pick and shovel throwing up huge piles of earth. They were uncovering a small portion of that ancient buried city and were finding the foundations and floors and hypocausts of Silchester's public baths; also some broken pottery and trifling ornaments of bronze and bone. The workmen in that bitter wind were decidedly better off than the gentlemen from Burlington House in charge of the excavations. These stood with coats buttoned up and hands thrust deep down in their pockets. It seemed to me that it was better to sit in the shelter of the wall and watch the birds than to burrow in the crumbling dust for that small harvest. Yet I could understand and even appreciate their work, although it is probable that the glow I experienced was in part reflected. Perhaps my mental attitude, when standing in that sheltered place, and when getting on to the windy wall I looked down on the workers and their work, was merely benevolent. I had pleasure in their pleasure, and a vague desire for a better understanding, a closer alliance and harmony. It was the desire that we might all see nature—the globe with all it contains—as one harmonious whole, not as groups of things, or phenomena, unrelated, cast there by chance or by careless or contemptuous gods. This dust of past ages, dug out of a wheatfield, with its fragments of men's work—its pottery and tiles and stones—this is a part, too, even as the small birds, with their little motives and passions, so like man's, are a part. I thought with self-blame of my own sins in this connection; then, considering the lesser faults on the other side, I wished that Mr. St. John Hope would experience a like softening mood and regret that he had abused the ivy. It grieves me to hear it called a 'noxious weed'. That perished people, whose remains in this land so deeply interest him, were the mightiest 'builders of ruins' the world has known; but who except the archaeologist would wish to see these piled stones in their naked harshness, striking the mind with dismay at the thought of Time and its perpetual desolations! I like better the old Spanish poet who says, 'What of Rome; its world-conquering power, and majesty and glory—what has it come to?' The ivy on the wall, the yellow wallflower, tell it. A 'deadly parasite', quotha! Is it not well that this plant, this evergreen tapestry of unnumerable leaves, should cover and partly hide and partly reveal the 'strange defeatures' the centuries have set on man's greatest works? I would have no ruin nor no old and noble building without it; for not only does it beautify decay, but from long association it has come to be in the mind a very part of such scenes, and so interwoven with the human tragedy, that, like the churchyard yew. it seems the most human of green things.

W. H. HUDSON, *Afoot in England*, 1909, The Royal Society for the Protection of Birds and The Society of Authors

BRAMPTON URNS

I thought I had taken leave of urnes, when I had some Years past given a short Account of those found at Walsingham, but a New Discovery being made, I readily obey your Commands in a brief Description thereof.

In a large Arable Field, lying between Buxton and Brampton, but belonging to Brampton, and not much more than a Furlong from Oxnead Park, divers Urnes were found. A Part of the Field being designed to be inclosed, while the Workmen made several Ditches, they fell upon divers Urnes, but earnestly, and carelessly digging, they broke all they met with, and finding nothing but Ashes, or burnt Cinders, they scattered what they found. Upon Notice given unto me, I went unto the Place, and though I used all Care with the Workmen, yet they were broken in the taking out, but many, without doubt, are still remaining in that Ground.

Of these Pots none were found above Three Quarters of a Yard in the Ground, whereby it appeareth, that in all this Time the Earth hath little varied its Surface, though this Ground hath been Plowed to the utmost Memory of Man. Whereby it may be also conjectured, that this hath not been a Wood-Land, as some conceive all this Part to have been; for in such Lands they usually made no common Burying-places, except for some special Persons in groves, and likewise that there hath been an Ancient Habitation about these Parts; for at Buxton also, not a Mile off, urnes have been found in my Memory, but in their Magnitude, Figure, Colour, Posture, &c., there was no small Variety, some were large and capacious, able to contain above Two Gallons, some of a middle, others of a smaller Size; the great ones probably belonging to greater Persons, or might be Family Urnes, fit to receive the Ashes successively of their Kindred and Relations, and therefore of these, some had Coverings of the same Matter, either fitted to them, or a thin flat stone, like a Grave Slate, laid over them; and therefore also great Ones were but thinly found, but others in good Number; some were of large wide Mouths, and Bellies proportionable, with short Necks, and bottoms of Three Inches Diameter, and near an Inch thick; some small, with Necks like Juggs, and about that Bigness; the Mouths of some few were not round, but after the Figure of a Circle compressed; though some had small, yet none had pointed Bottoms, according to the Figures of those which are to be seen in Roma Soterranea, Viginerus, or Mascardus.

In the Colours also there was great Variety, some were Whitish, some Blackish, and inclining to a Blue, others Yellowish, or dark Red, arguing the Variety of their Materials. Some Fragments, and especially Bottoms of Vessels, which seem'd to be handsome neat Pans, were also found of a fine Coral-like red, somewhat like Portugal Vessels, as tho' they had been made out of some fine Bolary Earth, and very smooth; but the like had been found in divers Places, as Dr. Casaubon hath observed about the Pots found at Newington in Kent, and as other Pieces do yet testifie, which are to be found at Burrow Castle, an Old Roman station, not far from Yarmouth.

Of the Urnes, those of the larger Sort, such as had Coverings, were found with their Mouths placed upwards, but great Numbers of the others were, as they informed me, (and One I saw myself,) placed with their Mouths downward, which were probably such as were not to be opened again, or receive the Ashes of any other Person; though some wonder'd at this Position, yet I saw no Inconveniency in it; for the Earth being closely pressed, and especially in Minor-mouth'd pots, they stand in a Posture as like to continue as the other, as being less subject to have the Earth fall in, or the Rain to soak into them; and the same Posture has been observed in some found in other places, as Holingshead delivers, of divers found in Anglesea.

Some had Inscriptions, the greatest Part none; those with Inscriptions were of the largest Sort, which were upon the reverted Verges thereof; the greatest part of those which I could obtain were somewhat obliterated; yet some of the Letters to be made out: the Letters were between Lines, either Single or Double, and the Letters of some few after a fair Roman Stroke, others more rudely and illegibly drawn, wherein there seemed no great Variety, NUON being upon very many of them; only upon the inside of the bottom of a small Red Pan-like Vessel, were legibly set down in embossed Letters, CRACU-NA. F. which might imply *Cracuna figuli*, or the Name of the Manufactor, for Inscriptions commonly signified the Name of the Person interr'd, the Names of Servants Official to such Provisions, or the Name of the Artificer, or Manufactor of such Vessels; all which are particularly exemplified by the Learned Licetus, where the same Inscription is often found, it is probably, of the Artificer, or where the Name also is in the Genitive Case, as he also observeth.

Out of one was brought unto to me a Silver Denarius, with the Head of Diva Faustina on the Obverse side, on the Reverse the Figures of the Emperor and Empress joining their Right Hands, with this Inscription, *Concordia*; the same is to be seen in Augustino; I also received from some Men and Women then present Coins of Posthumus and Tetricus, two of the Thirty Tyrants in the Reign of Gallienus, which being of much later Date, begat an Inference, that Urne-Burial lasted longer, at least in this Country, than is commonly supposed. Good Authors conceive, that this Custom ended with the Reigns of the Antonini, whereof the last was Antoninus Heliogabalus, yet these Coins extend about Fourscore Years lower; and since the Head of Tetricus is made with a radiated Crown, it must be conceived to have been made after his Death, and not before his Consecration, which as the Learned Tristan Conjectures, was most probably in the Reign of the Emperor Tacitus, and the Coin not made, or at least not issued Abroad, before the Time of the Emperor Probus, for Tacitus Reigned but Six Months and an Half, his Brother Florianus but Two months, unto whom Probus succeeding, Reigned Five Years.

There were also found some pieces of Glass, and finer Vessels, which might contain such Liquors as they often Buried in, or by, the Urnes; divers Pieces of Brass, of several Figures; and in one Urne was found a Nail Two Inches long; whither to declare the Trade or Occupation of the Person, is uncertain. But upon the Monuments of Smiths, in Gruter, we meet with the Figures of Hammers, Pincers, and the like; and we find the Figure of a Cobler's Awl on the Tomb of one of that Trade, which was in the Custody of Berini, as Argulus hath set it down in his Notes upon *Onuphrius, Of the Antiquities of Verona*.

Now, though Urnes have been often discovered in former Ages, many think it strange there should be many still found, yet assuredly there may be great Numbers still concealed. For tho' we should not reckon upon any who were thus buried before the Time of the

Romans (altho' that the Druids were thus buried, it may be probable, and we read of the Urne of Chindonactes, a Druid, found near Dijon in Burgundy, largely discoursed of by Licetus), and tho', I say, we take not in any Infant which was *Minor igne rogi*, before Seven Months, or Appearance of Teeth, nor should account this Practice of burning among the Britains higher than Vespasian, when it is said by Tacitus, that they conformed unto the Manners and Customs of the Romans, and so both Nations might have one Way of Burial; yet from his Days, to the Dates of these Urnes, were about Two Hundred Years. And therefore if we fall so low, as to conceive there were buried in this Nation but Twenty Thousand Persons, the Account of the buried Persons would amount unto Four Millions, and consequently so great a Number of Urnes dispersed through the Land, as may still satisfy the Curiosity of succeeding Times, and arise unto all Ages.

The bodies, whose Reliques these Urnes contained, seemed thoroughly burned; for beside pieces of Teeth, there were found few Fragments of Bones, but rather Ashes in hard Lumps, and pieces of Coals, which were often so fresh, that one sufficed to make a good draught of its Urne which still remaineth with me.

Some persons digging at a little Distance from the Urne Places, in hopes to find something of Value, after they had digged about Three-Quarters of a Yard deep, fell upon an observable Piece of Work. The Work was Square, about Two Yards and a Quarter on each Side. The Wall, or outward Part, a Foot thick, in Colour Red, and looked like Brick; but it was solid, without any Mortar or Cement, or figur'd Brick in it, but of an whole Piece, so that it seemed to be Framed and Burnt in the same Place where it was found. In this kind of Brick-work were Thirty-Two Holes, of about Two Inches and an Half Diameter, and Two above a Quarter of a Circle in the East and West Sides. Upon Two of these Holes, on the East Side, were placed Two Pots, with their Mouths downward; putting in their Arms they found the Work hollow below, and the Earth being clear'd off, much Water was found below them, to the Quantity of a Barrel, which was conceived to have been the Rain-water which soaked in through the Earth above them.

The upper Part of the Work being broke, and opened, they found a Floor about Two Foot below, and then digging onward, Three Floors successively under one another, at the Distance of a Foot and Half, the Stones being of a Slatty, not Bricky, Substance; in these Partitions some Pots were found, but broke by the Workmen, being necessitated to use hard Blows for the breaking of the Stones; and in the last Partition but one, a large Pot was found of a very narrow Mouth, short Ears, of the Capacity of Fourteen Pints, which lay in an inclining Posture, close by, and somewhat under a kind of Arch in the solid Wall, and by the great Care of my worthy Friend, Mr. William Masham, who employed the Workmen, was taken up whole, almost full of Water, clean, and without Smell, and insipid, which being poured out, there still remains in the Pot a great Lump of an heavy crusty substance. What Work this was we must as yet reserve unto better Conjecture. Meanwhile we find in Gruter that some Monuments of the Dead had divers Holes successively to let in the Ashes of their Relations, but Holes in such a great Number to that Intent, we have not anywhere met with.

About Three Months after, my Noble and Honoured friend, Sir Robert Paston, had the Curiosity to open a Piece of Ground in his Park at Oxnead, which adjoined unto the former Field, where Fragments of Pots were found, and upon one the Figure of a well-made Face; But probably this Ground had been opened and digged before, though out of the Memory of Man, for we found divers small Pieces of Pots, Sheeps Bones, sometimes an Oyster-shell a Yard deep in the Earth, an unusual Coin of the Emperor Volusianus, having on the Obverse the head of the Emperor, with a Radiated Crown, and this Inscription, *Imp.Caes.C.Volusiano Aug.*; that is, *Imperatori Caesari Caio Vibio Volusiano Augusto*. On the Reverse an Human Figure, with the Arms somewhat extended, and at the Right Foot an Altar, with the Inscription *Pietas*. This Emperor was Son unto Caius Vibius Tribonianus Gallus, with whom he jointly reigned after the Decii, about the Year 254; both he, himself, and his Father, were slain by the Emperor Æmilianus. By the radiated Crown this Piece should be Coined after his Death and Consecration, but in whose Time it is not clear in History.

Sir Thomas Browne, *Concerning Some Urnes found in Brampton-Field, in Norfolk, anno: 1667*, 1683

GAMESMANSHIP

Dr. Buckland [was] working in these graves [on Breach Down] with his coat off, and a red silk handkerchief tied round his head, his hat covered with chalk, and his black nether garments white, ludicrously white. The Professor made an amusing picture in the grave, from which he carefully collected two handkerchiefs' full of different sorts of black kind of dust and earth. In this grave the Professor attempted to play off a trick upon Lord A. Conyngham's man 'Charles' who was the operator in these barrow diggings. Drawing from his finger an old fashioned ring with a zigzag ornament in bold relief, and well daubing it with chalk-earth, unseen by any individual, he slyly slid it into the ground near the spot where 'Charles' was scraping and peering, who on arriving at the ring and giving it one look, and with his pecker, jerked it off onto the waste heap with the debris.

'What's that', quoth the Professor.

'Oh, 'twon't do for me' was the reply.

'Well, but it's a ring I've picked up'.

'Yes, but you put it there first'.

To this man great credit is due—he has evidently been thoroughly imbued with a 'barrow-opening' mania, and so conversant is he with the features they present, that no object, however minute, can escape his searching glance. The praiseworthy conduct of the juvenile peasantry deserves also to be noticed. In every nook and cranny where they could possibly creep, there were they to be found, as closely and as eagerly poring after relics as any Archaeologist present . . . and in years yet to come will they relate the proceedings of that day, and will impress on the minds of their progeny, that the works of bygone ages are not wantonly to be destroyed.

Report of the Proceedings of the First General Meeting of the British Archaeological Association at Canterbury in 1844. Edited by Alfred John Dunkin, 1845

FINDING AND KEEPING

A bone Dagger 3500 years old was found in the Thames during dredging operations near Staines.

Roman tiles and a Roman wall were also found at Cranbrook, Kent.

Evening Standard, November 11, 1954

A 16-inch 'spike' ploughed up ten years ago by Mr H. Spalding of Swaffham (Norfolk) and used by him for odd jobs on the farm has been identified as a *Bronze Age rapier*, over 3,000 years old.

It is being placed in the Norwich Museum.

Star, May 6, 1957

Nearly 90 *Bronze Age burial urns* have been uncovered in a field at Ardleigh, Essex.

Evening Standard, November 28, 1957

Four ancient *British gold armillae* (bracelets), of the Iron Age, have been dug up in the garden of a new bungalow at Caister-on-Sea, near Great Yarmouth.

Evening Standard, December 12, 1957

A *flint arrowhead* 4500 years old was found by a boy on an allotment at Bury St. Edmunds.

Evening Standard, February 15, 1955

A pot containing a hoard of about 300 *Roman copper coins* has been dug up by a Bromley (Kent) schoolboy, Harold Horne, 14, of Holbrook Way, Bromley.

He was helping to dig a long-jump pit on the Raglan-Hayesford Secondary School playing field in Hayes Lane, Bromley.

Fired with enthusiasm by a history lesson, schoolboy Kenneth Frusher of Upwell, Cambridgeshire, called in two of his chums and began to dig for bones on his father's allotment. Three feet below the surface they found a complete skeleton, believed by local archaeologists to be 800 years old.

London evening papers, 1957

THE UNLUCKY SERGEANT

Willcocks Goldworthy McKenzie of 10, Southern Road, Thame, a lorry driver, said that on 21st April he went for a walk along the bank of the River Thame in company with his wife. His dog got into some weed and started to scratch about, and while watching the dog he saw something shining. This was the larger ring, and going to the spot they poked the soil about and found the remainder of the rings and the coins. He later took these finds to the police.

Police Sergeant Hermon stated that he had examined the spot and the river level was about 5 feet below the bank. The soil was of a clayey nature, and deposited on the bank when the river was dredged last year.

The Revd J. F. Rowlands said that three of the rings were certainly church rings worn by bishops, abbots or other church dignitaries. They may have been lost or hidden there during the time of the Reformation or, as the spot was near the Prebendal, they may have been deposited there for security.

A Juryman asked if any further search had been made.

Police Sergeant: 'Yes, but I've been unlucky'.

Coroner's Inquest at Thame, Oxon, 31st May, 1940 on the discovery of 10 silver groats, (1351–1457) five gold rings, and a reliquary ring

A KING'S RING

Lord Radnor communicated a piece of gold found about August 1780, in a field near Salisbury in the parish of Laverstoke. By the account of William Petty the finder it appears to have been prest out of a cart-rut sideways, as it lay on the surface of the mould adjoining to the rut. It was carried down to Mr Howell, a silversmith in Salisbury, who having proved it in the usual manner, gave the man thirty-four shillings for it as the value of the gold, and from Mr Howell lord Radnor purchased it. Its weight is eleven pennyweights fourteen grains, height one inch and a half, circumference two inches seven eights. The metal is as near as may be agreeable to the standard of the present English currency.

Its age may be ascertained by the very legible superscription:
[ETHELWULF R]
Whether it was or was not designed to be the cap or covering of any little statue, or the locket of a scabbard, or, which is thought most probable, a ring, is submitted to the Society.

Archaeologia VII, 1785

(*This fine massive gold finger-ring enriched with niello belonged to Ethelwulf of Wessex (839–58), father of Alfred the Great, and is one of the treasures of the British Museum.*)

A QUEEN'S RING

The Revd W. Greenwell, F.S.A., Local Secretary for the County of Durham, exhibited the gold ring of Æthelswith, Queen of Mercia . . . [married 853].

The ring is one of the most remarkable relics of antiquity that has appeared in our rooms for many years past.

It was ploughed up in Yorkshire, between Aberford and Sherburn, in the West Riding, and it is said that the fortunate finder attached it to the collar of his dog as an ornament.

Proceedings of the Society of Antiquaries of London, 2nd series, VI, 1876

(*A York jeweller subsequently exchanged it for table-spoons, and the ring passed by way of Canon Greenwell, the noted barrow-explorer of his day, to Sir Wollaston Franks and thence in the munificent Franks Bequest to the British Museum.*)

A BISHOP'S RING

A gold enamelled ring, supposed to have been the property of Alhstan, bishop of Sherburne [817–67].

The ring was found by a labourer on the surface of the ground, a common, at a place called Llys faen, in the North East corner of Carnarvonshire.

Communicated to the Society of Antiquaries by DR SAMUEL PEGGE, December 2, 1773. *Archaeologia*, IV, 1786

(It was once worn on the neck-tie of the finder but in the course of years found a home in Edmund Waterton's famous Collection which is now in the Victoria and Albert Museum.)

UNSKILLED AND IGNORANT?

Let us go back three thousand years, for somewhere about the year 1,000 B.C., that is in the Late Bronze Age, a soldier—not a Roman, for the Legions had not come to Britain then—dropped or threw a sword in the vicinity of Wear Bay, Folkestone.

Who the soldier was we shall never know, nor perhaps for whom he fought, but certain it is that he lived somewhere on the East Cliff, maybe was buried there.

The sword is of bronze, beautifully shaped and in excellent preservation, one of the lugs of the hilt being still in position when it was first brought to me. . . . The sword was trawled up in the nets of the Folkestone fishing-vessel F.E. 169 off the Roman Remains site in East Wear Bay, about 40 yards from the shore. No particular value was attached to it by the crew . . . but Mr G. F. Finn, of Fairlight Road, Hythe, happened to be in the Fishmarket when the catch was being dealt with, and he noticed the sword. The shape of it took his eye; he thought it might be Roman. So interested was he in it that he went to the trouble of sending it to the British Museum for examination [where it was identified as a typical leaf-shaped sword of the late Bronze Age, *circa* 1000–500 B.C.].

The incredible thing about the sword is that it should have been so beautifully made by people whom we are apt to look upon as totally unskilled and ignorant.

Folkestone and Hythe Herald, April 14, 1951

THE AMERICAN'S ROMAN EAGLE

Two thousand American airmen were asked yesterday: 'Have you bought a metal eagle from a boy in Colchester?'

Experts believe that the eagle is a bronze emblem broken off a Roman legion's standard two thousand years ago, and of great value.

An American bought it for half-a-crown.

The curator of Colchester and Essex Museum, Mr. M. R. Hull, said last night that the boy found the eagle in Sheepen Field, off the Colchester by-pass.

'Dream find'

'It could be the first find of a Roman legionary eagle—the archaeologist's dream. If it is, it will be worth a very large sum of money.'

An 18-year-old labourer, John Withers, of Sussex Road, Colchester, said: 'I only knew the boy, Brian, slightly, but two years ago we found the eagle—about eight inches square—in a trench in the field while drainage work was going on.

'He had it in his garden and thought no more about it. Then I saw him again the other day and he told me he sold it to an American airman for half-a-crown. I told Mr. Francis Jarman.'

'Worst thing'

Mr. Jarman, an antique dealer in the same road, told the curator.

'From what I can gather this is an authentic eagle's head,' Mr. Jarman said. 'It was encrusted with a green patina and I understand the boy put it in vinegar—the worst thing for bronze.'

Mr. Hull added: 'If it is a genuine Roman eagle it would fetch a very large price.'

Meanwhile, the Americans at the Wethersfield air base 20 miles away were looking for an eagle that existed as a symbol long before the United States version came into being.

News Chronicle, Sept. 16, 1958

7—PRINTLESS FEET
OR, FABLE AND LEGEND

PRINTLESS FEET
OR, FABLE AND LEGEND

A kind of awful reverence
Helmets-full of Earth
Elf-arrows and Danes'-pipes
Danes' Blood
The White Owl of Tiverton
Robin Hood's Butts: Monuments of Vulgar Error
Ancient Britons and All That
Minoan Margate?—
   —or Gematrian Margate?
A Figtree blocke sometime I was
The Shippe Swalower
A Golden Corselet
Better than Precious Ointment?

A KIND OF AWFUL REVERENCE

Thursley, or Thirsley, is an extensive parish in the county of Surrey and hundred of Godalming. The village is mean and straggling, standing in a dry, healthy situation, pleasant in summer, but, from its high, unsheltered situation, exposed to the north-east winds, very cold in winter. On the heaths between Thursley and Frinsham are three remarkable conic-shaped hills, called the 'Devil's Three Jumps,' the eastern hill (or jump) being the largest in circumference and height, the centre hill the least and lowest. They are composed of a hard rock, barely covered with a light black mould, which gives a scanty nourishment to moss and stunted heath. Their bases are nearly surrounded by a foss, which in some places appears to be artificial. In the fosses are constant springs of water, which assist in forming near them a large piece of water called Abbot's Pond, formerly part of the possessions of the neighbouring abbey of Waverly. The country people, particularly the aged, relate many tales of these eminences, and hold them in a kind of awful reverence (the revels of the fairies yet linger in the tales of the aged rustick). It was formerly customary for the country-people on Whit-Tuesday to assemble on the top of the eastern hill to dance and make merry. If I might be permitted to risk a conjecture on the probable etymology of the name of the parish, Thursley, or Thirsley, that is, Thir's field, this spot was formerly dedicated to the Saxon god Thir, and his image was erected on the eastern eminence. On the introduction of Christianity, it is reasonable to suppose it acquired its present name from having been appropriated to the service of an heathen idol. These circumstances may have given rise to the legendary tales and awe for the spot, which is now scarcely erased from the memory of the neighbouring villagers.

The Gentleman's Magazine, November, 1799

HELMETS-FULL OF EARTH

Here *Selbury*, a round hill, riseth to a considerable height, and seemeth by the fashion of it, and by the sliding down of the earth about it, to be cast up by men's hands. Of this sort are many to be seen in this County, round and copped, which are call'd *Burrows* or *Barrows*, perhaps raised in memory of the Soldiers there slain. For bones are found in them; and I have read that it was a custom among the Northern People, that every soldier escaping alive out of Battel, was to bring his Helmet full of earth toward the raising of Monuments for their slain Fellows. Tho' I rather think this *Selbury*-hill to be placed instead of a Boundary, if not by the Romans, yet by the Saxons, as well as the ditch call'd *Wodensdike*, seeing there were frequent battels in this country between the *Mercians* and the *West Saxons* about their limits; and *Boetius*, and the Writers that treat about Surveying, tell us, that such heaps were often raised for Landmarks.

WILLIAM CAMDEN, *Britannia*, 1586, ed. Gibson, 1695

ELF-ARROWS AND DANES'-PIPES

The flint arrow-heads, of which so many have been collected in different parts of Ireland, and preserved in our antiquarian museums, are supposed by the commonalty to have been shot at cattle, which are objects of aversion to the fairies. This is one of their peculiar sports. The flints are popularly called 'elf-arrows', despite the different nomenclature and theory of our most distinguished antiquaries. What the peasants call an 'elf-arrow' was frequently set in silver and worn about the neck. It was used as an amulet to preserve the person from an elf-shot. Small and oddly shaped smoking instruments sometimes found, and termed 'Danes' pipes', are thought to have been dropped by the 'good people' in a variety of instances. Shoes are also lost on their travels. It is thought to be very lucky to find a fairy's shoe of tiny shape and mould, and to keep it concealed from the eye of mortal. If seen by a third person, the luck vanishes. Many other antique objects are supposed by rustics to have been forgotten by the 'wee people'. These articles are unfortunately often destroyed to avert the dreaded consequences of retaining property that might afterwards be discovered or claimed by their supposed previous owners.

The Gentleman's Magazine, October, 1865

DANES' BLOOD

And in those parts of this county which are opposite to Cambridgeshire, lyes *Barklow*, famous for four great Barrows, such as our ancestors us'd to raise to the memory of those Soldiers that were kill'd in battel, and their bodies lost. But when two others in the same place were dugg up and search'd, we are told that they found three stone Coffins, and abundance of pieces of bones in them. The Country-people have a tradition that they were rais'd after a battel with the Danes. And the *Wall-wort* or *Dwarf-elder* that grows hereabouts in great plenty, and bears red berries, they call by no other name but *Danes'-blood*, denoting the multitude of Danes that were slain.

WILLIAM CAMDEN, *Britannia*, 1586, ed. Gibson, 1695

THE WHITE OWL OF TIVERTON

Many attempts have been made by poor workmen, who frequently left their daily employ, to discover money supposed to be hid near this chapel, but without success; it was therefore proposed, that some persons should lodge in the chapel, for a night, to obtain preternatural direction respecting it. Two farmers, at length, complied with my wishes, and ventured one night, about nine, aided by strong beer, to approach the hallowed walls: they trembled exceedingly at the sudden appearance of a white owl, that flew from a broken window of the building, with the solemn message, that considerable treasures lay hid in certain fields of the barton; that if they would carefully dig there, and diligently attend the labourers, to prevent purloining, they would undoubtedly find them. The farmers attended to the important notice, instantly employed many workmen in the fields described, and I was lately informed had discovered the valuable deposit.

R. Dunsford, *Memoirs of Tiverton*, 1790

ROBIN HOOD'S BUTTS: MONUMENTS OF VULGAR ERROR

We are favoured by a correspondent with the following facts concerning these monuments of vulgar error.

They are situated on Brown Down, near the road from Chard to Wellington. . . . A few days ago, a party of gentlemen from Chard explored one of them, the foundation of which was formed of very large stones, disposed in a perfect circle. Upon these was raised a mound, eight feet high, of alternate layers of black soil, found in the Somersetshire moors, and fine white sand. Ashes, intermixed with bones which had evidently undergone the action of fire, together with a quantity of charcoal, were found gathered up in the centre. Thence, the tumulus consisted only of the black bog earth, and rose more abruptly to the height (in all) of thirteen feet. It was surrounded, at a distance of six feet, by a circumvallation about two feet high.

A jaw, and several small bones, as white as ivory, were found very perfect, and there was a large portion of a skull. The bog earth, had, through so many centuries, preserved its appearance unaltered; and was cut out, like soft soap, but immediately turned to dust, on exposure to the air. On the top of each barrow was a small excavation like a bowl, which I have also found in several barrows on the Dorset Downs.

This hollow was sagaciously alleged by a neighbouring farmer as a proof that the popular tradition whence these monuments have derived their name was well founded. 'Robin Hood and Little John,' said he, '*undoubtedly* used to throw their quoits from one to the other (distance a quarter of a mile); for there is the mark made by pitching the quoits!'

The Taunton Courier, 1818

ANCIENT BRITONS AND ALL THAT

Every perambulator ought to keep a page in his note-book to record the prize bits of misinformation which come his way. The page will not be filled very quickly, except perhaps in Ireland, but that it should have any entries at all is surely remarkable in these days of universal aunts.

It would be hard to beat the story of King Arthur's Sword which was told me by that indefatigable topographer, Edmund Vale. Above the door of a farm-house at Llansannon in Denbighshire is a stone lintel which is nothing more or less than a medieval grave-slab which has evidently been robbed from a church. It bears a common decorative feature, a carved floriated cross on a stepped base and another piece of carved ornament which seems to be a sword of an early type. Both have been improved in modern times with additions of black paint and the sword in particular has been given a fanciful sort of open hilt. Near the house is a prehistoric earthwork—a burial mound or a hill-top camp—which has long been known as Arthur's Table: what more natural than that the sword should also be a relic of that great king, and so to-day you will hear it described. Excalibur, with a basket-hilt. It was Edmund Vale, too, who shattered a fond belief in the famous Bargain Stone in the parish churchyard at Wolverhampton. A prehistoric stone it must be, with its perforation something like the port-hole entrance to a megalithic cist. Bargains were sealed in the olden days by the clasping of hands through the hole. What an interesting piece of folk-memory it all was. But the stone happened to be a medieval gargoyle removed from the chancel roof in an early twentieth century restoration and left in the churchyard.

Not all of us can record such fine bits of nonsense, but the following examples, some of them heard recently in a tour of Kent and Sussex, ought to be of help to those who wander in the byways of archaeology and history. Several came from a bus conductor who, between the punching of tickets, became a self-appointed guide. Please be quite clear that he was a kindly, gentle man: for all we know he may have been that very Gilbertian bus-conducting man who

154

> . . . has auburn hair,
> His wife is far from plain.

Rye is a Cinque (pronounced, correctly, Sink) Port. It is so called—
though there is some doubt about it—from the marble fittings in the
Catholic church there. They were made by Belgian refugees in the
last (1914–18) war.

The timbers of Brookland church—we are now crossing Romney
Marsh—are the beams of Roman and Saxon galleys which sunk in the
sands. More interesting, though, is the font which has figures on it in a
language which no one, not even the parson, can read. Our guide
wouldn't be surprised if it turned out to be Egyptian. The Rector, we
know, would gladly have shown him the Lombardic lettering which
describes the Signs of the Zodiac and the Occupations of the Months
on this famous twelfth-century lead font. But now we were really for
it—and yes, we feared so, Winston Churchill. This is it. In Lydd
church they used to lock the font up (the staple marks are there, certainly) so that the gypsies could not steal Holy Water and sell it to
Mother Shipton who lived in a hovel close to Lydd—and she was a
Marlborough and therefore a relative of Mr Churchill. There is more
than a little truth in this remarkable statement, though it can be
known to but few people who have not read Miss Anne Roper's
Guide to Old Romney Church. A certain Frances Jennings, who lived for
many years at Agney, a manor between Brookland and Lydd which was
anciently a holding of Christ Church, Canterbury, was said to be a
sorceress and was referred to as 'The Famous Mother Shipton': she
was the 'Mother Haggy' of *The Saint Alban's Ghost* published in 1712,
as Miss Roper kindly reminds me, and was outrageously slandered by
Swift. Frances' daughter Sarah married John Churchill, Duke of
Marlborough. Did our busman chance to see Miss Roper's little book?
He hoped to get more time to read it all up in the books and we hope
(in a friendly way) that he does.

Surely, said someone, Mr Churchill is Lord Warden of the Cinque
Ports. Our bus-conducting guide refused to commit himself on this
point, but volunteered that 'they' had built Winston a place out the
other side of Deal, though he didn't live in it. Walmer Castle was Top
Secret in 1538, but there seems little harm in saying now that it is the
Lord Warden's official residence.

We went again to that pleasant little eighteenth century garden con-
ceit, the shell grotto at Margate. 'There is something not exactly high-
class in the name of Margate,' wrote Miss Marie Corelli in one of her
short pieces, and 'If the curious and beautiful subterranean temple of
which I am about to speak existed anywhere but at Margate, it would

155

certainly be acknowledged as one of the wonders of the world, which it undoubtedly is'. This is how the Wonder Chamber and Shrine, the Dome and Hindu Temple, the Sacred Turtle and the Seven Trumpets of Jericho are described in an advertisement leaflet:

> Alluring, Archaeological, Architectural, Antiquarian, Astronomical, Baccusgodical, Conchological, Cruxansatical, Egyptological, Educational, Fylfotical, Ganeshgodical, Geometrical, Geological, Holocryptical, Incomprehensible, Inconceivable, Inexplicable, Inexpressible, Inimitable, Inscrutable, Magical, Mathematical, Mystical, Phallussignical, Problematical, Shellmosaical, Symbolical, Symmetrical, Serpentical, Subterranical, Sungodical, Unexplainable, Unbelievable, Unfathomable, Unforgettable, Uranical, Whisperphonical, Zodiacal.

Mr. Beresford, of Fulham, says it is 'The one place in Margate worth visiting', but Dreamland with its magic mirrors that day must have been shut. Please do not think the Proprietor is unwilling to help you make up your mind. He suggests that his grotto is 'A Temple built by wandering Phoenicians or a Mastaba or funerary chambers built by Cretans' and that it exhibits 'early Creto-Egyptian influences'. The Greek certainly has a word for it, though it is one which would not be printed by the Editor of this review. See and hear for yourself one day: it costs but a shilling.

On the downs at Chilham, near Canterbury, close to the long barrow which Camden christened Jullieberrie's Grave, is a circular earthwork which was for long something of a puzzle to archaeologists. It is quite regular in form and, rather unusually, is a ring-work with its ditch enclosed by a bank. It was marked 'Earthwork' on the Ordnance Survey maps in the familiar Old English type which is used to denote pre-Roman remains. We were told in the village that it was an Ancient British Camp and a schoolmaster went so far as to assure us that the Ancient Britons used to shoot their arrows from this ring into the Castle, a truly remarkable flight of three-quarters of a mile.   Flinders Petrie, a well-known authority of his day, claimed it as a disc-barrow— 'its object must have been religious or sepulchral'. An excavation in 1938 proved it to be of relatively modern date, but we were quite unprepared to learn in casual conversation with a farmer two years later that it was remembered as a colt-breaking ring and to come across an estate record which suggests that it was made between 1774 and 1791. The spurious legend has not yet died, for only this year we heard with avidity that the ring covered the golden treasure of the chieftain who was buried in Jullieberrie's Grave.

It was in a pub at Snodland in the Medway Valley that we saw a thunderbolt. So hot was it that when 'our George picked it up in the pit it burnt him so bad he had to go up to Dr. Carter's'. A nodule of iron pyrites, marcasite, delicately gleaming in the evening sunlight: a piece of 'Fool's Gold', a natural concretion in the chalk in which it was found.

The Medway Valley is noted for its megaliths—Kits Coty, The Countless Stones, Coldrum and the others—imposing remains of sarsen stone burial-chambers which belong in the main to our neolithic civilization. All of them are deservedly tourist trophies. But there are also many sarsens, now isolated, which may or may not be prehistoric monuments. About one, the White Horse Stone, there is a fair measure of agreement: it was once part of a burial-chamber. Added to this it has a further attraction, for it is none other than the Western Sphinx and upon it the Saxons raised their standard of a White Horse after the Battle of Aylesford. It must be so, for a local authority announced it in 1906. The Kentish Standard Stone, his first choice, was unfortunately destroyed by roadmakers. But the White Horse Stone remains for us all to see and moreover it is officially protected as an Ancient Monument.

RONALD JESSUP, *Time and Tide*, August 26, 1950

MINOAN MARGATE?—

For over a century there has been a dispute as to the nature and origin of the Grotto at Dane Hill, in the centre of Margate, which was discovered accidentally by excavators in 1835. Some have said the Grotto's shell mosaic panels were Phoenician. Others dismissed them as fake or fancy eighteenth-century work.

For a year a Ramsgate resident has been at work in the Grotto photographing the mosaics and, as he puts it, breaking down their symbolism. His conclusion, announced yesterday at a private meeting of interested parties in the town, is that the Grotto is the central chamber of a Cretan king, or priest-god's tomb, dating from 2000–1500 B.C.

It is, of course, news to Margate people—and many others—that Cretans were burying kings in their borough such a long time ago, but the Corporation and other representatives present at yesterday's meeting were so impressed by this exposition that a committee is being set up to pursue the investigation further.

The Observer, July 10, 1949

—OR GEMATRIAN MARGATE?

A profound probe into the secrets of the Shell Temple at Margate, popularly known as the Grotto, has opened up an interesting new line of thought.

157

Previous scholars who have tried to solve the mysteries of this unique subterranean structure have mainly concentrated on the symbolism of the intricate shell mosaic.

The Shaws have regarded the patterns in the panels as subsidiary and searched deeper for hidden meanings. And their work has been fruitful. On the theory that the Grotto is of Mithraic origin Mr Shaw states that Mithraic temples were orientated east, and contained sculptures or pictures of Mithras, bulls, etc.

In the Shell Temple, which is orientated south, there are no such figures, because, claims Mr Shaw, the original builders, a certain ancient Hebrew sect, were forbidden on principle to portray them.

By a system of Gematria—a cabbalistic method of interpreting the Hebrew scriptures by interchanging words whose letters have the same numerical value when added—he has translated the messages of the entire 100 panels.

Kent Messenger, November 7, 1958

A FIGTREE BLOCKE SOMETIME I WAS

But now if I shoulde thus leave Boxley, the favourers of false and feyned Religion would laugh in their sleeves, and the followers of Gods trueth might iustly cry out and blame me.

For, it is yet freshe in minde to bothe sides, and shall (I doubt not) to the profite of the one, be continued in perpetuall memorie to all posteritie, by what notable imposture, fraud, Iuggling, and Legierdemain, the sillie lambes of Gods flocke were (not long since) seduced by the false Romish Foxes at this Abbay. The manner whereof, I will set downe, in such sorte onely, as the same was sometime by themselves published in print for their estimation and credite, and yet remaineth deeply imprinted in the mindes and memories of many on live, and to their everlasting reproche, shame, and confusion.

It chaunced (as the tale is) that upon a time, a cunning Carpenter of our countrie was taken prisoner in the warres betweene us and Fraunce, who (wanting otherwise to satisfie for his raunsome, and having good leysure to devise for his deliveraunce) thought it best to attempt some curious enterprise, within the compasse of his owne Art and skill, to make himselfe some money withall: And therefore, getting togither fit matter for his purpose, he compacted of wood, wyer, paste and paper, a Roode of such exquisite arte and excellencie, that it not onely matched in comelynesse and due proportion of the partes the best of the common sort: but in straunge motion, variety of gesture, and nimblenes of ioints, passed al other that before had been seene: the same being able to bow down and lifte up it selfe, to shake and stirre the handes and feete, to nod the head, to rolle the eies, to wag the chaps, to bende the browes, and finally to represent to the eie, both the proper motion of each member of the body, and also a lively, expresse, and significant shew of a well contented or displeased minde: byting the lippe, and gathering a frowning, froward, and disdainful face, when it would pretend offence: and shewing a most milde, amyable, and smyling cheere and countenaunce, when it woulde seeme to be well pleased.

So that now it needed not Prometheus fire to make it a lively man, but onely the helpe of the covetous Priestes of Bell, or the aide of some craftie College of Monkes, to deifie and make it passe for a verie God.

This done, he made shifte for his libertie, came over into the Realme, of purpose to utter his merchandize, and laide the Image upon the backe of a Iade that he drave before him. Now, when hee was come so farre as to Rochester on his way, hee waxed drie by reason of travaile, and called at an alehouse for drinke to refreshe him, suffering his horse neverthelesse to go forwarde alone along the Citie.

This Iade was no sooner out of sight, but hee missed the streight westerne way that his Maister intended to have gone, and turning Southe, made a great pace toward Boxley, and being driven (as it were) by some divine furie, never ceassed iogging till he came at the Abbay church doore, where he so beat and bounced with his heeles, that divers of the Monkes heard the noise, came to the place to knowe the cause, and (marvelling at the straungenesse of the thing) called the Abbat and his Covent to beholde it.

These good men seeing the horse so earnest, and discerning what he had on his backe, for doubt of deadly impietie opened the doore: which they had no sooner done, but the horse rushed in, and ran in great haste to a piller (which was the verie place where this Image was afterwarde advaunced) and there stopped himselfe, and stoode still.

Now while the Monkes were busie to take off the lode, in commeth the Carpenter (that by great inquisition had followed) and he challenged his owne: the Monkes, loth to loose so beneficiall a stray, at the first made some deniall, but afterward, being assured by all signes that he was the verie Proprietarie, they graunt him to take it with him.

The Carpenter then taketh the horse by the head, and first assayeth to leade him out of the Church, but he would not stirre for him: Then beateth hee and striketh him, but the Iade was so restie and fast nailed, that he woulde not once remoove his foote from the piller: at the last he taketh off the Image, thinking to have carried it out by it selfe, and then to have led the horse after: but that also cleaved so fast to the place, that nothwithstanding all that ever he (and the Monks also, which at

159

the length were contented for pities sake to helpe him) coulde doe, it would not be mooved one inche from it: So that in the ende, partly of wearinesse in wrestling, and partly by persuasion of the Monkes, which were in love with the Picture, and made him beleeve that it was by God himselfe destinate to their house, the Carpenter was contented for a peece of money to go his way, and leave the Roode behinde him. Thus you see the generation of this the great God of Boxley, comparable (I warrant you) to the creation of that beastly Idoll Priapus, of which the Poet saith,

Olim truncus eram ficulnus, inutile lignum,
Cum faber incertus SCAMNUM FACERETNE PRIAPUM,
MALUIT ESSE DEUM: Deus inde ego furum, &c.

> *A Figtree blocke sometime I was,*
> *A log unmeete for use:*
> *Till Carver doubting with himselfe,*
> *WERT BEST MAKE PRIAPUS,*
> *OR ELSE A BENCHE? resolvd at last*
> *To make a God of mee:*
> *Thencefoorth a God I am, of birdes*
> *And theeves most drad, you see.*

But what? I shall not neede to reporte, howe lewdly these Monkes, to their own enriching and the spoile of Gods people, abused this wooden God after they had thus gotten him, bicause a good sort be yet on live that sawe the fraude openly detected at Paules Crosse, and others may reade it disclosed in bookes extant, and commonly abroad. Neither will I labour to compare it throughout with the Troian Palladium, which was a picture of wood that could shake a speare, and rolle the eies as lively as this Roode did: and which falling from heaven, chose it selfe a place in the Temple, as wisely as this Carpenters horse did: and had otherwise so great couvenience and agreement with this our Image, that a man would easily beleeve the device had beene taken from thence: But I will onely note, for my purpose, and the places sake, that even as they fansied that Troy was upholden by that Image, and that the taking of it awaye by Diomedes and Ulysses, brought destruction (by sentence of the Oracle) upon their City: So the town of Boxley (which stoode chiefly by the Abbay) was through the discoverie and defacing of this Idoll, and another (wrought by Cranmer and Cromwell) according to the iust iudgement of God, hastened to utter decay and beggerie.

And now, since I am falne into mention of that other Image which was honoured at this place, I will not sticke to bestowe a fewe wordes for the detection thereof also, as wel for that it was as very an illusion as the former, as also for that the use of them was so linked togither, that the one cannot throughly be understood without the other: for this was the order.

If you minded to have benefit by the Roode of Grace, you ought first to bee shriven of one of the Monkes: Then by lifting at this other Image (which was untruly of the common sort called S. Grumbald, for Sainct Rumwald) you shoulde make proofe whether you were in cleane life (as they called it) or no: and if you so found your selfe, then was your way prepared, and your offering acceptable before the Roode: if not, then it behoved you to be confessed of newe, for it was to be thought that you had concealed somwhat from your ghostly Dad, and therefore not yet woorthie to be admitted Ad Sacra Eleusina.

Now, that you may knowe, how this examination was to be made, you must understande, that this Sainct Rumwald was the picture of a pretie Boy Sainct of stone, standing in the same churche, of it selfe short, and not seeming to be heavie: but for as much as it was wrought out of a great and weightie stone (being the base thereof) it was hardly to be lifted by the handes of the strongest man. Neverthelesse (such was the conveighance) by the helpe of an engine fixed to the backe thereof, it was easily prised up with the foote of him that was the keeper; and therefore of no moment at all in the handes of such as had offered frankly: and contrariwise, by the meane of a pinne, running into a post (which that religious impostor standing out of sight, could put in, and pull out, at his pleasure) it was, to such as offered faintly, so fast and unmoveable, that no force of hande might once stirre it. In so much, as many times it mooved more laughter than devotion, to beholde a great lubber to lift at that in vaine, which a young boy (or wench) had easily taken up before him.

I omit, that chaste Virgins, and honest married matrones, went oftentimes away with blushing faces, leaving (without cause) in the mindes of the lookers on, great suspicion of uncleane life, and wanton behaviour: for feare of whiche note and villainie, women (of all other) stretched their purse strings, and sought by liberall offering to make S. Rumwalds man their good friend and favourer.

But marke heere (I beseech you) their policie in picking plaine mens purses. It was in vaine (as they persuaded) to presume to the Roode without shrifte: yea, and money lost there also, if you offered before you were in cleane life: And therefore, the matter was so handled, that without treble oblation (that is to say) first to the Confessour, then to Sainct Rumwald, and lastly to the Gracious Roode, the poore Pilgrimes could not assure themselves of any good, gained by all their labour. No more than such as goe to Parisgardein, the Bell Savage, or Theatre, to beholde Beare baiting, Enterludes, or Fence play, can account of any pleasant spectacle, unlesse they first pay one pennie at the gate, another at the entrie of the Scaffolde, and the thirde for a quiet standing.

WILLIAM LAMBARDE, *A Perambulation of Kent*, 1576

THE SHIPPE SWALOWER

For close on a thousand years men have speculated upon the nature of the Goodwin Sands. And for the greater part of that time, perhaps, has a dread of the 'shippe swalower' been a familiar enough feeling in the hearts of all seafarers who made voyage round the coast of Thanet. It is not surprising therefore to find that the literature of the Goodwins is both large in volume and widely spread in publication, and as a great deal remains unedited, the task of the general reader who hopes for some sort of historical background to his store is indeed formidable. . . . There is, too, in this great welter of the written word not a little that is inaccurate, and much that is frank legend and popular hearsay. Writer copied uncritically from writer, and in the quiet seclusion of cloister and library far removed, it may be, from the coast of Kent, the swirl of the tide over the sands was but a faint remembrance. Romance took pride of place. . . .

The first mention of the Island of Lomea is to be found in a book written by John Twyne (1501–81), a schoolmaster-antiquary who settled in Canterbury and became in turn Sheriff, Alderman and then Member of Parliament for the City. His learned work in Latin, *De Rebus Albionicis Britannicus*, was published posthumously by his son Thomas in 1590, and as his is the earliest mention of the Island by name, we shall translate an extract in which it occurs.

> 'Of Lomea,' he writes, 'or as it is now called Godwin Sands . . . this isle was very fruitful and had much pasture; it was situated lower than Thanet from which there was a passage by boat of about three or four miles. This Island in an unusual tempest of winds and rain and in a very high rage of the sea was drowned, overwhelmed with sand, and irrecoverably converted into a nature between that of land and sea . . . sometimes it floats, while at low water, people may walk upon it.'

Of Lomea, he prefaces his remarks, 'take what I have read in some writers,' but neither he, Camden, the famous antiquary who published his *Britannia* in 1586, nor William Lambarde, the father of English topography, whose *Perambulation of Kent* first appeared in 1576, tells us anything further about these early sources. All rests upon John Twyne's recollection of his own reading of early chroniclers, or perhaps even upon his imagination. Lambarde puts it quite plainly:

. . . and that this his (Godwin's) land in Kent sonke sodainly into the Sea. Neyther were these things continued in memory by the mouthes of the unlearned people onely, but committed to writing also by the hands and pens of Monkes, Frears, and others of learned sort: So that in course of time, the matter was past all peradventure, and the things beleived for undoubted veritie. . . .

We may pause a moment to notice one point of interest. Twyne calls his island off the Thanet coast by the name of 'Lomea,' and it may be significant that part of the surface of the mainland of Thanet is to-day covered by a loamy soil. Thanet indeed gives its name to the Thanet Sand, the well-known light yellow sand which overlies the chalk and is prominently exposed, for instance, at Pegwell. The place-name 'Lomea' sounds as though it might be derived from the same Old English root as the word 'loam', and although no place-name like it now exists in Thanet (so far as we know), the possibility of a connection between the two remains an attractive speculation.

By the early years of the eighteenth century, the local tradition of a drowned island once the property of Earl Godwin had become firmly established. Had you visited a certain ale-house in Broadstairs in 1736, you could have played shove-ha'penny on an oak board which the landlord swore was made from a tree once growing on the island. In the encouragement of an interest in this story, the Kentish topographers had played an important part. Richard Kilburne in 1659 accepted it quite uncritically; in 1693 the more cautious William Somner is led to remark, 'I cannot possibly say, nor am scarce willing to conjecture least I seem to some too bold.' In 1719 John Harris felt able to accept the Godwin traditional story, though he did not support another entertaining legend, that of Tenterden Steeple being the cause of Goodwin Sands, a belief to which we shall return in a moment. John Lewis, 'Vicar of Mynstre and Minister of Mergate,' in 1736 tells us a great deal more about the sands themselves than any other writer until his time. His lively observations are at first-hand and therefore of much value, but so far as the legend of the island of Lomea is concerned, he is content to regard it as 'the common tradition hereabouts.' The best known historian of Kent, Edward Hasted, published his seventh volume in 1798: in it he describes the common traditions associated with the Goodwins, and discreetly wonders how far they are consistent with the truth. We need go no further than to notice the careful summary made in 1871 by Robert Furley when he wrote his *History of the Weald of Kent*. Almost without exception all the writers following him, especially those in the mode of romance and adventure, have quoted from earlier books.

There is also for our consideration the Kentish saying that 'Tenterden Steeple's the cause of the Goodwin Sands,' . . . A second version of the proverb runs:

Of many people it hath been said
That Tenterden Steeple Sandwich Haven hath decayed

It is usually linked with Sir Thomas More's alleged questioning of a rather self-satisfied old man, a real forerunner of the oldest inhabitant who nowadays might well give the same sort of answers into the travelling microphone of the British Broadcasting Corporation. Anyone interested in a mild piece of literary detection may like to try to trace its original form; it may be somewhere in the arid pages of Bishop Hugh Latimer's Sermons, or in Thomas More's *Dialogues* first published in a folio in 1529, and from one or the other of these sources the amiable Thomas Fuller perhaps took notes for his *Worthies* published in 1662 in London.

We do happen to know, on the sound evidence of testamentary documents by which people bequeathed money to its cause, that the present tower of Tenterden Church was being built in the decade between 1461 and 1471. On the whole there is not likely to have been an earlier tower, and the legend must be accepted as a local proverb and not in any sense as an authentic explanation of the cause of the Goodwin Sands. And we cannot allow the place-name experts to sway our opinion here. The name of Tenterden certainly supposes a connection with Thanet in that it denotes the swine-pasture of the people of Thanet, but it only means that Tenterden belonged to the religious of Minster-in-Thanet.

Here it is convenient to recall two other proverbs connected with the Goodwins. 'Let him set up shop on the Goodwin Sands' is generally understood to apply to shipwrecked mariners, while the meaning of the phrase 'no more thanks than there are pebbles on the Goodwins' is abundantly clear to anyone who has seen what the Reverend Mr. Lewis so aptly described as '. . . soft, fluid, porous, spongious, and yet withal tenacious Matter . . .' The latter saying comes, rather surprisingly, from John Phillips's *Don Quixote* (1687), while the former, as the learned Dr. Samuel Pegge recorded during his residence at Godmersham Vicarage in 1735, was just a piece of 'countrey wit.'

GEORGE GOLDSMITH CARTER, *The Goodwin Sands*, 1953 (from the Introduction, by R. F. JESSUP), Constable and Co. Ltd.

A GOLDEN CORSELET

Connected with this [discovery by workmen] it is certainly a strange circumstance that an elderly woman who had been to Mold to lead her husband home late at night from a public-house, should have seen or fancied, a spectre to have crossed the road before her to the identical mound of gravel, 'of unusual size, and clothed in a coat of gold, which shone like the sun', and that she should tell the story the next morning many years ago, amongst others to the very person, Mr John Langford, whose workmen drew the treasure out of its prison-house. Her having related this story is an undoubted fact.

Archaeologia, XXVI, 1836

(*The corselet is the famous ceremonial cape (or possibly a peytrell or pony-trapping) from Mold now in the British Museum.*)

BETTER THAN PRECIOUS OINTMENT?

Names of some of the prehistoric burial mounds, stone circles and standing stones in the British Isles.

Alderman's Ground, Arthur's Round Table, Baverse's Thumb, Bridestone, Cannon Rocks, The Two Captains, Carl Lofts, Cold Harbour, Crock of Gold, Culpepper's Dish, Deadman's Hill, Devil's Arrows, Devil's Dyke, Devil's Pulpit, Egmonds Howe, Fairy Toot, Five Lord's Burgh, Giant's Load, Grey Mare and her Colts, Grimsditch, Guggleby Stone, Hetty Pegler's Tump, Holy Stone, Hulleys Slack, Hurdlow, Julliberrie's Grave, King's Stone, Kits Coty House, Knot Low, Ladstones, Long Meg and her Daughters, Lowfield, Matlow Hill, Men-an-tol, Men-skrfa, Money Tump, Music Barrow, Ned and Grace's Bed, Nine Maidens, Noggar Noise, Old Man at Mow, Pancake, Pots and Pans, Ringstone, Robin Hood's Bed, Rise Hill, Sazzen Stone, Shipley Hill, Skellow, Skirt-full-of-stones, Solomon's Thumb, Sleepy Lowe, Soldiers' Ring, Warrior's Grave, Whispering Knights, Willy Howe, Wolf Fold.

8—FOUR BREVITIES

FOUR BREVITIES

The Olde Discipline of Englande
Purviaunce made for King Richard
Cloaths of My Lord Buckingham, 1625
Layd out for John Dalyson—A Kentish Schoolboy, 1633–4

THE OLDE DISCIPLINE OF ENGLANDE

Consider with thy selfe (gentle Reader) the olde discipline of Englande, mark what we were before, and what we are now: . . . cast thine eye backe to thy Predecessors, and tell mee howe wonderfully wee have been chaunged, since wee were schooled with these abuses. *Dion* sayth, that english men could suffer watching and labor, hunger and thirst, and beare of al stormes with hed and shoulders, they used slender weapons, went naked, and were good soldiours, they fed uppon rootes and barkes of trees, they would stand up to the chin many dayes in marishes without victualles: and they had a kind of sustenaunce in time of neede, of which if they had taken but the quantitie of a beane, or the weight of a pease, they did neyther gape after meate, nor long for the cuppe, a great while after. The men in valure not yeelding to *Scithia*, the women in courage passing the *Amazons*. The exercise of both was shootyng and dancing, running and wrestling, and trying such maisteries, as eyther consisted in swiftnesse of feete, agilitie of body, strength of armes, or Martiall discipline. But the exercise that is nowe among us, is banqueting, playing, pipyng, and dauncing, and all suche delightes as may win us to pleasure, or rocke us a sleepe.

Oh what a woonderfull chaunge is this? Our wreastling at armes is turned to wallowyng in Ladies laps, our courage, to cowardice, our running to ryot, our Bowes into Bolles, and our Dartes into Dishes. We have robbed *Greece* of Gluttonie, *Italy* of wantonnesse, *Spaine* of pride, *Fraunce* of deceite, and *Dutchland* of quaffing. Compare *London* to *Rome*, and *England* to *Italy*, you shall finde the Theaters of the one, the abuses of the other, to be rife among us. *Experto crede*, I have seene somewhat, and therefore I thinke may say the more.

STEPHEN GOSSON, The Schoole of Abuse, 1579

PURVIAUNCE MADE FOR KING RICHARD

Being with the Duc of Lancastre, at the Bishop's Palace of Durham, at London, the xxiii Day of September, the Yere of the King aforesaid. [1388]

First beginning for a chatry

		xiii	Calvys
xiii	Oxen lying in salte	cxi	Pigge
ii	Oxen fresh	ccc	Marribones
xxvi	Carcas of shepe freysh		Of larde and grece eynough
xxvi	Hedes of shepe freysh	iii	Ton salt venyson
xii	Bores	iii	Does of freysh venyson

The pultrey

l	Swannes
ccx	Gees
l	Capons of hie grece
viii	Dussen other capons
lx	Dussen harries
cc	Copull conyny
iiii	Fesaunts
v	Herons and bitors
vi	Kidds
v	Dussen pullayn for gely
xii	Dussen to roste
c	Dussen pejons
xii	Dussen parterych
viii	Dussen rabettes
x	Dussen cerlews
xii	Dussen brewes
	(*forsan* grouse)
xii	Cranes
	Wildefowle ynough
xxvi	Galons milke
xii	Galons creme
xl	Galons cruddes
iii	Boshel appelles
xi	Thousand egges

The first course

A potage called viand bruse
Hedes of bores
Grete fleshe
Swannes rosted

Pigges
Crustade lumbarde in paste
a soltite

The seconde course

A potage called gele
A potage de blandsore
Pigges rosted
Fesaunts rosted
Cranes rosted
Herons rosted
Chekenes rosted
Breme
Tartes
Broke braune
Conyng rosted
A soltite

The thirde course

Pottage bruette of almond
Stewed lumparde
Venyson rosted
Rabettes rosted
Parterych rosted
Pejons rosted
Quailes rosted
Larkes rosted
Playne puffe
a dish of jely
Long frutors
A soltite

British Museum *MS. Harley* 4016, 1

CLOATHS OF MY LORD BUCKINGHAM, 1625
For a Journey to Paris to bring over Queen Henrietta Maria

His Grace hath for his body, twenty-seven rich suits embroidered, and laced with silk and silver plushes; besides one rich white satin uncut velvet suit, set all over, both suit and cloak, with diamonds, the value whereof is thought to be worth fourscore thousand pounds, besides a feather made with great diamonds; with sword, girdle, hat-band and spurs with diamonds, which suit His Grace intends to enter Paris with. Another rich suit is of purple satin, embroidered all over with rich orient pearls; the cloak made after the Spanish fashion, with all things suitable, the value whereof will be 20,000*l* and this is thought shall be for the wedding day in Paris. His other suits are all rich as invention can frame, or art fashion. His colours for the entrance are white pwatchett, and for the wedding crimson and gold. . . .

British Museum MSS Harley 6988, 2

(*Letters of the Royal Family of England in the Reign of Charles I from 1625 to 1648.*)

LAYD OUT FOR JOHN DALYSON— A KENTISH SCHOOLBOY, 1633–4

Shirts 24s; a coat 17s; hatt and gloves 9s	£002	10	00
Sendinge horse and man seuerall tymes to Islington	000	04	00
Tronke carredge and other things for Islington	000	02	00
Stockings, bands, coffes, handkerchers, shooes, and gloues	001	04	00
Garters and shoe strings	000	03	04
Bringinge a tronke and other things from London to Grenewich; and servants charges in byinge theise things	000	03	06
Carredge of them from Grenewich to Croydon and a mans and horse hire to goe with it	000	03	00
Giuen him at seuerall tymes	000	05	00
A dosen of napkins, towells, capps and makinge	001	05	00
His parte in a syluer boule giuen Mrs Webb [*wife of his tutor*]	001	10	00
Sendinge for them from Croydon and giuen the servants	000	04	00
Payd Mr Webb monye layd out for mending his clothes, bookes, and schoole dutyes	001	03	00
His parte in a yard ½ of laune for Mrs Webb	000	05	03
A sute of aparrell	002	15	00
His halfe yeares dyett due at the Annunciation 1634	008	00	00
	£019	17	01

Dalison Documents, Archaeologia Cantiana, XV, 1883

9—THE GRAMMAR OF ANTIQUITY

The science of archaeology
The influence of antiquity
The Relique
The Ruines of Time
To Promote the Work
A Society to be sett up—
   —its Nature and Extent
Virtue and Vice, Science and Errour
After the Universal Deluge
Mr. Rowland's better Method
Curiosities at Home (1)
Curiosities at Home (2)
Crop-marks at Richborough
The Antiquities of Britain
To make a Respectable Figure
Chymeras of Virtuosi?
Antiquity in the cause of History
The development of our Subject
The Barrow Diggers
Prehistory and the Romantic Movement
The First of the Moderns
Dating these Grave-hills
Every detail to be recorded
The everyday life
Behind the things themselves
Archaeology in Sussex—
   —and in Dorset
At the Inaugural Meeting of the Kent Archaeological Society, 1858
The scope and object of our Design
The First Archaeological Congress
Notes for Beginners
Archaeology and Society
The British Museum
Non Extinguetur

THE SCIENCE OF ARCHAEOLOGY

Do not look on archaeology as merely a digging into the past; it is a science of how to manage the future. It is a science which shows us what happens under varying situations and man's reactions to those situations. It shows us what man has done to conquer the obstacles in his path, where he has failed and where he has succeeded.

SIR CYRIL FOX, Opening Address to a *Conference on the Future of Archaeology*, London, 1943

THE INFLUENCE OF ANTIQUITY

Never probably has the steadying influence of antiquity been more needed than it is to-day, when amid the bewilderment of new aims, new methods and standards, the one point of common agreement is the revolt against all conventions in art. The results are seen in the eccentricities, the disharmonies, that prevail; in the unflagging efforts after a capricious and assertive self-expression; and in the attempts at rendering all things new, and most things violent, in art. To an age perplexed antiquity comes with its teaching of other things. It suggests that art is a blend of both representation and expression; that its true ends are attained when there is a balance of free creation and control; and, further, that its appeal is directed neither to an individual nor to an age, but to something elemental and universal in man. And in these ideas and counsels are summed up not the least of the findings of antiquity. They are the considered judgments of sane and fastidious critics; and in art, as in life, it is the part of wisdom to let the ages instruct the years.

J. W. H. ATKINS, *Literary Criticism in Antiquity*, 1934, Cambridge University Press.

THE RELIQUE

When my grave is broke up againe
Some second ghest to entertaine,
(For graves have learn'd that woman-head
To be to more then one a Bed)
And he that digs it, spies
A bracelet of bright haire about the bone,
Will he not let'us alone,
And thinke that there a loving couple lies,
Who thought that this device might be some way

175

To make their Soules, at the last busie day,
Meet at this grave, and make a little stay?
    If this fall in a time, or land,
    Where mis-devotion doth command,
    Then, he that digges us up, will bring
    Us, to the Bishop, and the King,
      To make us Reliques; then
Thou shalt be a Mary Magdalen, and I
    A something else thereby;
All women shall adore us, and some men;
And since at such time, miracles are sought,
I would have that age by this paper taught
What miracles wee harmelesse lovers wrought.
    First, we lov'd well and faithfully,
    Yet knew not what wee lov'd, nor why,
    Difference of sex no more wee knew,
    Then our Guardian Angells doe;
      Comming and going, wee
Perchance might kisse, but not between those meales;
    Our hands ne'r toucht the seales,
Which nature, injur'd by late law, sets free:
These miracles wee did; but now alas,
All measure, and all language, I should passe,
Should I tell what a miracle shee was.

                  JOHN DONNE, 1572–1631

THE RUINES OF TIME

It chaunced me on day beside the shore
Of siluer streaming Thamesis to bee,
Nigh where the goodly Verlame stood of yore,
Of which there now remaines no memorie,
Nor anie little moniment to see,
By which the trauailer, that fares that way,
This once was she, may warned be to say.

I was that Citie, which the garland wore
Of Britaines pride, deliuered unto me
By Romane Victors, which it wonne of yore;
Though nought at all but ruines now I bee,
And lye in mine own ashes, as ye see:

Verlame *I was; but what bootes it that I was*
Sith now I am but weedes and wastfull gras?

O vaine worlds glorie, and unstedfast state
Of all that liues, on face of sinfull earth,
Which from their first untill their utmost date
Tast no one hower of happines or merth,
But like as at the ingate of their berth,
They crying creep out of their mothers woomb,
So wailing backe go to their wofull toomb.

To tell the beawtie of my buildings fayre,
Adornd with purest golde, and precious stone;
To tell my riches, and endowments rare
That by my foes are now all spent and gone:
To tell my forces matchable to none,
Were but lost labour, that few would beleeue,
And with rehearsing would me more agreeue.

High towers, faire temples, goodly theaters,
Strong walls, rich porches, princelie pallaces,
Large streetes, braue houses, sacred sepulchers,
Sure gates, sweete gardens, stately galleries,
Wrought with faire pillours, and fine imageries,
All those (O pitie) now are turnd to dust,
And ouergrowen with blacke obliuions rust.

They are all gone, and all with them is gone,
Ne nought to me remaines, but to lament
My long decay, which no man els doth mone,
And mourne my fall with dolefull dreriment.
Yet it is comfort in great languishment,
To be bemoned with compassion kinde,
And mitigates the anguish of the minde.

But me no man bewaileth, but in game,
Ne sheddeth teares from lamentable eie:
Nor any liues that mentioneth my name
To be remembred of posteritie,
Saue One that maugre fortunes iniurie,
And times decay, and enuies cruell tort,
Hath writ my record in true-seeming sort.

177

Cambden *the nourice of antiquitie,*
And lanterne unto late succeeding age,
To see the light of simple veritie,
Buried in ruines, through the great outrage
Of her owne people, led with warlike rage.
Cambden, *though time all moniments obscure,*
Yet thy iust labours euer shall endure.

EDMUND SPENSER, *Complaints: The Ruines of Time,* 1591

TO PROMOTE THE WORK

Queries in order to the Geography, and Antiquities of the Country.

First therefore Information is desired of the *Name* of the Parish; both according to the Modern Pronunciation and the Oldest Records, (which would be also very convenient as to all other Places whatever) and whence 'tis thought to be deriv'd. Also whether a *Market-Town, Town-Corporate,* or *Village.*

II. In what Comot or Hundred *Situate?* How *Bounded?* Of what *Extent,* and what Number of *Houses* and *Inhabitants?* To what *Saint* is the Church dedicated, and whether a *Parsonage, Vicarage,* or both?

III. An Enumeration and brief Description of the *Towns, Villages, Hamlets, Castles, Forts, Monasteries, Chappels of Ease, Free-Schools, Hospitals, Bridges,* and all *Publick Buildings* whatever within the Parish, whether Ruinous or Entire; or whose Names only are preserv'd: When, and by whom Founded, Endow'd or Repair'd.

IV. *Sanctuaries* or Places of Refuge; Places memorable for *Battels, Births,* or *Interment* of *Great Persons, Parliaments, Councils, Synods,* &c.

V. Seats of the Gentry; with the Names and Quality of the present Proprietors, and their Arms and Descent.

VI. A Catalogue of the *Barrows,* or those Artificial Mounts distinguish'd by the several Names of *Krigeu, Gorsedheu, Tommenydh, Beili,* &c as also of the *Camps,* and all old *Entrenchments* whatever.

VII. Roman *Ways, Pavements, Stoves,* or any Under-ground Works: Crosses, Beacons, Stones pitch'd an (sic) end in a regular Order; such as *Meinihirion* in *Caernarvonshire, Karn Lhechart* in *Glamorgan,* and

178

Buarth Arthur in the County of *Caermardhim*: As also all those rude Stone-Monuments distinguish'd by the several Names of *Bêdh, Gwely, Karnedh, Kromlech, Lhêch yr âst, Lhêch y Gowres, Lhêch y Wydhan, Koeten Arthur, Kist vaën, Preseb y Vuwch Vrech,* &c.

VIII. The Old *Inscriptions* in the Parish, whether in the Church, or elsewhere; a Collection of all being intended to the Time of King *Henry* the Eighth.

IX. Old *Arms, Urns, Lamps, Pateræ, Fibulæ,* or any other Utensils; where, and when discover'd?

X. *Coyns, Amulets, Chains, Bracelets, Rings, Seals,* &c where, and when found; and in whose Possession at Present?

XI. *Manuscripts*: Of what Subject and Language; In whose Hands; Whether Ancient or Late Copies.

XV. The *Customs*, and peculiar *Games* and *Feasts* amongst the Vulgar in the Parish, Hundred, County, or any part of *Wales*: Together with the *Vulgar Errors* and *Traditions*. . . .

Having thus propounded what *Queries* occur to my Thoughts; nothing remains, but that I own to the Publick, that in case this Paper meets with a kind Reception (as from this last Summer's Travels, I have great Hopes it may) if the Undertaking be ill perform'd, 'twill be wholly my own Fault; the Gentry of the Country having in all respects done more than their Part, and afforded such an Encouragement towards it, as might sufficiently require the labours of a Person far better Qualified for such a *Design*: But of this, a particular Account (as is necessary) shall be given hereafter. So I shall only add here; that as to these *Queries*, besides *Wales*, I entreat the favourable Assistance of the Gentry and Clergy in those other Countries mention'd in the former Proposals: and that in all Places, they who are dispos'd to further the Design, would please to communicate this Paper where they think fit, amongst their Neighbours; interpreting some *Queries* to those of the Vulgar, whom they judge Men of Veracity, and capable of giving any the least Information towards it, that may be pertinent and instructive.

Edward Lhwyd, 'Keeper of the Ashmolean Repository in Oxford,' Broadsheet advertisement for Parochial Queries for a Geographical Dictionary . . . of Wales, [1697] Bodleian MS. Ashmole 1820a, folios 76–7

A SOCIETY TO BE SETT UP—

In Obedience to your Commands I here humbly present to you such Heads, as at present occur to my Thoughts, of what I believe in time may be done by a Society of nobles and Gentlemen meeting in Order to Improve and Cultivate the History and Antiquities of Great Britain; wherein many most excellent Monuments are still to be found, which for want of due Care, go more and more to decay and Ruin.

The last Ages have Employed the Learned and Curious, Cheifly in the Consideration of the Greek and Roman Antiquities, from whence the Voluminous Collections of Gronovius and Graevius have arisen; which tho' large, yet have not taken in all that has been Publish'd, or Written in that Way.

But as the History of a man's own Country is (or should be) dearer to him than that of Foreign Regions; so there have been very many who have been inquisitive after the Laws, Customs and Ways of Living used by their Ancestors and the Remains left by them. And for this Reason most of the Great Cities and Churches of Italy, Spain, France and Germany have been described in Print; whilst the English, tho' they have not been wholly Silent on these Subjects, have yet (as 'tis said) published less to the World than other Nations.

This is not to be attributed to the Inadvertence or Sluggishness of our people (who are known to be as Curious and Industrious as others) nor to a want of fit Matter to entertain the World with; since the Monasticon Anglicanum, and Mr. Rymer's Leagues (books treating of single subjects) seem to shew how many noble Memoirs have been buried in dust and Corners, and what may be recovered relating to the same or other Subjects, when a general search shall be made into the Libraries, Archives, and other Repositories of the Kingdom.

But as this must be a work of great Charge and Constant Application, and far too great for one purse, 'tis to be wish'd that a Society of Antiquaries might be sett up, from whose united endeavours, the world might receive compleat volumes Relating to Our Native Countrey, to Our Kings, Our Church, and Our People, with others of a Miscellaneous nature.

British Museum *MS. Harley* 7055, 1. Wanley Papers

—ITS NATURE AND EXTENT

Such a Society would Bring to Light and Preserve All old Monumental Inscriptions, and other pieces of Antiquity yet remaining.

Architecture, Sculpture, Painting, Engraving, Music, etc. will come under their Consideration, and the Antient Methods being retrieved, perhaps many things may be used afresh to good Purpose.

They will be also able to explain not only most of the Obscure places in our Historians and other Writers, but others in the Roman and Greek Authors, and consider of their other Antiquities.

In Order to this, they will find it necessary to maintain a Correspondence with the Learned and curious men in each County and with the most eminent Persons abroad.

They will send fitt Persons to Travel, throughout England, and also in Other Countries, whose Business might be to Inspect the Books, Writings and other Rarities, which the Owners would be loth to send to Town; to take the Prospects of Antient Fortifications, Castles, Churches, Houses, etc. To take Draughts of Tombes, Inscriptions, Epitaphs, Figures in Painted Glass, etc. To Collect all Material Notices pertaining to History and Antiquity, from the Relations of Persons of known Worth and Veracity; and if need by (sic) to buy up the most curious and useful pieces of Antiquity, of all kinds, at the Charge of the Society.

Such a Society seems to be reserv'd for her Majesty, and the Establishment of it would be one of the Remarkables of her most Glorious Reign.

The Meeting, Library and Repository, an Ease and Satisfaction to Her Majesty's Officers, Foreign Gentlemen and others Attending.

Will promote the ends of the Union, since a Communication and Correspondence with the Scotch will ensue, which begets mutual Love.

'Twill be a School where in the antient Constitution, Laws and Customs of this Kingdom will be best learn'd, and usefully declar'd and mentioned in Parliament; whereby ma[n]y innovations and troublesome Debates may be prevented; as we have seen great Quarels have arisen thro' the Inexperience of Persons in our Antiquities and antient Constitution, which by the Authority of such a Society would have died in their very birth.

British Museum *MS. Harley* 7055, 1. Wanley Papers. [1707]

(*These papers relate to the revival or re-institution of the Society of Antiquaries. The extracts are from a draft memorandum to Lord Harley, his patron, from Humfrey Wanley, secretary of the Society.*)

VIRTUE AND VICE, SCIENCE AND ERROUR

There is no study more instructive and entertaining than that of Ancient and Modern History; and, though the latter may be more interesting, easy, and pleasant, yet the former is also a most necessary part of Knowledge, as it enlarges our prospects, furnishes us with a great variety of examples both of Virtue and Vice, produces frequent instances of Science and Errour, discovers the manner in which great actions have been conducted, and great attempts have miscarried.

Now, the study of Antiquity is the study of Ancient History; and the proper business of an Antiquary is, to collect what is dispersed, more fully to unfold what is already discovered, to examine controverted points, to settle what is doubtful, and, by the authority of Monuments and Histories, to throw light upon the Manners, Arts, Languages, Policy, and Religion, of past Ages.

Antiquities may be either considered as Foreign or Domestic; such, I mean, as relate to other people and countries, or are peculiar to our own.

It is the usual observation of Foreigners, that the English Travellers are too little acquainted with their own Country; and so far this may be true, that Englishmen (otherwise well qualified to appear in the world) go abroad in quest of the rarities of other countries, before they know sufficiently what their own contains; it must likewise be acknowledged that, when these foreign tours have been compleated, and Gentlemen return captivated with the Medals, Statues, Pictures, and Architecture, of Greece and Italy, they have seldom any relish for the ruder products of Ancient Britain. Thus what is foreign gets the start of what is at home, and maintains its prepossession. My situation in life (whatever my inclinations might be) confined me to a different track; I saw myself placed in the midst of Monuments, the Works of the Ancient Britans, where there were few Grecian or Roman Remains to be met with; my curiosity, therefore, could only be gratified by what was within its reach, and was confined to the study of our own Antiquities; and these papers are the fruits of that study.

THE REVD WILLIAM BORLASE, *Antiquities, Historical and Monumental, of the County of Cornwall,* 1754, 1769 ed.

AFTER THE UNIVERSAL DELUGE

ARCHAEOLOGY, or an Account of the Origin of Nations after the Universal DELUGE, admits of two ways of Enquiry, either beginning at BABEL, the Place of Mankind's Dispersion, and tracing them downwards to our own Times by the Light of Records, which is HISTORY, and of Natural Reason, which is INFERENCE and CONJECTURE; or else beginning from our own Time, and winding them upwards, by the same Helps, to the first Place and Origin of their Progression; both which Ways are usually taken by HISTORIANS and GENEALOGISTS, and are equally to be allow'd in their manner of proceeding. By the former which I have in the following SECTIONS adventured through some of the darkest Tracks of Time, to calculate the ARCHAEOLOGY, and to fetch out and put together some rude Stroaks and Lineaments of the ANTIQUITIES of the Isle of ANGLE-SEY, from its first Planting, to the Time of the Roman Conquest, mostly in an Hypothetical Way, or a rational Scheme of Enquiry.

A Method (I confess) very unusual, viz. to trace the Footsteps of Historical Actions any other way, than by that of Antient MEMOIRS and RECORDS. But where those lights are wanting, what shall we do? Shall we lie down and wallow with our Forefathers in the general Slumber, blaming the past AGES for leaving us in the Dark; or like the Men of Egypt, shall we only confine our View to the praeterfluent Stream of Nile, and resolve to look no higher, because ('tis said) its Fountain-Head lies hid beyond the Mountains of the Moon? No, that were to act unfaithfully with the Designs of Nature; Knowledge is her Gift from GOD unto us; and we ought to employ all the Means and helps She affords, to improve and enlarge it.

The Main and Principal Helps to walk through the dark Recesses of Time, are the Testimonies of unexceptionable RECORDS, and such Consequences as are naturally deducible from them. These are like the Solar Rays, where there are Holes and Crannies to let them in there is sure and perfect Light, and the Motion guided by them is even, steady and regular.

There are other Things, as Analogy of Antient Names and Words, Antient Laws, Constitutions, and Customs: Coins and Medals: Erections, Monuments, and Ruins: Ædifices and Inscriptions: The Appelations of Places: The Genius and Tempers, and Inclinations and Complexions of People; and a Variety of such REMARKS, which afford here and there little strinkling Lights, to be cautiously and warily made use of, and which we ought likewise to scan and examine jointly and severally, and from them extract such Secondary Supplies and Assistances, as may help to fill up, and enlighten those obscure Chasms and interlinary Spaces of Time, which interpose the brighter Stroaks, and more undeniable Certainties of RECORDS. And in this manner, by a just proportionate Disposal of the Lights and Shadows of TRUTH, we may undertake to represent the Accounts and Transactions of the remotest Times, though not certain, yet what is next to it, that is, highly probable, coherent and intelligible.

THE REVD HENRY ROWLANDS, *Mona Antiqua Restaurata*, 1723

MR ROWLAND'S BETTER METHOD

The Reverend Mr Rowland [in *Mona Antiqua Restaurata*] took a better method to advance this kind of Learning; he examined a great variety of Druid Monuments in Anglesea, has described them as particularly as he could (though his Drawings are extremely short of the rest of his performance), and gives the world many pertinent observations upon them. He understood the British, and learned Languages, and has made a proper application of both, in order to give light to his subject.

THE REVD WILLIAM BORLASE, *Antiquities, Historical and Monumental, of the County of Cornwall,* 1754, 1769 ed.

CURIOSITIES AT HOME (1)

The intent of this Treatise is to oblige the curious in the Antiquities of Britain: it is an account of places and things from inspection, not compiled from others' labours, or travels in one's study. I own it is a work crude and hasty, like the notes of a traveller that stays not long in one place; and such it was in reality. Many matters I threw in only as hints for further scrutiny, and memorandums for myself or others: above all I avoided prejudice, never carrying any author along with me, but taking things in the natural order and manner they presented themselves: and if my sentiments of Roman stations, and other matters, happen not to coincide with what has been wrote before me; it was not that I differ from them, but things did not so appear to me. . . . The whole is to invite Gentlemen and others in the country, to make researches of this nature, and to acquaint the world with them: they may be assured, that whatever accounts of this sort they please to communicate to me, they shall be applied to proper use, and all due honour paid to the names of those that favour me with a correspondence so much to the glory and benefit of our country, which is my sole aim therein.

It is evident how proper engravings are to preserve the memory of things, and how much better an idea they convey to the mind than written descriptions, which often not at all, oftener not sufficiently, explain them: beside, they present us with the pleasure of observing the various changes in the face of nature, of countries, and the like, through the current of time and vicissitude of things. . . .

I know not whether it will be an excuse, or a fault, if I should plead the expedition I used in the drawing part; but I may urge, that a private person, and a moderate fortune, may want many useful assistants and conveniences for that purpose. It is enough for me to point them out: to show things that are fine in themselves, and want little art to render them more agreeable, or that deserve to be better done; or any way to contribute toward retrieving the noble monuments of our ancestors;

in which case only, we are behind other the learned nations of Europe. It is not that we have a less fund of curiosities than they, were the descriptions of them attempted by an abler hand, and more adequate expence. . . .

The numerous plates I have given the reader, of ground-plots and prospects of Roman cities, I thought contributed much towards fixing their site, and preserving their memory: they may be useful to curious inhabitants, in marking the places where antiquities are found from time to time, and in other respects. . . .

WILLIAM STUKELEY, Preface to *Itinerarium Curiosum*, 1724

CURIOSITIES AT HOME (2)

The love I had for my own country, in my younger days, prompted me to visit many parts of it; and to refuse great offers made to me, to go into foreign and fashionable tours. I was sensible, we abounded at home with extraordinary curiosities, and things remarkable, both in Art and Nature; as well as most valuable Antiquities in all kinds; most worthy of our regard; and which it must become us to take cognisance of.

WILLIAM STUKELEY, Preface to *An Account of Richard of Cirencester*, 1757

CROP-MARKS AT RICHBOROUGH

But now age has eras'd the very tracks of it; and to teach us that Cities dye as well as men, it is at this day a corn-field, wherein when the corn is grown up, one may observe the draughts of streets crossing one another, (for where they have gone the corn is thinner) and such *crossings* they commonly call *S. Augustine's cross.* Nothing now remains, but some ruinous walls of a tower, of a square form, and cemented with a sort of sand extremely binding. One would imagine this had been the *Acropolis*, it looks down from so great a height upon the wet plains in *Thanet*, which the Ocean, withdrawing itself by little and little, has quite left. But the plot of the City, now plow'd, has often cast up the marks of it's Antiquity, gold and silver coyns of the Romans.

WILLIAM CAMDEN, *Britannia*, 1586, ed. Gibson, 1695

(*This is perhaps the earliest record of an archaeological site being defined by crop-marks, elusive clues upon which the modern archaeologist often relies.*)

185

THE ANTIQUITIES OF BRITAIN

The Antiquities of Great Britain are, beyond dispute, far more numerous and more curious than those of any other nation in the habitable world, not even excepting Italy itself, whose ruins are so much glorified by the legendary traveller. But, upon examination, it will be found that Italy is famous only for the remains of its own ancient people, the descendants of Romulus; while England, on the contrary, can boast not only of the works of its aborigines, but those of its conquerors and invaders; of distant people, varying in manners from each other, as much the invader from the invaded; and we join to the massive rudeness of the Briton, the elegance of the Roman, and the clumsy ornament of the Saxon.

To go a day's journey in any part of this kingdom without meeting with a variety of ruinated structurs, is next to impossible; either some hoary altar, towered castle, or gothic abbey presenting themselves in almost every scene and diversifying every prospect.

Nor (whatever may have been the ridicule thrown on the studious in antiquity) is the contemplation of these venerable piles without its use. We not only learn from them the vicissitude of worldly greatness, and how frail the works of men's hands prove when opposed to the rage of war, or the more powerful ravages of time; but we are furnished by them with a retrospective view of the character and actions of our forefathers. Who can gaze on the rude altar of the Druid, without tracing in his mind our present established religion through its several stages, to that remote period when human sacrifices smoked on the very spot he is contemplating? Who can walk over the beautiful pavement, or grass-grown cities of the Romans, without feeling himself affected with the character of that people, and comparing to such mouldering fragments the declension of their once noble empire? In the castle we have a history of our ancient war, and, reviewing the feuds which once distracted this country, console ourselves with these happy days that need no such strong holds to defend us against the violence of the intestine party. The solemn ruins of the abbey strike the mind with reverential awe and serious reflection; and the sculptured tomb, appearing from among rank weeds and scattered columns, cannot fail reminding us of the short duration alloted to mortals and their works.

JOHN COLLINSON, *The Beauties of British Antiquity*, 1779

TO MAKE A RESPECTABLE FIGURE

It has long been the fashion to laugh at the study of Antiquities, and to consider it as the idle amusement of a few humdrum plodding fellows, who, wanting genius for nobler studies, busied themselves in heaping up illegible Manuscripts, mutilated Statues, obliterated Coins, and broken Pipkins! In this the laughers may perhaps have been somewhat justified, from the absurd pursuits of a few Collectors: But at the same time, an argument deduced from the abuse or perversion of any study, is by no means conclusive against the study itself: and in this particular case, I trust I shall be able to prove, that, without a competent fund of antiquarian learning, no one will ever make a respectable figure, either as a Divine, a Lawyer, Statesman, Soldier, or even a private Gentleman, and that it is the *sine qua non* of several of the more liberal professions, as well as of many trades; and is, besides, a study to which all persons, in particular instances, have a kind of propensity; every man being, as Logicians express it, 'Quoad hoc,' an Antiquarian.

FRANCIS GROSSE, The Antiquarian Repertory, 1775

CHYMERAS OF VIRTUOSI?

Amongst all the Varieties, which present themselves before us, in prosecuting of this grand and necessary Work, those Studies which are the most Improving, deserve our greatest Application: In the Number of which, *Antiquity* claims a great Share, particularly *Archiology*, which consists of Monuments, or rather Inscriptions, still subsisting; in order to prove demonstratively those Facts which are asserted in History; which being the Mirror that reflects to Posterity, the objects of Past Ages, by the Discoveries made from such Parts of Antiquity, we have often True History distinguish'd from Falsehood and Imposture, and its Narratives either confirmed or condemned.

I know, that there are People to be found, and it is to be regretted, some of them of Birth and Fortune, who expose their own Ignorance, in discountenancing this kind of Knowledge, giving out, that Antiquity, and such like Branches of Learning are but the *Chymeras* of *Virtuosi*, dry and unpleasant Searches; so, because they themselves are blind, and uncapable to relish such Pleasures, they have the Impudence to betray their own Weakness to the World. Hence we Observe, That Things which are in their Nature rough, unpolish'd, vicious and cruel, these fit their Genius the best; violent Hunting, Bear-Gardens, Gaming-Tables, Quarrelling and Midnight Revellings, are their Daily Delights.

ALEXANDER [SINGING SANDY] GORDON, Itinerarium
Septentrionale, 1726

ANTIQUITY IN THE CAUSE OF HISTORY

If the study of antiquity be undertaken in the cause of History, it will rescue itself from a reproach indescriminately and fastidiously bestowed on works which have been deemed frivolous. In proportion as this study has been neglected by antient or modern historians, authority will be found to deviate from conjecture, and the eye of reason more or less taught to discern the fable which the pomp of history has decorated; it should, therefore, instead of being accounted the dreg, be styled the alembic, from which is drawn the purity or perfection of literature.

The inscription or the medal are the only facts which can obviate error, and produce the substitutes for deficiency of antient records: when these are wanting, in vain will the human mind be gratified by the most acute investigation; incredulity will arise in proportion as the judgement is matured.

By contemplating the relics discovered in our antient sepultures, the historian may have an opportunity of comparing them with similar relics found in different places, and on which arguments have been grounded by authors who have written on the antient inhabitants of Britain. If a medal or inscription be found in a sepulture among other relics, the undoubted characteristic of the customs of a people at the time of the deposit, and the superscription on the medal or the inscription evincing a low period, it will be a self-evident position, that similar relics under similar forms of sepulture, discovered in other parts of the island, cannot apply to a period more remote; hence the most trifling fact will invalidate many received opinions, and history be reduced to a more critical analysis. . . .

No position in the work has been assumed on mere conjecture; and when deductions have been made, they have been founded on a scrupulous comparison of facts; but, free to form his own opinion, the work has been arranged under such heads, that the reader may form his own conclusions, without any apprehension of being involved in the confusion of self-opinionated theory.

All nations deriving their origin apparently from one common stock, have used, in many respects, the same funereal customs; but the progress of society having evidently produced many specific distinctions, they may be methodically arranged, and the identity of a people recognised.

JAMES DOUGLAS, Preface to *Nenia Britannica*, 1793

(*Douglas, a Captain of the Royal Engineers before he became a divine, excavated many Saxon burial mounds in Kent, and his work marked a notable progress in the method of archaeology.*)

THE DEVELOPMENT OF OUR SUBJECT

The development of our subject in recent times is certainly some-what remarkable. Camden was the person who first arranged, with great skill, the topics of the ancient history and geography of our island from such information as his times supplied, and gave them much of their due shape and consistency.

The discoveries of the subsequent two centuries and a half afforded chiefly elucidations, and displaced comparatively little; but of late years the materials which have been derived from the labours of modern investigators, or from other sources, are copious and striking, and often indeed so conclusive in the illustrations they afford, as to render in many places a re-arrangement, or rather a re-construction of the subject indispensable.

The new acquisitions are required to be taken into it, and many points to be exhibited in other lights than have been accustomed, in order to correspond with facts now ascertained. . . .

BEALE POSTE, Preface to *Britannic Researches*, 1853

THE BARROW DIGGERS
Persons Represented

ANTIQUARIUS   THREE BARROW DIGGERS
DISCIPULUS   LOOKERS ON
SCENE: *A Barrow on a Common*
Enter Three Barrow Diggers with Spades, Shovels, etc.

IST BAR. DIG. Is this a Roman, or a British Barrow?

2ND BAR. DIG. I tell thee 'tis a British Barrow, therefore straightways open it; Antiquarius hath set on it, and finds it British Burial.

IST BAR. DIG. How can that be, if Roman Ornaments and Arms should here be found?

2ND BAR. DIG. They may be found.

IST BAR. DIG. It must be Roman, it cannot be British Burial. For here lies the point; if Roman Arms and Ornaments are found in it, it argues a Roman Act; and a Barrow Act hath three Branches, to Act, to Dig, to Shovel; we go to work willingly.

3RD BAR. DIG. Nay; but hear you good friend!

IST BAR. DIG. Give me leave. Here is a Common; good; here is the Barrow; good; if the Barrow contains Roman Arms, or Urns, it must be a Roman Barrow; mark you that; but if spear heads made of flints, and British Arms are here, it must be a British Barrow; if nought but an empty Cist tumulus inanis. He that is not inclined to dig, shortens not our work.

2ND BAR. DIG. But is this Barrow Law?

1ST BAR. DIG. Ay, marry is't Antiquarius's Barrow Law.

2ND BAR. DIG. Will you ha' the truth on't. If this had been a Roman relic of funeral pomp, it would have been a very different sort of Burial. The Romans raised not Barrows o'er their Dead.

1ST BAR. DIG. Why there thou say'st; and the more pity that great folks shall countenance the grandeur of gaudy funerals, more than their poorer neighbours. To my mind they are mighty like representations of Death carrying off his wealthy victims in Triumph. Come my spade. There are no antient gentlemen; but Gardeners, Geologists, and Barrow Diggers; they hold up Adams profession.

3RD BAR. DIG. Was he a Gentleman?

1ST BAR. DIG. He was the first that ever bore Arms, a Mattoc, Shovel, and a Spade.

2ND BAR. DIG. Why, he had none.

1ST BAR. DIG. What, art a heathen? How dost thou understand the Scripture? The Scripture says, Adam digged. Could he dig without arms? I'll put another question to thee; if thou answerest me not to the purpose, confess thyself.

3RD BAR. DIG. Go to work.

After having taken an observation with a Compass, and marked out a Section, they commence opening the Barrow.

1ST BAR. DIG. What is that earthly form all skin and bone, which eludes the Sexton, the Mason, and the Carpenter?

2ND BAR. DIG. The Living Skeleton, for that fragile frame outlives a thousand Harry's.

1ST BAR. DIG. Now where is he?

2ND BAR. DIG. Eating Soup Maigre!

1ST BAR. DIG. Eating Soup Maigre! Where?

2ND BAR. DIG. Not where fat Kings are eaten: a certain convocation of politic worms are e'en at them. Your worm is your only Emperor for diet; we fat all creatures else to fat us; and we fat ourselves for maggots: Your fat King and your lean Skeleton is but variable service: two dishes, but to one table that's the end.

1ST BAR. DIG. Alas! Alas! Shall I feed worms when I am dead?

2ND BAR. DIG. Ay, and a living Skeleton may fish with the worm that hath eat of a King: and eat of the Fish that hath fed of that Worm.

1ST BAR. DIG. What dost thou mean by this?

2ND BAR. DIG. Nothing; but to show you how a King may go a progress through the carcase of a living Skeleton.

1ST BAR. DIG. I like thy wit well in good Fath: To't again; Come, what is this Barrow.

2ND BAR. DIG. Cudgel thy brains no more about it; for your dull ass will not mend his pace with beating: and when you are asked this question next say 'tis a British Barrow; a house that will last till doomsday. Go get thee to Shapwicke and fetch me a stoup of liquor.

1st Bar. Dig. continues Digging and Sings:

> *Britons rais'd an earthy mound,*
> *Whene're their Chieftains died,*
> *And I am digging underground,*
> *Where delvers have not tried.*

Antiquarius and Discipulus Enter

ANT. Has this fellow no feeling of his business, he sings at Barrow opening?

DIS. He knows not that he treads on hallow'd Mould!

ANT. Tis e'en so, the hand of Antiquaries only hath the Barrow Sense.

1st Bar. Dig. continues Digging and Sings:

> *Clasps, Celts, and Arrow-heads, I'll try*
> *To claw within my Clutch,*
> *And if a Shield I should espy,*
> *I'll vow there ne'er was such.*

> *With Popish Tricks, and Relics rare,*
> *The Priests their Flocks do gull;*
> *In casting out the earth take care,*
> *Huzza! I've found a Skull.*

Carefully takes up the Skull

ANT. That skull had a tongue in it and could sing once. How the knave jowls it to the ground, as if it were a slave's jaw-bone or that of the first Murderer! That might be the pate of a Druid, which this ass now o'erreaches; one that would gorge his Deities with human blood: might it not?

DIS. It might.

ANT. Or of a Warrior, who could say kill and burn captives to appease the Dead. Or a Chieftain that prais'd another Chieftain's horse, when he meant to beg it.

191

DIS. Ay, Antiquarius! or it might be a Slave's!

ANT. Why e'en so; and now my lady Worm's chapless and knocked about the mazzard with a Sexton's shovel. Here's fine revolution an we had our spectacles to see't. Prodigious to think on't.

1st Bar. Dig. continues Digging and Sings:

> *A Mattoc, Shovel, and a Spade,*
> *Will dig up human bones;*
> *To play at Marbles Britons made,*
> *Some small round Portland Stones.*
>
> *If Casqes we find, or iron Arms*
> *Of curious form and make,*
> *Why surely they's Roman charms,*
> *Your British Creed to shake.*

ANT. Cease prattler cease! Why should they not be the Casques; Arms; or Bosses of British Chieftains in Roman service? No golden filagree work nor carved ivory; No Amethystine Beads, nor Chrystal Balls, No Coins, No Medals, No well-formed Urns, nor colour'd Stones from Rome will here be found; but Tin, Glass, or Amber Beads, the Tusks of Boars, or Unbaked Urns of rudely shape with limpet shells will denote 'tis a British Barrow.

1st Bar. Dig. continues Digging, and comes to a Cist, and Sings:

> *This Cist of chalk just like a grave*
> *For such a guest is meet,*
> *As if asleep here rests the brave,*
> *Below the Turf three feet.*

ANT. How independent the knave is! we must speak by the card. By the little Lord, Discipulus, since the passing of the Reform and Municipal Bills, I have taken note of it; that the toe of the Democrat comes so near the heel of the Aristocrat, he galls his kibe. How long hast thou been a Barrow Digger?

1ST BAR. DIG. Of all the Ages of the World I came not to't in that Age when the whole Earth was in a state of Fusion.

ANT. How long's that since?

1ST BAR. DIG. Cannot you tell that! Every Mechanic can tell that. It was that very day that young Pluto was born: he that was a Geologist. He that gave a New System by Posting through the bowels of the Earth in his chariot drawn by four Horses.

ANT. Ay marry! how did he do that?

IST BAR. DIG. With Lucifer Matches.

ANT. Why?

IST BAR. DIG. Because he was mad after Proserpine!

ANT. How came he mad?

IST BAR. DIG. Very strangely they do say.

ANT. How strangely?

IST BAR. DIG. Faith e'en with loosing his wits.

ANT. Upon what ground?

IST BAR. DIG. Why here upon this ground that's gradually elevating itself. Cant you perceive its motion upwards? How dizzy I do feel!

ANT. Peace I pray you! How long will the jaws of a Leviathan or the Bones of a Megatherium lie in the earth e'er they crumble into dust.

IST BAR. DIG. Faith if they be not fused in Pluto's crucible for many thousand years.

ANT. Good! But tell me again how long will a man lie i' the earth e'er he rot?

IST BAR. DIG. Ay. Geology and Zoology like man and wife are one in the delvings of bone grubbers. If he be not rotten before he die he will last you some Eight years, or Nine years, a Tanner will last you Nine years.

ANT. Why he more than another?

IST BAR. DIG. Because, Antiquarius, his hide is so tanned with his trade, that he will keep out water a great while; and your water is a sore decayer of the dead body of your libertine. Here's a skull (*Takes one from a Green Baize Bag*) I've chang'd or filch'd that hath passed through various hands for Nine and Seventy Years. By Bumps, and Lumps, I judge 'twas not a Murderer's. The Crowner's Quest did err. The finding should have been a harmless Slayer of man. Whose was it?

ANT. Nay, I know not.

IST BAR. DIG. A pestilence on him for a Dominie that was gibbetted. Anxious to obtain a relic of the man, a learned Leech chopp'd off his head and pickled it. This same skull was Eugene Aram's skull. 'The schoolmaster abroad'.

DIS. Why may not that be the skull of one that opened Barrows?

IST BAR. DIG. Where is the grave organ of Acquisitiveness?
I smell it not. (*Smells the Skull*)

DIS. I'll taste it not. Thou art a Phrenological Nonpareil.

IST BAR. DIG. By the feel, by the taste, by the smell, by all that's wonderful I vow that 'twas the skull of Eugene Aram.

ANT. This? (*Takes the Skull*)

IST BAR. DIG. E'en that.

DIS. That, that's a woman's skull!

1st Bar. Dig. rests on his Spade, and Sings:

Now by that skull sage Inglis swore,
That Spurzheim ranks with dolts,
And Simpson thinks with Dr. Bore,
That 'twas a dangerous colts.

While Granville, Knott and Dr. Fife,
Th' Identity decry,
Shrewd Hindmarsh says upon his Life,
The Proofs he'll flat deny.

I learn from men, I learn from Books,
That skulls are void of brains;
Behold the print of iron hooks,
And Eugene hung in chains.

ANT. Eugene Aram, I've heard of him Discipulus. He was a Pedagogue and how abhorred in my imagination he is, my gorge rises at him. He received a Murderers judgment, and by that Name he died. He suffered for his crime at fifty-four, his guilt or innocence is chronicled on high. His body has moulder'd into dust. Upon his skull no certain mark has been put except the mark of Cain. Faith I hold not with Phrenology. Surely this skull belong's to one, who liv'd not Thirty Years. Now get you to my Lady Rosa, and tell her, let her paint an inch thick to this favor she must come at last, will she smile at that? Pry'thee, Discipulus, tell me one thing?

DIS. What's that Antiquarius?

ANT. Dost thou think Discipulus, the British Chieftain looked of this fashion i' the earth?

DIS. I do.

ANT. And smelt so earthy? Pah! (*Returns the Skull to 1st Bar. Dig.*)

DIS. Ee'n so Antiquarius.

ANT. To what quaint uses we may return Discipulus, the Unbaked Urn perchance contains the Noble Chieftain's ashes, and why may not imagination trace his dust till we find it stopping a Mousehole?

DIS. 'Twere to consider too curiously, to consider so.

ANT. No, Faith, not a jot, but to follow him thither with modesty enough, and likelihood to lead it, as thus. The Chieftain died. The Chieftain returneth to the Dust. The Dust is Earth, and why of that Earth whereto he was converted might not a Mouse-hole be stopped?

194

The British Chieftain dead, and turned to clay,
Might stop a hole to keep the wind away.
Oh! that the Earth, which kept vast Tribes in awe,
Should strive in vain to check a Mouse's paw.

DIS. How oft to day, Have we consorted with the dead?
ANT. Peace to their Manes, hear me my good friend, That yonder Sun
   now scarcely lends his light To grubs and eyeless skulls.
DIS. E'en so Antiquarius.
ANT. How long have we been here?
DIS. Eight day's. No more be done!
IST BAR. DIG. Must there no more be done? We've made an inverted
   Cone.
ANT. No more be done,
   Respect sepulchral rites, inhume those bones
   Shards, Flints, and Earth replace, and heap up here
   A pile of dust upon the sleeping dead,
   Till of this flat a mountain you have made
   To o'er top old Badbury, and prepare
   To conduct our fair guides unto their homes.
   The heavens do low'r upon us for ill
   Obey my mandate.

The Barrow Diggers commence closing the Barrow.

DIS. 'Tis Cold Antiquarius.
ANT. 'Tis very cold, the wind is Northerly.
DIS. Your cloak to its right use; 'tis for the outer man. (*Discipulus assists*
   Antiquarius in cloaking)
ANT. Thank you Discipulus.
IST BAR. DIG. To't again, Come.
2ND BAR. DIG. Who builds stronger than a Mason, or a Carpenter?
IST BAR. DIG. Ay! tell me that, and shovel away.
3RD BAR. DIG. Marry now I can't tell.
2ND BAR. DIG. A Cist maker.
ANT. Get you home womankind go!

1st Bar. Dig. Shovels, and Sings:

Fairies dance round the mystic rings,
In hare-bells oft they lie;
To say that they are changing things,
Oh! fie, Oh! Maro fie.

195

When secret fear our heart alarms,
And cares the mind oppress;
Then women with their playful charms
Are quick to lend redress.

ANT. This Barrow Digger is a merry knave.

DIS. Come we'll not tarry, but carry off our Treasures, More Anti-
quorum.

2ND BAR. DIG. Dust to Dust farewell.

---

*(The small book from which this is an extract was written by the Revd Charles
Wools (or Woolls), M.A. of Pembroke College, Oxford, and Curate of Sturminster
Newton, Dorset, in which parish the barrow at Shapwick which he describes was
situated. He was a contemporary of Charles Warne, the Dorset antiquary, who
mentions this book in his* Ancient Dorset *(1866) and in* Celtic Tumuli *of Dorset,
also published in 1866.*

It shows some similarity to Barrow Digging by a Barrow Knight, *the same
sort of poetic antiquarianism applied to barrows opened in Derbyshire and Stafford-
shire. The latter was published in 1845 anonymously by the Revd Stephen Isaacson.)*

PREHISTORY AND THE ROMANTIC MOVEMENT

By now Archaeology and Romanticism walked hand in hand,
familiar twin figures in the English scene. How inevitable that Higgins's
Celtic Druids (1829) should have a lithographed title-page whereon a
blasted oak flanks a crumbling stone inscribed 'And like the baseless
fabric of a vision . . .', overgrown with nettles, thistles and toadstools,
while in the background Stonehenge is outlined against the sunset.
It is without surprise that one finds Mr. Miles, describing *The Deverel
Barrow* (1826), indulging in sweetly melancholy meditations—'On a
spot so hallowed by the Wing of Time, the imagination may vividly
depict the rude but solemn rites attendant on the burial; the blazing pile
flinging its lurid beams around . . .' and so on, with 'mystic songs of
bards', 'frantic yells' and 'wild and piercing shrieks of expiring
victims'. And at this point I may perhaps touch on a curious aspect of
the early barrow-diggers' mentality which I believe is reflected in their
works. A morbid interest in graves and skeletons is well known as a
psychological phenomenon which has often been exploited in literature
and art. In English literature perhaps the most famous example is
Blair's *Grave*, written before 1731, and we have the authority of Dean
Farrar that 'few essays have had wider circulation among admiring
readers than the vicious and tawdry rhetoric of Harvey on the Tombs'

(*Meditations among the Tombs*, 1746). This feeling was inevitably latent in certain aspects of the Romantic Movement—it comes out for instance in Bentley's designs to Gray's poems, and in a thousand other places, notably in the 'Tale of Terror' type of story beginning with the *Castle of Otranto* and continuing in the works of Lewis, Mrs. Radclyffe, and others—and I cannot but detect traces of conscious gloating over the paraphernalia of Death in some of the early archaeological records. It is implicit in that curious effusion *The Barrow Diggers*, 'written in imitation of the Grave-Diggers in Hamlet' (1839). Is it to this mental attitude, probably more often unconscious than deliberate, that we are to attribute the fact that until scientific excavation began with Pitt-Rivers, prehistoric settlement sites remained almost entirely neglected in favour of wholesale barrow-digging? One has of course to reckon with the strong acquisitive instinct of the collector . . . which would be better satisfied with the complete grave-furniture than with the broken scraps from a midden, but I think this other factor must be allowed some weight.

STUART PIGGOTT, 'Prehistory and the Romantic Movement',
Antiquity, March, 1937

THE FIRST OF THE MODERNS
We Speak from Facts, not Theory

Such is the motto I adopt, and to this text I shall most strictly adhere. I shall not seek among the fanciful regions of romance, an origin for our Wiltshire Britons, nor, by endeavouring to prove by whom, and at what period, our island was first peopled, involve myself in a Celtic or Belgic controversy; neither shall I place too much reliance on the very imperfect traditions handed down to us by former antiquaries on this subject. I shall describe to you what we have found; what we have seen; in short, I shall tell you a plain unvarnished tale, and draw from it such conclusions as shall appear not only reasonable, but even uncontradictable.

SIR RICHARD COLT HOARE, Introduction to *The Ancient History
of South Wiltshire*, 1812

DATING THESE GRAVE-HILLS

I have abstained from any attempt to assign a date to these grave-hills, because no one can do so with any degree of certainty. Attempts of this kind have been too common and have often been based upon insufficient data. The only way of approximating to it is to compare the results of barrow diggings in different parts of the country. Unfortunately excavations have been conducted in so many places so carelessly and unscientifically that no safe conclusions can be drawn from them. The mere treasure-seeker has done irreparable injury to the cause of science. The employment of paid labourers to do the work which should be done by the Antiquary himself is always unsatisfactory. No one should undertake barrow-digging who fears blistering his hands. The eye of the explorer should be directed to every spadeful of earth, and he should carefully note the manner in which the mound is constructed and the interments are deposited.

One of the most extensive grave-diggers that England has ever produced (Sir R. Colt Hoare, Bart.), who has left behind him a very costly record of his labours in Wiltshire, exemplifies this remark. No volumes could contain less useful information in proportion to their bulk. We search through them almost in vain for intimations as to the materials of the barrows, the mode of their construction, and the position of the skeletons; and we are lead to the conclusion that the principal, if not the sole, object of the investigator was the possession of the articles which had been deposited with the human remains. The object of barrow-openers should not be mere gratification of curiosity, nor the accumulation of ancient works of art. A museum of antiquities is comparatively worthless if the history of the discovery of each particular specimen is not accurately known and recorded. These examinations should be made with the sole view of throwing light upon a dark period in the history of those who have occupied the soil of England.

THE REVD W. C. LUKIS, *The Yorkshire Archaeological and Topographical Journal*, Vol. I, 1870

EVERY DETAIL TO BE RECORDED

Excavators, as a rule, record only those things which appear to them important at the time, but fresh problems in Archaeology and Anthropology are constantly arising, and it can hardly have failed to escape the notice . . . on turning back to old accounts in search of evidence, the points which would have been the most valuable have been passed over from being thought uninteresting at the time. Every detail should, therefore, be recorded in the manner most conducive to facility of reference, and it ought at all times to be the chief object of an excavator to reduce his own personal equation to a minimum.

LT-GEN. PITT-RIVERS, *Excavations in Cranbourne Chase*, i, 1887

THE EVERYDAY LIFE

Our knowledge of the weapons and implements of prehistoric times, has so much improved of late, owing to the researches of Evans, Greenwell, Franks, Lubbock and others, in this country, that there is hardly any difficulty in determining at a glance, the period to which any such object should be assigned, but our ignorance of the towns, villages, habitations, etc., in which the people who used these weapons lived is still very great, and the reason is not far to seek. The weapons, tools, and implements are for the most part obtained from graves. A tumulus is easily dug into, and the relics obtained from it are of value, whereas the examination of a town or encampment is a costly undertaking, and the relics seldom have any intrinsic value, consisting mainly of common objects that have been thrown away by the inhabitants. It is for this reason that our knowledge of prehistoric and early people is derived chiefly from their funeral deposits, and for all we know of their mode of life, excepting such information as has been obtained from lake-dwellings, and crannoges, they might as well have been born dead. Yet the everyday life of the people is, beyond all comparison, of more interest than their mortuary customs.

Lt-Gen. Pitt-Rivers, *Excavation in Bokerly and Wansdyke, Dorset and Wilts*, iii, 1892

BEHIND THE THINGS THEMSELVES

The distributional aspect of the subject (of prehistoric archaeology) has been almost as completely ignored as the evolutionary. This is partly because most prehistorians have been essentially townsmen and so out of touch with nature; they are the last people to understand the conditions of prehistoric life. This is why some of the articles in the leading archaeological journals of the last century are so amazingly deficient in the commonsense of the country dweller; and why the proceedings of small country field clubs are often far ahead of them in showing a true appreciation of prehistoric problems. The townsman, and his brother the collector, rarely get behind the things themselves to the people who made them.

O. G. S. Crawford, an unpublished note to a paper in *Geographical Journal* (1912)

ARCHAEOLOGY IN SUSSEX—

The first meeting [of the Sussex Archaeological Society] took place on June 18th, 1846, at the suggestion of a few gentlemen in the town and neighbourhood of Lewes, who, observing the interest excited by some recent antiquarian discoveries, were anxious to promote a readier acquaintance among persons attached to the same pursuits, and to combine their exertions in illustration of the History and Antiquities of Sussex. . . .

The objects of this Society embrace whatever relates to the Civil or Ecclesiastical History, Topography, Ancient Buildings, or Works of Art, within the County, and for this purpose the Society invite communications on such subjects, especially from those Noblemen and Gentlemen who possess estates within the County, and who may materially assist the completion of the County History, now very imperfect, by the loan of Ancient Documents relating to Estates, Manors, Wills, or Pedigrees, and of any object generally connected with the Ancient History of Sussex.

The Society will collect Manuscripts and Books, Drawings and Prints, Coins and Seals, or copies thereof, Rubbings of Brasses, Descriptive Notices and Plans of Churches, Castles, Mansions, or other Buildings of Antiquarian interest; such Collection to be preserved and made available for the purposes of the Society, by publication or otherwise.

Sussex Archaeological Collections, vol. I, 2nd ed., 1853

—AND IN DORSET

Much delving and poking about in odd corners are found necessary to unearth the riches of antiquity, and our papers show that, at least, the society has commenced the work in an honest and liberal spirit. . . .

Proceedings of the Dorset Natural History and Antiquarian Field Club,
Vol. I, 1877

AT THE INAUGURAL MEETING OF THE KENT ARCHAEOLOGICAL SOCIETY, 1858

Steam is the great innovator. I do not mean to depreciate its use; but it is no respecter of antiquity. In our own county it has ruthlessly swept from the earth the remains of the old Priory at Tunbridge, and the Castle would have shared no better fate had it happened to stand in the way. In a county with which I am well acquainted (Dorsetshire), it was with great difficulty that the relics of a splendid Roman amphitheatre were wrested from the 'appropriation clause' of a railway company; and memory, in calling back the patience and courage of the venerable martyr awaiting his fate from the wild beasts of the Circus, and shuddering not at their roar,—memory, I repeat, would be put to

the blush on the same spot in hearing the shrieks and groans of a much
more powerful monster, the railway engine.

THE REVD W. M. SMITH MARRIOT

There is one word I do not see in this Resolution, but which I am
sure was in the minds of those who drew it up. This Resolution calls
upon Members to contribute original papers, drawings, etc. Under
that 'etc.' is concealed something which is more valuable than all the
original drawings in the world—I mean photography. The invention
of this art gives a new life and a new meaning to the study of Archaeology. The very best drawing is infinitely inferior to the realities of any
building; and many of the most interesting questions may hang on
what no draughtsman's skill can give—some peculiarity in the geology
of the material, something in the masonry, some small change in the
tone of the material. Now all these things come within the range of
photography—the art which tells the truth, whether we wish it to be
told or not. Artists 'were deceivers ever,' whether depicting fair ladies
or old buildings, but photography is the honest friend who always
comes out with the whole truth.

ALEXANDER J. B. BERESFORD HOPE, *Archaeologia Cantiana*,
Vol I, 1858

THE SCOPE AND OBJECT OF OUR DESIGN

If it be asked what is the scope and object of our design, we shall best
answer in the words of the philosopher [Bacon] which we have chosen
for the motto of our work. From the memory of things decayed and
forgotten, we propose to save and recover what we may, for the present
generation and for posterity, of the wrecks still floating in the ocean of
time, and preserve them with a religious and scrupulous diligence.
We propose to gather into one the neglected fragments and faint
memorials that remain to us of ages long gone by; to reclaim and
preserve the memories of men who, with common passions like ourselves, have stood and laboured on this soil of Kent; to save from the
submergence of oblivion their manners and their traditions, their
names, their lineage, their language, and their deeds. To reproduce the
past in its full integrity is perhaps impossible; yet for those who have
hopes somewhat beyond the present,—vision and affections somewhat
more extended than the narrow shoal of earth and time on which they
stand,—it may be sufficient if we can collect some feeble and scanty
remnants, which, failing to ensure a higher purpose, may help them in

some degree to link the present to the past, and serve as stepping-stones to bridge over the broad chasm and torrent of time.

Upon the importance of such a work as this it is hardly needful for us to enlarge. To the archaeological researches of scholars during the last and the preceding centuries, history and criticism are more indebted than to any other studies. From the labours of the archaeologist, from coins, monuments, inscriptions, and etymologies, the modern historian of Rome has been enabled to throw a steadier light, not merely on the obscure originals of that imperial city,—a clearer and brighter light than the Roman himself ever enjoyed,—but to hold up a torch to all history, and teach mankind to thread those paths with safety which they had trodden blindfold before. Why should not similar fruit be expected from similar labours? Why should not the toil of the archaeologist, when applied to our own county, prove as beneficial to English history? Why should not the light thus upheld on the distant past, kindle into a steadier blaze for the history of nearer times? In all that constitutes such memorials as these, in the bulk and salvage of these wrecks, England is incomparably richer than Greece or Rome. Here civil wars and foreign invasions have less obliterated the traces of ancient laws, institutions, families, and races; the barrows and burial-grounds of long-forgotten generations remain unviolated; the manor-house and the farm bear upon their faces the legible records of the past as clearly as the promises of the future; the very shells and incrustations through which the internal life of the nation has passed have been religiously preserved in all its varied forms. We can trace, from step to step, from age to age, the infant sallies, the march and progress, the maturer counsels and ripened institutions of the land. We can point to the mine from which they were dug, the shadows where they reposed at noon.

THE REVD J. S. BREWER, *Archaeologia Cantiana*, Vol. I, 1858

THE FIRST ARCHAEOLOGICAL CONGRESS

. . . the Canterbury Meeting has gone off brilliantly—notwithstanding numerous complaints of bad management and sundry petty evils, all seemed to agree that these were merely little roughnesses in the road which had not had time to settle, but not worth mentioning, the Machine had pace and vigour enough to have overcome far greater obstacles. The papers in general were valuable and interesting, the cream of the whole being Willis's paper on the [Canterbury] Cathedral which was admirable and delighted every body even those quite ignorant of Architecture.

Mr Godwin's paper on Mason's Marks was mere rubbish ... they are just such marks as are convenient to make with the chisel to distinguish one man's work from another and there is no need of any mystery at all about them—Mr Bloxam's paper on Saxon Architecture was not read for want of time. No great loss I suspect, as his opportunities of observation have not been sufficient for what he attempts to prove. Mr John Britton's paper was also withdrawn—he being in high dudgeon because he was not made enough of, and could not have it all his own way. I was really sorry for the old man, but nothing would pacify him. . . . No one had prepared anything on the local Antiquities of the place and neighbourhood which are highly interesting. . . . I believe that the ransackers of the graves of their ancestors were very well pleased with the results of their proceedings and Dr Traupott's museum was said to be splendid. I was too busy with the Cathedral to attend to these things. The Quadrille Band at the Conversatione set all the young ladies longing for a ball which they succeeded in getting up on Friday evening—after the Mummy had been cut open— for the pitch would not allow the wrapper to be unravelled—this was a very popular show and I suppose very edifying, tho' not in my line. I had some sleep during Mr Pettigrew's lecture and heard that several others did the same.

JOHN HENRY PARKER to ALBERT WAY, September 15, 1844.
Society of Antiquaries Correspondence, 1844–8

NOTES FOR BEGINNERS

. . . Archaeology is a most difficult subject. Skill and proficiency can only be acquired by experience. On the other hand, the beginner, if he can adapt himself to its discipline, can be sure to find it a satisfying pursuit; and it will give him the opportunity of making real and original contributions to knowledge whether as a professional or as an amateur, once he has gained the necessary experience. Nowadays there is as great a need as ever for skilled and experienced amateur archaeologists, whose intensive local or specialised knowledge is vital to progress; moreover, professional posts in archaeology are sometimes filled from among those who have made a reputation as amateurs.

No site should be excavated just for pleasure. Excavation is hard and exacting work, often a bitterly fought compromise on which lack of time, bad weather, and personal shortcomings all leave their mark. It can only be of value if done with meticulous effort on a thoroughly professional basis.

An archaeological site is a priceless and unique monument. Once excavated it has been ripped in pieces and can never again be mended. In part, or whole, it has ceased to exist. So much the more worthy then is the excavation of sites which are doomed to destruction in any case, by open-cast workings, housing, road-construction, &c; and, since the excavator of such sites is bound to realize that all that will ever be known about them depends on his efforts, he has a real incentive to work properly.

Excavation brings many worries and responsibilities and is not lightly to be indulged in except when necessary. Where sites are in no danger of destruction, a campaign of field-work is a much better and more satisfying proposition for the beginner starting on his own. The field-worker is far less likely than the excavator to be hampered by circumstances beyond his control, and his work can provide just as great an increase in knowledge, and without a risk of loss. It should, of course, be systematically planned with a precise objective. It can include the tracing and planning of roads and earthworks and field-systems, the identification and inspection on the ground of sites which have been discovered and photographed from the air, and the regular examination of gravel-pits, quarries, and other commercial excavations where archaeological material may be expected to occur. Any discovery should be reported immediately to the nearest museum.

Notes on Archaeological Technique, first issued by the Oxford University Archaeological Society, 1940, 3rd ed., The Ashmolean Museum, Oxford, 1950

ARCHAEOLOGY AND SOCIETY

It may be concluded that archaeology deserves to be cultivated in a free society first and foremost as an end in itself, as a form of that 'disinterested intellectual curiosity' which G. M. Trevelyan has recently proclaimed 'the life blood of real civilization'. The primary task of archaeologists is to enlarge and deepen man's knowledge of his own development. The results of their labours, wisely used, may subserve great social ends, fostering love of country and in the end promoting a deeper realization of human solidarity, but the motive of their researches ought to be no more and no less than the acquisition of knowledge. There is a very real sense in which archaeologists can only discharge their highest social function by ignoring society. Certainly it is true that society can expect to profit most from the cultivation of archaeology if the subject is allowed to develop freely and without reference to any extraneous considerations, however worthy in themselves. For this reason any movement to entrust the State with a monopoly or even with extensive powers over research in this field ought to be resisted. The proper task of the State in relation to archaeology is the provision of essential services, such as the safeguarding of monuments and sites, the classification and display of archaeological material in public museums and the recording of ancient sites on the Ordnance Survey maps. Yet it would be wrong to draw a hard-and-fast line between research and the provision of these services, and it is indeed evident that ampler opportunities should be allowed to archaeologists in public employment; in this respect we have much to learn from the Danes and the Scandinavians, not to mention the Germans and the Swiss. Further, it seems no less essential that, at a time when the cultivated classes are facing economic eclipse, if not extinction, the State ought to share the burden of maintaining civilization by subsidizing the arts and fields of study, economically useless, but culturally valuable, such as archaeology. If society is to remain free as well as equalitarian, and civilized as well as free from want, it may be necessary, as in France, to support private associations from public funds, while refraining from restrictive control. One may end by reflecting that the standing of archaeology within a society is one index of its degree of civilization.

GRAHAME CLARK, *Archaeology and Society*, 1947 ed. Methuen and
Co. Ltd.

THE BRITISH MUSEUM
'Fourmillante cité, cité pleine de rêves'

A figure with no sense of history
strolls, without due reverence, through the ages,
stares at the bulls and goddesses,
but does not see their mystery.

Down the long arcades of the museum,
the massive incrustations of the past,
Assyrian, Egyptian, Greek,
he walks, pursued by boredom.

The winged and monumental bull,
the cracked detritus of the Parthenon,
to other men said everything,
but, with no message now at all,

elude his curiosity.
He leaves them there, descends the steps,
and goes into the lamp-lit world
to wander through an inhabited city.

For they are real, not ghosts, who walk this street.
The past is dead.
                    Yet as he turns away he hears
remembered syllables of Greek.
The past is dead, but still we live in it.

This is a world of ghosts. We are the past,
One day this megalithic town will be unearthed:
historic data, empty of all ghosts,
and dry as Thebes or Cnidos at the last.
                    Bernard Bergonzi, *The Times Literary Supplement*,
                                        August 6, 1954

NON EXTINGUETUR

The visits to Laplain's shop [a curiosity dealer in Maidstone]
continued until 1857. In that year Harrison was one day watching the
progress of some drainage operations that were being carried out on
land belonging to his father at Ivy Hatch—a short distance from Rose
Wood.

'Old Bob Jessup', a workman, picked from an excavation a
smooth flint, with the remark, "Ain't it a queer one? It's like a whet-
stone". Thanks to his visits to Laplain, Harrison at once recognised
the stone as a flint celt.

From Benjamin Harrison's Notes:

        12.7.1869 Old Bob Jessup died in the night.

                    Sir Edward Harrison, *Harrison of Ightham*,
                                Oxford University Press, 1928

AUTHOR INDEX, WITH NOTES

BLOUNT, ED.   11
1588?–1632. A London printer,
stationer and translator best known as
one of the printers of the Shakespeare
first folio.

BODLEIAN LIBRARY MS   179
Ashmole 1820a.

BORLASE, THE REVD WILLIAM
181, 183
1695–1772, Cornish antiquary; made
a Fellow of the Royal Society in 1750.

BRACTON, HENRY DE   81
Died about 1268, judge and the author
of the best work on English law
written in the Middle Ages.

BREWER, THE REVD J. S.   201
At the time this article was written,
Professor of History in King's College
in the University of London.

BRITISH ARCHAEOLOGICAL
ASSOCIATION   25, 80, 143
Founded in 1843 by certain dissatisfied
Fellows of the Society of Antiquaries
and others.

BRITISH MUSEUM MSS
Harley 4016   169
Harley 6988   170
Harley 7055   180

BROWNE, SIR THOMAS   139
1605–82. Physician with a bent towards the study of antiquities. This is
possibly the earliest excavation report.

BROWNSALL, THOMAS   7

CAM, HELEN M.   43
Fellow of Girton College, Cambridge,
and a leading authority on the Hundred and the Hundred Rolls, the records of its ancient Courts. Died 1968.

CAMDEN, WILLIAM   47, 55, 98,
151, 185
1551–1623, historian and antiquary
whose name was made famous by the
publication of his *Britannia* in 1586.
He endowed the Camden professor-

ship of ancient history at Oxford, and
the Camden Society was founded in
his honour in 1883.

CARTER, G. G.   162
Has spent almost all his life at sea and
is an authority on lightships and navi-
gation.

CAWTHORN, JAMES   22
1721–61. A minor poet who as a
schoolboy launched his own periodi-
cal. He married the daughter of a
Soho Square schoolmaster and eventually became Headmaster of Ton-
bridge. His poems were collectively
published in 1771.

CLARK, GRAHAME   204
A leading British prehistorian, now
Disney Professor of Archaeology in
the University of Cambridge.

CLAY, HENRY   21

COLLIER, THE REVD CHARLES
124
A theologian elected F.S.A., 1860.
Died 1890. Contributed much to the
Gentleman's Magazine.

COLLINSON, THE REVD JOHN
186
A historian of Somerset, elected
F.S.A., 1784, the year of his death.

CONYNGHAM, LORD ALBERT
43
A nineteenth-century peer much
interested in excavation work from
which he amassed a large collection of
antiquities. F.S.A., 1840.

CRAM, R. A.   108
His best known book was *The Gothic
Quest* published in 1907.

CRAWFORD, O. G. S. 56, 121, 123,
199
A geographer whose work as Archaeology Officer of the Ordnance Survey
and Editor of *Antiquity* laid one of the
corner-stones in the study of archaeology in Great Britain and abroad.

His mild eccentricities, foreshadowed in one extract, endeared him to his many friends who still mourn his death in 1957.

descended from a Spitalfields silk-worker and a German tobacco manufacturer, who illustrated many archaeological works and was elected F.S.A. in 1844.

FAUSSETT, THE REVD BRYAN
31, 65, 67
An East Kent parson-antiquary who excavated very many Saxon grave-mounds between 1757–73. His collections and his careful day-to-day Journal are among the chief treasures of Liverpool Public Museum. F.S.A., 1763.

FAUSSETT, THOMAS GODFREY
68
A distinguished Kentish archaeologist, great-grandson of The Revd Bryan Faussett, and an active member of his County Society. F.S.A., 1859.

FIRBANK, RONALD   111, 132
1886–1926. A novelists' novelist whose roots were in the *fin-de-siècle*.

*FOLKESTONE AND HYTHE
HERALD*   147

FOX, SIR CYRIL   175
A Past President, and Gold Medallist of the Society of Antiquaries, 1952, and author in 1932 of *The Personality of Britain*, a famous synthesis of British prehistory. Died 1967.

FRANZERO, C. M.   60
A journalist with a flair for Roman history who dedicated this book, by his kind permission, to Benito Mussolini.

FREEMAN, R.   97
A Kentish poet who himself published a two-volume anthology of Kentish poets in 1821.

FRERE, JOHN   4
The paper from which this extract is taken is one of the most notable landmarks in the study of prehistory. F.S.A., 1775.

FULLER, THOMAS   7, 38, 40, 93
1608–61. Divine and antiquary, and an amiable character. This book, published posthumously, is of particular interest in its early use of a county basis for antiquarian study.

G., D.   135

GENTLEMAN'S MAGAZINE 7, 8,
12, 39, 43, 76, 77–8, 80, 81, 85, 101,
124, 126, 127, 131, 135, 151, 152
Founded in 1731 by Edward Cave and noted for its antiquarian information. It lasted in various forms until 1914.

GORDON, ALEXANDER   187
1692–1754. A Scottish antiquary who toured widely abroad and in Scotland and northern England. He was Secretary to the Society of Antiquaries 1735–41 and later to the Egyptian Society.

GOSSON, STEPHEN   169
1554–1624. An Elizabethan actor and poet who turned satirist and later entered the church.

GREENWELL, CANON WIL-LIAM   70
His *British Barrows*, 1877, was a practical synthesis of the subject. He died, still working, in 1917, at the age of 98, and his "Greenwell's Glory" is still known to some fly-fishermen.

GROSE, FRANCIS   109, 186
1731–91. A draughtsman who became Richmond Herald and spent much of his time travelling in Great Britain in antiquarian research. His topographical books are well known, and he was elected F.S.A. in 1757.

HARRIS, JOHN   80
1667–1719. A Kentish ecclesiastic of great abilities in mathematics, history and lexicography, but notwithstand-

ing his substantial preferments he was often in distress and died insolvent.

HARRISON, SIR EDWARD 1872–1960   206
Harrison of Ightham was Benjamin Harrison, Sir Edward's father, the noted protagonist of eoliths, the flints which some prehistorians still regard as the first traces of human activity. The character named in this extract had a nose for a flint, and private research suggests that he added regularly to the population of his village without blessing of clergy.

HAWKES, JACQUETTA   83
A well-qualified archaeologist who has the very rare gift of combining imagination with scholarship.

HOARE, SIR RICHARD COLT   197
A pioneer of scientific archaeological excavation in Great Britain, though his written reports often show a romantic streak, as would be expected from a member of the Society of Dilettanti to which he was elected in 1792. F.S.A. in the same year.

HOPE, A. J. BERESFORD   200
A distinguished Member of Parliament for Maidstone who, by purchasing the site of the Abbey of St Augustine at Canterbury, ended its existence as a public-house. He was a founder-member of the Kent Archaeological Society in 1857. F.S.A., 1847.

HUDSON, W. H.   138
1841–1922. A field naturalist who imposed his South American background on his vivid interpretation of the English countryside.

HUGHES, EVELYN   28
A member of a Welsh family well known for its interest in archaeology.

HUGHSON, DAVID   116
HUNTER, THE REVD JOSHUA   105

ISAACSON, THE REVD STEPHEN   See p. 196

JACKSON, THE REVD WILLIAM   94, 95
A Fellow of Worcester College, Oxford. F.S.A., 1861.

JESSUP, R. F.   60, 154, 162

JONES, BARBARA   130
This book, by a very accomplished modern artist, is a masterly evocation of the melancholy and genial extravagance in which the temperamental vagaries of the English aristocracy found expression.

KENNETT, WHITE   10
An industrious antiquary who was Bishop of Peterborough when he wrote this Life of Somner in 1726. F.S.A., 1720.

KENT ARCHAEOLOGICAL SOCIETY   29, 200
A flourishing County society founded in 1877.

KENT MESSENGER   157

LAMBARDE, WILLIAM   158
1536–1601. A distinguished lawyer whose Perambulation of Kent, said to have been completed in 1570, was the first history of any county.

LELAND, JOHN   4, 42, 45, 55, 135, 138
1506–52. He was given a commission to travel England in search of records and antiquities, on which task he spent six diligent years. His records, which he was unable to digest, have nevertheless formed a great source for other workers in the same field.

LHWYD, EDWARD 178
1660–1709. Keeper of the Ashmolean Repository at Oxford. He was an indefatigable collector of antiquarian information for a geographical dictionary of Wales and Celtic lands, and an early field archaeologist.

LUKIS, THE REVD W. C. 197
A Cornish antiquary who in 1879 was given a grant by the Society of Antiquaries for research into the prehistoric monuments of his county. He also studied megaliths in other parts of the British Isles, in Holland and in Brittany, and was the authority of his day.

MEASOM, GEORGE 37
A prolific writer of English and French railway guide-books in the middle years of the nineteenth century.

MELVILLE, HERMAN 73
1819–91. An American novelist and poet, a pioneer in the literature of the South Seas.

MILES, W. A. 69
A Dorset antiquary who excavated the famous Deverel barrow in 1825. His name is forgotten, but the Deverel-Rimbury culture of the late Bronze Age finds mention in every book on British prehistory.

MITCHELL, JULIAN 87

MORRIS, WILLIAM 91, 109
1834–96. It has been well said of him that he can be numbered with the saints who in the days of triumphant commercialism strove unweariedly against its crimes. F.S.A., 1894.

MORTILLET, GABRIEL DE 121
A famous Conservator of the prehistoric collections in the French Museum of National Antiquities who in 1867–69 produced an archaeological classification of the Stone Age

using as a basis variations in the types of weapons and techniques.

MURRAY'S HANDBOOKS 38, 100
These were 'Works of Sound Information and Innocent Amusement, printed in large Readable Type, and suited for All Classes', in the terms of their own advertisements, and they may still be consulted with much profit.

NEWS CHRONICLE 147
NOTTINGHAM EVENING POST 137
NOVIOMAGIAN CLUB 9, 27, 98
For a note on this Dining Club, see p. 9.

OBSERVER 83, 117, 157
OXFORD UNIVERSITY ARCHAEOLOGICAL SOCIETY 204

PARKER, JOHN HENRY 202
An Oxford publisher and bookseller, a leading specialist in architecture, who became Keeper of the Ashmolean Museum. F.S.A., 1849. Died 1884.

PAYNE, GEORGE 69
A brewer and banker who became an energetic field antiquary in Kent and Secretary of the Kent Archaeological Society 1889–1904. He had a keen nose for discovery but no head for business. F.S.A., 1880. Died 1920.

PEERS, SIR CHARLES 82
A most distinguished occupant of the office of Chief Inspector of Ancient Monuments in the Ministry of Works. He was awarded the Gold Medal of the Society of Antiquaries in 1938 and was its President 1929–34. He died in 1952.

PEGGE, DR SAMUEL 12
Shortly after his death in 1796 he was

described as an ecclesiastical climber with a taste for antiquity, but this Kentish parson had no reason to be ashamed of his many contributions to various branches of antiquarian study. F.S.A., 1750.

language. The misfortunes of Laud, his patron, prevented the completion of his projected History of Kent.

the first President of the Society of Antiquaries to become a television personality. It may be doubted whether any of his predecessors could have taken the opportunity had it been offered them.